Essential Moments

Essential Moments

Dr. Antonio L. Carvajal

Library of Congress Control Number:		2009900654
ISBN:	Hardcover	978-1-4415-0560-6
	Softcover	978-1-4415-0559-0

This book was printed in the United States of America.

To order additional copies of this book, contact:
Xlibris Corporation
1-888-795-4274
www.Xlibris.com
Orders@Xlibris.com
57242

Contents

To my grandchildren,

Taylor Maté and Alexander Kabacy

Living on the margin either bums you out and kills you, or it turns you into a dreamer . . . . If these dreamers are liberated, if they are brought back into the arms of society, they become the architects of the new community.

—Judith Snow,

Acknowledgements

The abundant love and support that inspired the writing of this book was enormous. I am thankful for the words of encouragement my wife Joanie shared at the completion of each chapter and every step of the way.

My daughter Carmela Carvajal Kim provided her artistic editorial skills and talents as she scrutinized each passage and chapter with a meticulous flare. I am indebted to her for staunch and professional advice.

Jason Renouf, a devoted and loyal friend, remained the most valuable player in this project from beginning to end. His personal tenacity, clever and humorous reactions, technical skills, and appreciation for the cultural elements in the narrative gave me the inspiration I needed to continue the writing for numerous days from dusk to dawn.

My family, brothers, sisters, son and daughters, were constantly connected to the narrative. Each of them, in their own way contributed clarity of substance when specific passages of our family history were vague or unclear. I am grateful for their candor and sincerity.

I am deeply indebted for the traces of loving memories that my friends, students, and colleagues at every juncture of my personal and professional life impressed in my mind and heart. Without these significant relationships this book would not have evolved.

Finally, and extremely important, is the professional guidance the entire staff at Xlibris gave me throughout the last phases of the book. Their constant superior advise, expedient, thoughtful, and conscientious communications were constructive, professional, and most appreciated.

Part One:
Intimations of Immortality

There was a time when meadow, grove, and stream,
The earth, and every common sight,
To me did seem
Apparelled in celestial light,
The glory and the freshness of a dream.

—William Wordsworth

Author's note:
In many situations throughout this book, names have been changed to protect identity.

Chapter One

Years ago, my name was Antonio Lopez Ramirez Carvajal de la Plaza Brown. A huge name, indeed, for a puny five-year-old *chavalito* (child) who didn't weigh an ounce over forty pounds. My dad, in fact, nicknamed me Toñito el Flakito (skinny little Tony). It was a term of endearment that, when he used it, seemed to comment not only on my thinness, but also my sensitivity, clownish disposition, and neediness of him, all at once. Back then my world was very small. My house was close to everything. The grocery store was a hundred paces away; the Catholic church just six blocks. Brown Plaza, the center of our barrio, was the closest of all—about fifty paces from our doorstep. Our dear *placita* was the center of our universe. It felt as if it belonged to us and we to it. I once asked my dad why the placita was not named after him or me. He explained that many years ago, a man by the name of Mr. Brown had donated the land for the plaza to the community. Dad said that perhaps someday, when I made a lot of money and donated some of it to the city, they might change the name of the plaza to "Placita de Toñito." I liked the sound of that.

Our house was also only a few yards from San Felipe Creek. This powerful river—with its sparkling, translucent currents—was the pride of the barrio. I always wondered where the river started and where it ended. As a child, I would walk along the pebbles at the river's edge and talk to the fish that paraded under the shallow water. They would glide gracefully past my ankles, flapping me with their tails as if to say, *Catch me if you can!* Since the river ran through not just our part of town but the Anglo part as well, I hoped those other folks would find the same love and appreciation we had for it. It was central to our existence. The river's waters were a place for my family and neighbors to swim and fish, bathe and wash clothes. It was a refuge where people found relief from the intense heat of the day and tranquility after a hard day's work.

But the river could also be violent. At night, its sounds seemed to become loud and ravaging, and Dad warned us not to go near it after dark. Even in daytime, there were spots where the water was too deep and the current too strong. In these spots, my father repeatedly reminded us the river could swallow children within seconds and without mercy. But when Dad was away for a day or two, we kids would dare each other to plunge into the freezing waters to see who could stay underneath the longest (I was always the first one out). Though I heard many times the warnings of the river claiming children—and in the years to come, it did—I was rarely that scared of it. I always felt secure and protected by my family.

The river was a natural place for community and recreation, but the true center of the barrio was the placita. The placita was a perfect square plaza, one block by one block, lined with buildings. One day after I had learned to count, I counted all fourteen buildings in the placita: "Uno, dos, tres . . ." Half of these buildings were bars and cafes where my dad would meet his friends to enjoy cold drinks. In the middle of the square was a gazebo that looked like a huge ice cream cone. A statue of an eagle sat elegantly at the very top. This was the America I knew. This was my heaven on earth where the skies and my river were blue, and my love for life was abundant. At that time, I didn't realize there were other dimensions to life outside of my barrio. I guess the old proverb "Fish don't know they live in water" is indeed very true.

But as the years passed, I began to realize there was perhaps another America. Sometimes I would climb a tall tree by the river and see people walking across the bridge to where the Anglos lived. This is where my neighbors worked cleaning houses and making yards pretty. Here, the people drove nice cars and dressed in nice clothes. They too would cross the bridge when they came to pick up my dad and uncles to paint their homes. It was the job of the people I knew to make the beautiful world of the Anglos even more beautiful. The communities on each side of the river had their own culture, language, and definitions of money and wealth—or lack thereof.

The families from the other side were smaller, but their homes were bigger and their yards greener. Children were rich from the moment they arrived: born into wealth just like their parents and grandparents. My dad was born poor in the United States and remained uneducated throughout his life. My mom had been better-off. Her parents had owned a business in Mexico before fleeing for the United States with their two young daughters—my mom and her older sister, Manina—during the Mexican Revolution. They brought with them their entrepreneurial spirit and did well for themselves. But my mom and dad struggled to make ends meet for their own family. We did not have enough of many things. However, there were some things in which we were abundant: in songs, prayers, and language. Some things we had only the best of: my mom made tamales and tortillas better than anyone I knew.

My family lived on a compound that belonged to my grandparents. The huge plot was separated into three sections. I lived with my immediate family in one house; my aunt Amparo (my mom's younger sister) and uncle Raúl lived in another; my *abuelito* (grandfather), Antonio Ramirez, and *abuelita* (grandmother), Francisca, in the third. My grandparents were fortunate to have landed so near the placita. They strove to make a living by purchasing a building that they later remodeled and made into a successful Mexican restaurant. The restaurant sat near the river and had beautiful gardens of magnolias and bougainvilleas as well as excellent food. So picturesque was the setting by the restaurant that musicians and actors from various places in Mexico and the United States would come to entertain at the nearby casino.

There were nine of us in our house: me, my parents, and my four brothers and two sisters. My brothers Ramón and José and sister Magdalena were the oldest kids. Francisco, Raúl, and I were the younger brothers, each two years apart. The baby of the family was my sister Amparo. In many ways, my dad was a devoted father to all of us, but he sure had his favorites. José, because of his talent in boxing and football, was Dad's absolute favorite. Magdalena was his princess. The rest of us were simply acceptable. I tried desperately to get his attention so he would consider me special too. Sometimes my efforts paid off; most of the time, I was a pest. My dad worked from dawn to dusk as a housepainter and was proud of his job. Sometimes, after I begged to go with him to work, he would surrender and take me along. My job was to gather the paintbrushes and sweep the floors at the end of the workday. He would brag to his bosses about what a good worker I was—he was able to express many ideas in English. The money he earned gave us privileges other kids in the barrio didn't have: we could afford groceries and even buy ice cream cones. My dad bought a car that had shiny black tires and a very loud horn. It seemed to be able to fly.

While my dad worked and worked, my mom, Consuelo, known as Chelito to most, was busy with the rest of us. She took care of all our needs, always letting her pride for us shine through. She loved to show us off, and whenever there was a festivity, we were dressed in beautiful clothes made by a tailor in the plaza. She believed firmly that every one of us had to go to school: no compromise. When I was four, she enrolled me in a little schoolhouse called Jardín de Niños (Children's Garden). There were only six students. Here, I learned my colors and how to count in a new and strange language: English. But things at school were not easy. It wasn't that I didn't want to learn, it was that I didn't want to learn from Ms. Quack Quack. Our teacher's real name was Ms. Sophia, but to us, she was definitely Ms. Quack Quack because she talked like a duck and even walked like a duck. When she spoke, which was all the time and loud, she smacked her lips with self-importance as if she were eating a hamburger with hot sauce. I simply didn't like her, and I didn't like the school where there were no snacks or rest periods. Ms. Quack Quack taught colors by pointing to plastic fruit on her table. She warned us not to eat it. Red, brown, and yellow were easy to remember—these were colors used to paint the placita I knew so well. Green was more difficult. Ms. Quack Quack clenched her teeth to impress upon us how to say the word. She showed us the vibrant color of the trees and grass outside the window where we spent so much time. She said "green" as if she had discovered it herself. It was obvious she thought us rather slow.

I took to my lessons in counting in English because I had a need for it: I used my newfound skills to divide with my brothers the money we earned cleaning the placita. When Ms. Quack Quack asked us in English where we lived, I would say that my name was Toñito de la Plaza. But some of Ms.

Quack Quack's questions were harder. She wanted to know the year and date we were born. This was not a fair question: I didn't know! No one in my family kept papers of that sort of stuff. Ms. Quack Quack was appalled that I didn't know the difference between a year and a month. I thought that was supposed to be another lesson. After two months in this silly schoolhouse, I became the earliest dropout in the history of the barrio. I refused to learn from Ms. Quack Quack anymore.

As I faced my own school-day challenges, my dad struggled with his own problems. He didn't seem happy, and he began to drink more. Instead of coming home right after work, he would stop at a cantina. At first it was just for an hour; then, it became two. Eventually, he stayed out at the bars until they closed. Maybe providing for so many kids was too hard for him. He probably figured that if he was already in trouble with my mom, he might as well make the crime worth the punishment and spend more time with his pals.

Because I was the middle child, everything that happened in the household eventually landed in my space. One day, I heard a secret that I had to keep from those outside the family forever. My mother was speaking to my aunt Amparo, "I am going to have another baby that doesn't seem to be growing. I am tired all the time, and I am worried about the baby."

My aunt urged my mom to see a doctor in San Antonio, Texas, which was 150 miles away. Five days later, Mom returned with the horrible news that she had breast cancer and that unless her breast was removed, she would not only lose the baby, but she would also lose her life. Mom had her breast removed, and the baby almost grew to term. Born prematurely, my brother Francisco weighed only three pounds. He was so small that a shoe box was used as his first crib. His life had been spared, and life—challenging though it was—continued for Mom as well.

It was during this time that my parents became both verbally and physically abusive with each another. These episodes were extremely frightening to me. After things calmed down, my dad would hug me and make efforts to console me. The alcohol made him smell funny. One day, I opened the door to the old shack where he kept his paint buckets. A bottle filled with brownish liquid—whiskey, as I would later learn—fell on my shoulder. It smelled bad, like the sidewalks I swept in front of the cantinas. I ran back to the house and reported it to Mom. After that day, my dad was not allowed in the house. I felt ashamed to have caused so much trouble. Dad was starting to look as skinny as me. Each day he appeared sadder and more tired. He was constantly sick with a cold. I wanted to help him, but things just got worse.

Everywhere around me there seemed to be trouble. I watched as my mom continually berated and even hit my dad for coming home drunk. I would climb a tree and scout the war zone from above. I could hear the rage and fury spilling forth from her. I was there when the news arrived that doctors had told my dad he had a very bad flu in his lungs. I heard neighbors talk about my father's mom, dad, brothers, and sisters being sick with the same flu. The flu was called TB, but I thought they were saying, "TV," which we didn't have; only the Anglos had them in their homes. Everything was confusing.

After we found out my dad was ill, my siblings and I were farmed out to live with my aunt Manina and her family while my mom stayed to take care of Dad. Mom had to boil water in a trough to clean and disinfect his pajamas. She was the only one that could change his diapers and give him a bath. We stayed at my aunt's until after my dad's death, when the bad bugs in my home were also completely dead. Though my aunt was wonderful, these were very sad, lonely, and desperate days.

I was not there during my father's final days of illness and death. Though we did have a funeral, I was not there when my dad was buried: none of us were. Because of health precautions, the city didn't allow anyone to attend the burial for fear of the contagious disease he had suffered. Only my two older brothers were allowed to attend the funeral. Mom did not attend because she did not have shoes to wear. In the days after Dad left us, I had many moments of sadness. I would sit on an old apple crate he had painted for me, wondering where he had gone. During this painful time, I kept recalling very old Brazilian music Dad and I would listen to around the placita when people were preparing for grand celebrations called *jamaicas*. For some reason, the gleefulness and the joy was contagious all around. Dad seemed tremendously happy to be with me. I would make up lyrics from songs I didn't know just to make him laugh. He always responded with applause.

On one such day, as I waited for his return, I happened to look up at the wall where there hung a painting my aunt Amparo had given us after the funeral. The painting was of a little boy crossing a footbridge. The bridge was in bad shape: missing slats of wood here and there. Under the bridge was a roaring river. I thought, "If he's not careful and doesn't see that the bridge is broken, he'll fall in the water and drown." I knew this little boy would fall. Suddenly, I saw an angel with huge wings next to him. The angel was watching over the boy and guiding his steps, one by one. I knew the angel's job was to protect this little boy and keep him from falling. At that moment, I knew I needed someone like that to watch over me for the rest of my days. I remembered that on the afternoon of the funeral, a storm had brought thunder, lightning, and rain. My aunt had said that God's angels up in the sky were moving the furniture to make a happy home for Papa at last. Now as I stared at the picture on the wall, I believed in angels.

The days after the funeral were confusing, desperate, and empty. No one spoke. Mom began wearing black dresses every day—it was tradition that she wear them for a whole year, something that was confusing to me. She isolated herself in the kitchen and even slept there, not allowing anyone in. No one could enter except when it was time to eat the food she'd prepared. The silence continued as we ate, and then Mom retreated again to her isolation. Each day she looked worse than the day before. Her hair and teeth began falling out. Her clothes became tattered and smelly. Her very person seemed to be deteriorating. She would often cry through the night, sick with sorrow. Along with my brothers and sisters, I felt her sorrow, but communication with her was sealed off. I wondered if perhaps someday she'd recall one of her favorite songs "Cielito Lindo," which reminds us that music and songs make us happy and heal the soul.

Chapter Two

It's always been a talent of mine to dream of better days, training my mind to look beyond my problems and begin to solve them almost as if I were playacting. This is just what I did after Dad left us. I began to pretend I was a good father to my brothers and sisters. After several weeks of inconsolable grieving, Mom had no choice but to pull herself together and began looking for work to keep the family afloat. As she searched endlessly for jobs, I took the opportunity to experiment with my role as surrogate parent. My older sister Magdalena, who was called Maruca, grew frustrated with my naiveté, reminding me that Papacito was dead and buried, never to come back. "Now we need to know what we should do about it. Do you understand, flaco [skinny]?" I had to surrender the pretense: Maruca was right. I wasn't Dad.

But whether they knew it or not, my family needed me. I came to realize that my older siblings were impossible to protect or influence, so my game plan became to focus on the younger ones, who allowed me to pretend I was the big cheese. We all turned much of our attention to my two-year-old sister Amparo also known as Payito. Perhaps in our scrambling for solid ground, each of us felt the need for someone to love and protect. And it wasn't hard to love the sweet, adorable Payito. However, through our overindulgence, she was slowly evolving into *la consentida* (the spoiled one). Anything Payito wanted, she got. We couldn't move fast enough to please her. "*Quiero nieve* [I want ice cream], *dulce* [candy], *borregita* [pet lamb], and *gatito* [pet kitten], and *perito* [puppy]." Her minions were always at her beck and call. She knew she had all of us wrapped around her little finger. If we ignored her, she would pester us relentlessly. It was a situation we ourselves created. Fortunately, we didn't succeed in ruining her loving disposition, a wonderful gift that remains with her to this day.

Through the chaos of the early weeks without Dad, I hid my own pain. But I too needed someone to lean on for sympathy and consolation. No one seemed to come forward. One day, in my desperation, I rushed to the corner drugstore. I spent forty cents on Sangre de Chango, which is iodine, and I also bought bandages. I applied the deep red liquid to my ear, nose, forehead, and right arm and then wrapped my "wounds" in bandages. It was my way of making visible my personal agony. No one at home even noticed.

Next, I decided to visit a woman across the street, known as Clara la India, to see if she needed any errands run for her, which I would occasionally do for a few extra coins. Plenty of rumors about Clara swirled around the barrio. It was said that she was involved with black magic. Some believed that she could turn dogs into cats, goats into horses, mean boys and girls into rabbits, and sunshine into torrential storms. She even knew when people would die and where they ended up after they left. I believed a lot of the rumors, but doubted that Clara would ever hurt me. Her colorful dresses, dangling earrings, and huge bracelets fascinated me. I often wished my mother would dress a little more like her. Clara opened her door and looked down at me, shocked by my battered appearance. She didn't know the wounds were not real. Without hesitation, she invited me to come in and have *atole* (pudding) made from berries that grew in her backyard. Taking me in her arms, she offered her most sincere sympathy for the loss of my dad. I broke into tears. In this eccentric woman, I'd found what I needed most: a friend.

After that much-needed moment of consolation, it was somehow easier to see what lay ahead. I was determined to move beyond the awful place I had been in for so long. I threw myself into the role of teacher and advisor to my younger siblings. In fact, I started with my own school with three of the younger kids as my first students. Little Payito didn't meet the readiness criteria for admission, but I unilaterally waved the age requirement and accepted her. She was fortunate because my school was a delightful place to be. For snacks, I passed out mud cakes decorated with roly-poly beetles. We would take field trips to the river to gather berries for more realistic consumption. Indeed, snacks seemed to be a large part of the curriculum: I was no Ms. Quack Quack.

Since I had my own cash reserve from wages I earned as a sidewalk sweeper, plus whatever coins I found in the placita, I was able to design a reward system for my students: two cents for attending each day. It worked amazingly well, motivating my class to work hard and learn a lot. When other students in the neighborhood caught wind of our terrific school, they clamored for admittance. They were welcomed wholeheartedly. My ever-growing class became known as the "How and Why Club." No one knew what it meant, but we liked the way it sounded. The success of the How and Why Club was my first inkling that a teacher never really teaches anybody anything. What a teacher does is inspire students and get them to love school. By purposely going against everything she stood for, perhaps I'd learned from Ms. Quack Quack after all.

My career as an educator had begun, but there was still opportunity for other professional endeavors. As springtime bloomed, it became time for the *jamaicas*, three-day community festivals that were the highlight of the year. On festival days, the placita came alive with thunderous celebration. The sound of drums and trumpets mingled with music blaring from jukeboxes from the local bars. Attracted by the sound and excitement, men, women, boys, and girls from every corner of the barrio flocked to the placita, which was now decorated with red, white, and green streamers. Everyone participated: even goats and dogs turned up (though, for some reason, cats declined to attend). Everyone brought food to sell to make money for their families (Mom's famous tamales, enchiladas, and burritos were in high demand), and young and old alike performed songs and dances to entertain the crowds.

Needless to say, the morning after each festival day, the placita was a mess. I pretended I owned the square and put my brothers and sisters to work on cleanup duty. Though my labor force was unpaid, the nickels and dimes they found in the streets were pooled into a family fund. It was a terrific idea. The most lucrative spots were around the cantinas where older men hung around arguing and crying a lot. I didn't know what it was with these places, but I knew they had made my dad sick. Maybe they had served him bad water that made him feel ill in the mornings. My brother José branched out with a side business, sneaking inside the weeping caves to shine shoes. He almost became a millionaire. I helped out by keeping watch to see if Mom came around looking for him. For my role as sentry, I was paid twenty-five cents a pop.

Another job I had was to run errands for Mom. My task was to ask the grocers if I could buy things on credit. Mom would send a note with me with a promise to pay within a week. I would also make special trips to buy groceries for the old and unfit. They trusted me fully with their money, and I never let them down. While other boys and girls my age strolled around the plaza, talking, laughing, and making their first attempts at romantic flirtation, I was busy delivering food. One of my delivery customers was my friend Clara la India, who had trouble walking. Though I thought Clara's appearance was stunning, for the last year, she had been bandaging her feet from toes to ankles. My friends were always prodding me for information about the mysterious Clara's secrets, since I knew her so well and lived right across the street. But I was taught that people should mind their own business. Mother had zero respect for gossipers or "nosy rosies": meddling in other peoples' lives was strictly taboo. She always taught us kids to be fair, thoughtful, and kind to others and to never ever show disrespect to an adult (or we would get a spanking that could be heard from a block away). Besides, Mom always spoke kindly of Clara. I had no reason to give into my friends' goading questions, especially since Clara made me feel as if I was the golden boy of the neighborhood: the most awesome kid on the block. Yet I too became curious. What gruesome sight was Clara hiding beneath those foot bandages? It became an agonizing obsession. Finally, one day, my mother revealed the mystery: Clara had gangrene on her foot from the advanced stages of diabetes. My strange and unlikely advocate would eventually lose the foot and, a few years later, die of heart and kidney failure.

I had another delivery destination: the house on the other side of the placita where *Diablito* (little devil) lived. According to *chisme* (gossip), Diablito had been born from old parents who were paying for some crazy sins. Because of these sins, Diablito was their cross to bear. That cross was evidently too heavy because they passed it on to an aunt. The aunt's shack was nicer than Clara's: it even had an altar where she would pray for Diablito. One day, I was making my regular deliveries on bicycle. I was thinking how important I now was with so much work and responsibility when suddenly my pleasant reverie turned into horror: Diablito was right there, chasing my bike! He really did look like the devil—with a skinny body, wiry hands, watery eyes, a twisted stub of a nose, thick tongue, and sharp teeth. He grunted and growled as he ran because Diablito could not talk. When he caught up to me, he pushed me off my bike and threw me against a fence. He grabbed at my shoe, my cap, my ears, and my hair. Finally, he took off with my bike. I was out of there in flash, and within minutes, I was under my bed, praying for the first time in my life. I thought I had a lot of explaining to do to Mom, but when she heard what happened, she comforted me and prayed with me.

Later, I learned that Diablito was a real boy with a real name: Ramiro. He had been born with Down's syndrome. It was not intentional cruelty that led the people of my barrio to attribute such evilness to him. A lack of education in my corner of the world helped perpetuate misinformation and fear about many things. Little did I know that in the years to come, as destiny would have it, I would get the chance to help boys like Ramiro—when I began teaching children with Down's syndrome.

Chapter Three

Better days were emerging in the lives of the Carvajal family. Mom's angry energy was transforming into an obstinate sense of resiliency. Don Antonio Ramirez, my grandfather, who had visited only sporadically before Dad's death, had a hand in this. In time, my mother's sister and her family moved away from the compound, and my grandfather moved in with them. He reentered our lives quietly but unmistakably. Every Saturday morning, he would arrive on his bicycle, giving each of us kids five cents for treats. We ran to the store, already working out how we'd spend our loot. In the meantime, he could talk to Mom. He quickly became Mom's strongest advocate and source of security. One day, he and Mom called the four of us—Maruca, Francisco, Raúl, and I—together to announce that he would be taking us on a trip to San Antonio, a big city many miles away. How could any place be bigger than our barrio? We had to see this. We embarked on our trip—just Grandpa and us kids—on a Saturday morning, arriving in the city in late afternoon. He took us to a restaurant that had tables with red and white linens, forks and knives we had to use to eat, glasses for drinking water and pop, and the best hamburgers any of us had ever tasted. They even served fried potatoes! After we ate, we checked into a huge hotel. The room had freshly made beds, a tub to take a bath, soap, and lots of clean towels. It was incredible! Each morning we went to a diner for *pan dulce* (sweet bread) and the best hot chocolate in the world. After our meals, Grandpa Ramirez would take us to the park, the movies, and the church. He was a kind grandpa. We were gone for five wonderful days.

When we returned with presents for Mom, I had no doubt the beginning of a new and better life was here at last. I wondered why Grandpa had stayed away from us for so long. Later I learned that Don Antonio had harbored very little respect for my dad and the way he had lived. My grandfather knew the history of Dad's irresponsible behavior. He also knew that my mom had been tricked into marrying him in the first place. As it turned out, my dad had deceived Mom throughout their courtship, sending her love letters that Dad dictated but were actually written by a friend. Mom didn't realize that Dad couldn't read or write. By the time my grandfather found out, it was too late: the wedding had been planned, and the marriage took place. After that, my grandfather abandoned my mom and dad's relationship. Perhaps it wasn't fair, but it was what he chose to do.

Now back in the picture, Grandpa began to support Mom financially. He even drove her into Mexico to be fitted with a full set of dentures to replace her teeth, which she had lost almost entirely by this time due to poor health. The dental visits went on for months, but finally, one day, she came back with a radiant smile. She had also dyed her hair dark and wore a new dress, new shoes, and even a ring like Clara la India wore. We all agreed that Mom was indeed a beautiful gal. Grandpa also gave Mom money to rent a piano, which we later purchased. I thought having a piano was an extravagance of the greatest kind—even if nobody seemed to know how to play it.

Although we kids all stuck together, three different camps naturally began to emerge in the family: Maruca, Raúl, Francisco, and I became one; José and Ramón, now in high school, another. Payito enjoyed a status all her own. Now five, she was beginning to make her own impression on the family. Having her around brought a certain lightness to our daily chores. She herself had only to care of her many pets—dogs, cats, and a lamb named Nicky Bunger Ray—and to prepare for her first day of school.

In many ways, Mom was excluded from the daily proceedings of the family because of the long hours she worked. Because she had completed high school and one year of business school before she was married, she was able to get a job in a fancy department store across the river where the Anglos had their businesses. We couldn't wait for the days she got paid when she'd bring home a big load of groceries and even treats for us. The other benefit we saw to her job was that it left us free to do whatever we wanted around the neighborhood while she was gone under my less-than-stringent supervision. Before Mom went to work, however, she established a set of commandments: we should never steal, share family matters, go near the river in her absence, or lie to her when she got back. We kept all the commandments sacred except the business about the river—especially in the summer. Each morning, as soon as Mom started her long walk across the bridge and out of sight, we were swinging from tree vines and plunging into the water. I became Tarzan, king of the jungle. My brothers were alligators and monkeys, and Maruca was a wild woman who lived among the animals. Five hours later, before Mom arrived home from work, we snapped back to reality and prepared dinner for her and all the pets. Our bloodshot eyes drew her suspicion, but we were ready with credible explanations that did not involve being underwater. I guess we were convincing: she always bragged that other families didn't have children as good and obedient as hers.

One day, after hours of play at the river, I felt intense cramping and a wave of nausea. I broke out in a cold sweat and shivers all over my body. Whenever we kids got sick, it was not our first inclination to run home. You see, Mom had one other commandment: thou shalt not get sick. Her theory was simple: if you got sick, it was your own fault. She treated every ailment, no matter the kind, by giving us a few drops of *hepalina* (horse laxative). This, needless to say, caused incredible cramping. As a result of Mom's nursing tactics, we were inclined to avoid complaining about our physical condition at all costs. This is why, on this particular day, I crawled to my usual hiding place, reserved for just such occasions, underneath the foundation of the house. My stomach pain became so intense that I wondered what would happen if I died here and no one was able to find me. I shouldn't have eaten all those figs, I thought. Luckily, Francisco heard me screaming and quickly ran across the street to get Clara la India. Mom was not at home on that particular day—she was off cleaning houses for extra money. Clara gave me something that made me feel worse, but I still felt grateful I wasn't getting Mom's special remedy. Then everything went black. When I woke up, the face of a doctor loomed over me. Dr. Hyslop had performed emergency surgery on my ruptured appendix. I was amazed I had survived the experience. Unfortunately, though it seemed as if all was well again, the same horrific, near-death experience was to repeat itself later in my life: the doctor never actually removed my appendix!

After my recuperation, adventures with my siblings resumed as usual. But as much as we sought excitement around the neighborhood, nothing could have prepared us for the surprise awaiting us at home. Playing outside one day, we heard an unfamiliar sound coming from inside the house: it was music! We peeked through the window and couldn't believe our eyes: Mom was sitting at the piano, playing, just like some of our teachers did. She was amazing! She played with an energy and passion that no famous pianist could have equaled. She played the music to all the traditional Mexican dances, banging on the keyboard so hard we thought it would break apart. And she sang! "Ay, ay, ay, ay, canta y no llores, porque cantando se alegran, cielito lindo, los corazones" (Sing and don't cry because singing makes for a joyful heart). Her voice seemed to emerge from the depths of her soul. To us, it was a miracle, just like the nuns were always saying was possible when faith remained alive. In reality, it had been twenty years since Mom had touched a piano, longer than the lifetimes of any of us kids. After all this time, Mom and her instrument had begun to sing again.

To us, Mom's incredible talents seemed to come from thin air. But we were in for another surprise. One day, while Mom was at work, Francisco ran into the house with a wild look in his eyes. Stuttering even worse than usual, he got his message across. "Come with me, look in the casino!" he exclaimed. The old gray casino stood just a few blocks from our house near the placita. Once the toast of the town for gambling and entertainment, it was now abandoned and dilapidated. In fact, though boarded up, you could still sneak inside the building by crawling through broken planks at the foundation, though, of course, we were forbidden to do so. I followed Francisco through an opening under the building that led to a musty room full of framed photos. He grabbed my arm and stammered, "¡Mira, mira, mira!" (Look, look, look!) The photos were of beautiful men and women dancing together, the women in long white dresses and the men in black suits and ties. Francisco guided me to another room. There were still more pictures of the glamorous patrons and entertainers who had performed at the casino during its heyday. Then Francisco pointed to one particular photo. In it, among other people, was a very young and pretty girl who was dancing. Though all the photos were fascinating, there was something about this one—something unmistakably familiar. The girl in the photo was Mother.

We scampered out of the casino and then returned with Maruca, Raúl, and Payito. Everyone agreed it was Mom in the picture, but how? As we came to learn, Mom had once played piano at my grandparents' restaurant and later to accompany the performers at the casino. She even sang, danced, and acted on the casino's stage. That particular day, despite our excitement, we didn't utter a word about it to Mom when she got home. How could we, given the way we'd found out? But that didn't stop us from returning to the casino again and again where we'd dance and sing on the old stage, sure we'd become tomorrow's biggest stars.

As Mom's love for music and entertainment resurfaced, she eventually began to let us in on her exciting past. This is how we learned about her life as a young girl. She would share with us stories about the thrilling theatrical experiences she'd had as a young girl. We were in awe. However, what surprised us just as much as her hidden talent was how Mom had succeeded in cutting herself off completely from this important part of her life. She had always obeyed a mandate set down by our father never to play the piano or dance in public. She kept this promise throughout her eighteen years of marriage, focusing instead on her role as wife, mother, and homemaker. Perhaps it's difficult to understand a time when women were asked to make such heartbreaking choices. Yet I greatly admire Mom for the love that went into making this promise and stand in ovation to her for the unending sacrifices she made for all of us.

Chapter Four

"Faith in God is the bread of life." We heard it every week at mass, and now I was beginning to see it was so. A value instilled in me from a young age by my mother, prayer was becoming a sustaining factor in my life. After so much turmoil and pain, faith wasn't a choice but a necessity. I was around eight years old when a miracle happened: Mom decided to send all my siblings and me to Catholic school. Surely this would be the connection to heaven I'd been longing for. Mom had diligently saved up enough money for us to attend, in part by selling most of her clothes, old shoes, blankets, and furniture to a lady who bought and sold used goods.

The Catholic school was to have many rules and regulations, but life with Mom had prepared us. She could give orders like a drill sergeant and expected them to be carried out. Disobedience to her rules had quick and nonnegotiable consequences. "Yo no más una vez les digo, o me lo pagan" (I'll tell you only one time, or you'll pay for it), she would say. All punishments were carried out on Saturday mornings since she didn't have time to mess around with us during the week. It was the waiting that was most agonizing. With Mom, there were no apologies, no explanations, and no excuses. She was an inflexible officer, indeed. Sometimes, it was hard to understand that this was love.

In comparison, the type of discipline doled out by the Catholic nuns seemed like heaven. Yes, they did occasionally rap our knuckles with a ruler, but the ordeal just wasn't as harsh or intimidating as Mom's brand of justice. Sometimes after disciplining us, the nuns would help us pray for forgiveness. Often, our only penance for bad behavior was to go to Friday confession and admit our sins to a priest we never had to look in the eye. I loved it. I'd kneel in the little room with its dark silk curtain. From the other side, the priest would listen as I recounted my weekly transgressions. He had already heard from the nuns what I was there to confess. Then, speaking softly, he'd assign my penance, usually a set of ten Hail Marys and ten Our Fathers, a much better deal than facing Mom's wrath.

The priest also explained to me the different types of sin. Mortal sin worried me the most. This was the worst kind: the kind that could damn you to eternal hell the second you died. Mortal sin included not going to church on Sunday, stealing, lying, and having impure thoughts. Though it was a lesser offense, even going to public school was considered sinful. This caused me extreme emotional turmoil because at least two of my barrio buddies went to public school. I had to come to terms with the fact that they had chosen to be sinners. There was another type of sin that was most perplexing to me: original sin. This was the kind of sin from which there was no escape. It was all because a man and a woman ate an apple they weren't supposed to eat. A sneaky snake tempted them into taking a bite even though God had told them not to. Because of Adam and Eve's disobedience, every child from then on was born into original sin and would never be free from it their whole lives. So I marveled, all children were sinners. Even newborn babies who died before they were baptized were not worthy of going to heaven. They had to stay forever in a place called limbo. These things were very hard to understand.

In school, we learned that "blessed are the poor," an idea I found fascinating. The more humble and poor you were, the more God loved you, and the better chance you had of going to heaven. For me, this verse was convenient. More than just a comfort, it made me feel self-assured. I felt sorry for the Anglos with so much wealth. They simply didn't stand a chance of being rewarded when they were called by God.

Every day at school, I was gaining new knowledge and insight. And I had more reason to be proud. One day in catechism class, Mother Superior—Sister Anna—announced that I had been born on a very important day: December 8 was the day of the Immaculate Conception. One boy asked her why this was such a big deal, and she quickly replied that it was a holy day of obligation, and you had to go to mass just like on Sunday. But this kid insisted on having his question answered further. Cautiously, Mother Superior explained that Mary, the mother of Jesus, had been conceived and born without original sin. No person had ever been conceived this way before Mary. "But what does 'conceived' mean?" asked my classmate. Sister knew she had talked herself into a corner. She fumbled around, trying to evade the question before quickly ending the discussion. Later, when I could fully understand and appreciate its meaning, the Immaculate Conception was one of the greatest mysteries I had ever heard about. I made sure to explain it to my siblings and Mom until I was told to shut up.

For myself, I had to accept that I was just an ordinary person born with sin. But at least I could work on being a better Catholic by receiving the sacraments. I learned about all seven: baptism, first communion, penance, confirmation, marriage, holy orders, and last rites. I had already experienced the first one without even knowing it: as a baby, I was baptized into the church. Now in Catholic school, I prepared for my first holy communion. I remember vividly the day I finally received this sacrament. I was draped in the most elegant shirt and wore a pair of the best black trousers my mother could find. I was so proud of my achievement that I felt as if I was being knighted. Indeed, I had reached a superior level of knowledge and status in school. Soon after, Mother had me apply for the Society of Altar Boys. I was immediately accepted. It was then that my family changed my name from Toñito to Ony: Ony El Santito (dearest Tony, the saint). Whether meant sarcastically or not, I liked my new name. The nickname my father had given me was for little boys. Now with challenging and complex responsibilities, I would need my new more commanding title. I felt this name was a mandate handed down from God himself. After so much struggle, pain, and sorrow, I was now sure I really did have one of God's angels looking out for me and watching over my family.

In contrast to my home, the Catholic church was elegant. It was decorated in gold, and the altar draped in blue and white silk, making it look like a huge cake with lots of icing. Every day, parishioners brought flowers for the altar. It was a beautiful and serene sight. I knew it would please God: after all, it looked like heaven. Each morning before school, all the students went to mass. The nuns, ever vigilant, made mental notes of those who misbehaved. They didn't have to worry about me. When I was in church, all was right with the world. As an altar boy, I often got to assist the priest with the service, which gave me an incredible sense of honor and security. After all, I knew my elevated status made me one of the few chosen by God to go straight to heaven when my final day came. But on most days, I knelt with the other boys on one side of the church, the girls on the other. When mass was over, the boys went one way and the girls the other, marching in single file to their respective classrooms on opposite side of the building. The girls took their recess at 10:00 a.m., the boys at ten thirty. Lunch was taken separately as well. It all seemed quite ridiculous to me. I couldn't understand why the nuns made it seem as if it was always the boys who needed controlling. What were they scared we would do? Why didn't they just ship us off to another state if they were so worried? Whatever it was, it didn't matter much to me. Mom assured me that I was in God's heavenly graces.

One morning at mass, we heard a violent clap of thunder overhead. The angels may have been moving furniture, but they sounded truly angry. I prayed for Jesus to protect my mother and Payito. My other sister and brothers could run fast and would be able to hide from the storm. The rain didn't stop all week. I wondered when the priest would have to talk to us about building an ark. By the end of the week, I ran home to see the muddy water of the river rushing ferociously, gushing over its banks. Once before when it got like this, it had carried away our outhouse, but this time, it had taken even more. Our chickens, goats, and two of the neighbors' houses—closer to the river than ours—had been claimed. My horse, Jackie, was nowhere to be found. Things got even worse when a six-year-old boy was swept up in the river near our house. My brother Ramón fought the currents to save his life. Emerging with the little boy safe in his arms, Ramón was never forgotten by the family for his bravery and selflessness.

We all climbed onto the roof and watched the flood creep toward our house. From our vantage point, we could clearly see the raging river and all it had grabbed in its wake: tree branches and trunks, clots of land, even cars and trucks were being swept along by the river right before our eyes. We prayed to every saint we could remember to save our home. After hours of this horror, at last we saw the river begin to calm. Within a few hours, the water was in retreat.

Our house, built by my grandfather on higher ground and on stilts, fared well in the storm and had minimal damage. Jackie returned to me from out of nowhere like a faithful friend always does. But the experience of the flood had traumatized us all. How could our beautiful, peaceful river turn into such a savage and unmerciful beast? There was nothing to do but clean up the damage and move on, and everyone in the neighborhood participated in this effort.

Our family had survived the storm better than some, but we still had our share of problems. Mom continued to struggle to pay for our Catholic education, selling more of her belongings as well as her homemade tamales and tortillas. It was still barely enough to keep us in school or even meet our more basic needs. When things got desperate, Mom would send me around town to the different stores, getting a few items at each on credit. For some reason, I was never denied groceries. When no one was at the counter, I would immediately go to the rear of the store and rummage through the trash cans for discarded fruits and vegetables. I became addicted to rotten bananas.

Ultimately a realist, Mom finally had to admit that she simply couldn't afford our Catholic education anymore. Trying to come up with the tuition was causing far too much turmoil in our lives. One day, she swallowed her pride and asked Father Santos if he could waive the tuition for us. He quickly declined and warned her of the dire consequences we would experience if we did not continue in Catholic education. Deeply insulted, Mom stormed out of his office. That very day, she pulled us out of school, and the next morning, marched us to enroll in the nearby public schools. Father Santos had made the decision easy. We would all just have to forget we had previously regarded attending public school as a sin.

Mom still took us to mass the following Sunday as usual: my sisters in their best long dresses and my brothers and I in white shirts, dark pants, and fancy ties. But this Sunday was not to be a usual one. In fact, it was destined to be the most tragic day I had known since my dad's death. When we got to mass, one of the ushers asked Mom to follow him to a room on the side of the church. She gathered us together to wait close by. After a few minutes, the usher returned, pompously wielding a sign on which was printed: "La familia Carvajal está excomulgada de la Iglesia Católica por no seguir los mandatos de Dios" (The Carvajal family is excommunicated from the Catholic Church for not obeying the commandments of God). No one was even willing to offer us an explanation. There it was in black and white: we were no longer welcome in the house of Jesus. My soul crumbled. For the first time, my trust in the church had been broken. I knew I could never go back. Our family had survived the flood only to have the rain return again, beating us down and plunging us into despair.

Chapter Five

Still reeling from our humiliation, we were at least fortunate to have a free public elementary school one block from home. The school didn't have an official name but was known by the locals as *la escuela amarilla* (the yellow school). Though it was actually a dingy, washed-out color hardly resembling yellow, I knew where the name had come from. My father once told me that the school had, in fact, been a cheery yellow before it had weathered years of heavy rains. He would know since he himself had painted the school. This had struck me as quite an achievement. I was so proud of Dad when he told me this that I'd hugged and kissed him. Now I would be attending the school he once painted.

Truth be told, I had always watched the kids at the yellow school laughing and playing at recess, and it seemed as if they were having a pretty good time. I was nervous to go, but also proud to be attending such a big school. Francisco, Payito, and I were put in our respective grades. Maruca, Ramón, and José were enrolled in the public junior high school. Only Raúl, my youngest brother, refused to "sell out" and convinced Mom to enroll him at Sacred Heart, another Catholic school across the bridge. I was placed in the third grade. It was a tough year academically, especially since the emphasis on understanding English was much higher than at my old school. Socially, though, I was in heaven. I made seven new friends the first day.

That year, I also fell madly in love. This is something I didn't need or expect. I had far too many problems without this nonsense. Cipriana came into my life when my teacher Ms. Sunshine Humphrey assigned her to a seat in front of me. I became obsessed with her beautiful eyes, white teeth, and curly hair. I even loved the way she talked and dressed. To me, she was a princess of the highest royalty. I tried to impress her with my ability to spell: at least one area in which I could excel. (The Latin and French the nuns had taught me came in handy in this regard.) Cipriana thought I was a genius, and eventually, I won her over. I'd write perfectly spelled love notes to her. She made me feel cute and handsome. I started to comb a kiss-me-quick strand of hair over my forehead. The relationship was blossoming even under Ms. Sunshine's suspicious eye. Unfortunately, in the middle of the year, Cipriana moved with her family to another state. The day she said good-bye, I locked myself in the school bathroom and cried. The loss was enormous. I thought the pain would last forever. I cried for two minutes and then went out to recess.

Even with my ego inflated by the attentions of Cipriana, I couldn't stand up to the academic scrutiny of that year. Toward the middle of the year, Ms. Sunshine began to give me letters to take home to Mom, asking that she arrange a time for a conference. I threw the notes away. Switching tactics, Ms. Sunshine asked me to give her specific times my mom could come, but I always said, "Mom was sick." I sensed trouble. The last day of school, I finally paid the piper. Ms. Sunshine handed out our report cards, and there it was: FAIL stamped in big letters on the front. I had flunked the third grade. I felt sick. There was only one thing to do: refrain from giving Mom the report card. She didn't have to know everything. All my brothers and sisters, both individually and collectively, had devised just such schemes throughout the years to avoid spankings. Then I decided it would be better to simply change the ugly word on the sheet to PASS. I tried using chalk to white it out, but it was obvious what I'd done: Mom would see the grade *and* know that I'd tried to hide it. I guess she wouldn't be seeing the report card after all.

My fate was sealed. I walked home in a daze. The moment I opened the door, dear Mom was asking for my report card. "I lost it," I stammered, "but I passed to the fourth grade. I'm ready to work outside and do anything you want me to do. I'll feed the animals . . . I'll study every day . . ." As soon as I had uttered my litany of nonsensical pleas, Mom had gotten the idea. She put her shoes on, grabbed my arm, and dragged me back to school. I prayed to all the angels in heaven that Ms. Sunshine had already left. Then at least I would have the summer to figure out a way to gently break the news to Mom. But when we got to the school, the door to Ms. Sunshine's room was still open. I died a thousand times. I imagined myself now damned to purgatory for eternity, and I had earned it. Finally, Ms. Sunshine got to have her conference with Mom. It lasted three minutes. When we got home, Mom didn't disappoint: she gave me the biggest (and most well-deserved) spanking I had ever gotten. That day, for the first time, sin was not just theoretical. I truly understood the impact it could have on a person's life—my own. I felt intense shame and self-loathing for having betrayed my mother so profoundly. After Mom completed her punishment, she took me into her arms and consoled me. But because I was aware of how much I had hurt her, her love and forgiveness were almost harder to take than her fury.

After the fiasco of third grade, I decided to do what was respectable and responsible and buckle down to my academic endeavors. I repeated my entire year in the third grade. This experience, in conjunction with my previous exposure to Latin, made fourth and fifth grade a breeze. After graduating fifth grade, most kids started at the public junior high school across town. The thrill of this new mature endeavor was enough to keep us working hard as if we were preparing for admittance to college out of state. The excitement and fear of it actually made me nauseated, keeping me up many a night. I had reason to be scared. I had heard that the kids at the junior high were rich, smart, and mean. What's more, I heard they beat up new students, dragging them through the mud and setting them on fire. I heard the teachers were mean too and had a room reserved for beating kids who didn't do their homework. Rumor had it that the teachers would even call in parents to help with the beatings. This did not sound fair to me. What was worse, I had no reason to think these stories about my future school weren't true. After all, my older brothers and Maruca had all gone to school there, and they enjoyed using the worst of these stories to scare the living hell out of me. In my intolerable distress, I began to yearn for the relative safety of Catholic school and even thought for a second about begging Father Santos to take me back. But that was never going to happen: pride made it impossible. I had learned throughout my short life that people just have to take whatever lumps life deals out and adapt and assimilate into new realities.

Perhaps the thing that worried me most about the transition was showing up for my first day of school wearing the same khaki uniform I had worn not just through Catholic school, but also for my two years in third grade as well as fourth and fifth grade. It had served me well up until now, but it was demeaning to have to wear the same wardrobe for a new career. Mother even wanted me to wear the black tie with it. This was absolutely not going to happen: it would be asking to be killed by my new schoolmates—murdered in the first degree. The night before my first day of junior high, I dreamed that I had to go to school in my khaki uniform. The dream came true. I would continue to wear the same stupid pants and shirt again and again, minus the tie.

That morning, my first day of school, I jumped out of bed and hurriedly dressed in my starchy, disgusting outfit. Skipping breakfast, I was out the door, counting the steps to my death: *uno, dos, tres, cuatro.* I stopped at *cien* (one hundred). I thought it was obsessive to go beyond a hundred, so I turned instead to the *Padre Nuestro* (Our Father) and *Santa Maria Madre de Dios* (Hail Mary, Mother of God). It seemed to be working, at least to calm me down, when I came across another victim-to-be on my path. He seemed as unsure and bewildered as I was. He told me his name was Arturo, and it turned out that he was fresh out of the yellow school too. I introduced myself as Toñito since old habits die hard. How stupid of me! He sneered at me with heavy sarcasm. I immediately corrected myself and this time said my name was Antonio: a proud new name to endorse my new beginning. From then on, Arturo and I were destined to share many years of our lives navigating together through this brave new world.

Chapter Six

When we arrived at the junior high school, formally known as San Felipe School, what seemed like a million kids were hanging out in front. Sure enough, I was the one in a million wearing a uniform. When the bell sounded, loud and clear, we all filed into one of two buildings: the younger kids—like me—into the building for sixth through ninth grades, the older kids into a second building for high school where my older brothers and Maruca went. And so I, along with Arturo and thirty-five other sixth graders, began my adventure in another part of America. From the very first day, we began the inevitable process of navigating through, and forming for ourselves, a new social culture. The fact that 98 percent of my teachers at this new school were Hispanic and bilingual was a most welcomed reality.

With my new buddy Arturo at my side, I was assigned to the back row of class. It seemed like the largest kids were put up front near the teacher's desk. The school principal introduced Mr. Valen who was new to the school and would be our teacher for the year. Mr. Valen's face was beet red and dripping with sweat. If he was trying to hide his discomfort, he wasn't succeeding. He was the first Anglo teacher I had encountered that was totally ignorant of my language. I was shocked. I wondered how in the world this character had been allowed to cross the bridge and come into our world. It must have been a political appointment. He had three major strikes against him from the very beginning: he was white, he was nervous, and he had a delicate walk that looked to us as if he was tiptoeing through the tulips. This was a combination that would destroy any chances of success with this bunch of sixth graders. His fear of us was so apparent that it took no time at all for my classmates to catch on. Thirty minutes into his tenure, some of the rougher kids pushed him into a closet and locked the door. Hearing Mr. Valen's screams and the surrounding commotion, the janitor came to free him. After he had been rescued, Mr. Valen marched directly to the principal's office to turn in his resignation. We were without a teacher for two hours, and during that time, all hell broke loose. Immediately, another fight erupted between three of the largest boys in class. They fought as vigorously as the grown men I'd seen in front of the cantinas. I prayed to be home in my regimented world and even hoped that Sister Anna would make an appearance. *She* could tame these bullies into submission. She'd have them crying in no time. This was the level of respect she had always commanded: her faith was her armor. Mr. Valen, on the other hand, had been clueless as to what he was getting into. What judge had sentenced him to our class anyway? He had no idea of our needs, let alone how to begin addressing them. Unfortunately for him, it took minutes for us to sniff out his weaknesses. Fortunately for us, after Mr. Valen left, the more authoritative assistant principal Mr. Dias took over teaching the class.

My classmates weren't all a bunch of brutes: most of them were fantastic. That first morning, after the bullies had been escorted to the principal's office, we focused on learning each other's names and discussing where we lived. Several approached me to express their sincere compliments on the khaki outfit I detested. At morning recess, they asked me to join them for kickball, and in the afternoon, they invited me to join them to sing in the choir. Several of us had lunch together. I realized that some of my new friends must come from homes with refrigerators: they had fresh sandwiches and cold apples.

As always, birds of a feather flock together. The sixth-grade class soon started separating into cliques. I could see the kids starting to cluster according to their specific interests and talents. One group was going to pursue sports, another would gravitate toward music, another toward drama, and yet another would be the eggheads. Unfortunately, I didn't belong to any of the above, so I, along with kids in a similar situation, formed our own cluster. It was not necessarily a lonely place to be, just uncomfortable and awkward. I was not a member of *la crema* (the cream of the crop). Perhaps it would have been worse if school had been everything in my life. But even at this age, I had perspective on the world outside and experiences to draw upon that had nothing to do with school. I already sensed that I could learn in other ways and in other places than the classroom. Those who had loved and guided me had instilled in me a strong sense of self-awareness, self-discipline, and empathy for others, which kept me from placing too much importance on the ever-changing game of social acceptance. This was helping me survive, at least for now.

And as I was learning, relationships between people could certainly be complicated. One day, as our class was having study hall in the library, a teacher named Mr. Cal walked in with a gun. His plan was to shoot the school librarian who was also his wife. I remember we all raced out of there as fast as we could. Luckily, the police got there before he did any damage. He was arrested but evidently released temporarily because he came back to school to apologize to our class. It was then that he shared with us the outrageous chain of events leading up to his wild actions. It involved his wife's infidelity, whatever that meant. It all began when he found some love letters written and exchanged between his wife and a male student in the high school. But the affair hadn't stopped there: it ended up producing one child, one very hurt and angry husband, and a scandal that I didn't completely comprehend. I didn't even really understand why he was apologizing. What I did take from it, however, was that even adults make mistakes. And I had learned that sins should be forgiven.

Junior high breezed by. By the time I got to ninth grade, I was strongly rooted in my new world: so much so that it no longer felt new. My teacher in ninth grade was my cousin Teresita. I was pleasantly surprised to see her at the front of the classroom on the first day of the school year. Teresita was one of the five children of Aunt Manina, who had cared for my siblings and me when Dad had gotten sick. Manina had been not just an aunt but a surrogate mother. Teresita must have been only twenty-two years of age when she accepted a teaching position at my school. The impact her brilliant and talented manner of teaching had on me was lasting. I remember the admirable poise with which she articulated her expectations of her students and whatever concepts she was teaching. She made me a literary celebrity when she submitted a poem I had written for a contest sponsored by the local Lion's Club. It was selected as the best. The poem "Little Black Angels" was probably inspired by my need to express the racial tension I experienced in my own life. On the evening I received my award and prize money (five dollars), I read the poem slowly and calmly to the audience just as my cousin had instructed.

> Little black angels you never will see,
> Painted on churches or on green Christmas trees.
> You see just white angels so pure and so sweet,
> But little black angels, nowhere to see.
> Little black angels away from the white,
> We will not forsake you in your constant fight.
> I know that someday you'll win your place in the sky.

After the grand ceremony, we had punch and cookies. I accepted many expressions of congratulations. When I got home, I told Mom that I wanted to be a teacher just like my cousin and that I would write many books. There were two important insights I had gained from my experience. Through writing the poem itself, I began to understand the way in which people of color were not treated as a part of greater society. I also realized that I could write.

I was on a roll, so I decided to enter another writing assignment for a Lion's Club competition. It was to be an essay on fire prevention. A woman named Mrs. Evelyn Poag submitted the essay for me. She was one of my dad's past employers and the first Anglo I had ever met. She was also one of those people who are not even aware they are angels. Mrs. Poag had been not just an employer but an advocate of my family for years. Since the days of employing my father, she had hired José to work at one in a chain of movie theaters she owned around town. This one was a drive-in theater. She then hired Francisco, Raúl, and me to mow and tend to her elegant lawn. She would pick us up and drive us to her amazing two-story home and very thoughtfully explain her expectations for the job in detail. She spoke directly to me since she knew I was the foreman of the crew, making me feel extremely important and mature. She was always encouraging me in my studies and recognizing me for my creativity and insights.

On the days that we helped at Mrs. Poag's house, she never let us work too long without calling us in for a snack or some lunch. One day, I remember following Mrs. Poag toward the kitchen when one of her three maids interrupted her, letting her know she had a telephone call. As I waited for her return, I had a moment alone to just stand and take everything in. I scanned admiringly across the fabulous home and promised myself that someday I would have a house like hers. I would have green grass, flowers, and clean floors. I also promised myself that I would always have a refrigerator with plenty of food to feed anyone who came to my house, just like Mrs. Poag. I insisted to myself that this would not be just another dream, but that it would become a reality, just like many of the other wonderful things that had already happened to us. This was the beginning of my promise never to stay on the brink of failure but to step on toward success—whatever that meant, wherever that was.

As ninth grade flew by with school and work with Mrs. Poag, I also continued to fulfill my obligations at home. My main responsibility was to be accessible to my younger brothers and six-year-old Payito. I also had to keep an eye on Maruca, who had a strong tendency to always want to go somewhere. Many times, Mother would refer to her as *callejera* (one who is prone to hanging out in the streets). Mom would not allow Maruca to go anywhere without me as a guard. This made it very difficult for me, since I could not be at more than one place at the same time.

In the meantime, my older brothers were in high school and preparing for graduation. Ramón, the oldest, had just been recruited by the air force, and José was planning to attend junior college. Our economic situation hadn't changed much in the past couple of years; in fact, it had worsened, even with José working at the drive-in and my younger brothers and I working for Mrs. Poag. As Ramón was preparing to leave home to meet his military obligations, Mom started working more hours. Raúl and Francisco took additional jobs delivering groceries, and Raúl worked for a pharmacist delivering prescriptions on his bike around town. The days were difficult. Even as we fought to keep the family together, each of us scattered, searching in our own ways for solutions to our unmet financial and personal needs. As time went by, the household began to deteriorate as our separate and collective problems became all the more complex and difficult to solve. We still didn't have enough to eat, nor did we have money to pay the electricity or gas bill so we could stay warm on cold winter days. To my great shame, we still used an outhouse. It was impossible to invite my classmates over for a snack: invariably, they would ask to use the bathroom.

Another major embarrassment was to have my friends watch my brother José beat up on Ramón. The impact that my dad's death had on José had resulted in anger no one could control. He would assault anyone who so much as looked at him wrong. José's victim of choice, however, was Ramón. Perhaps my oldest brother's docile and submissive disposition gave José the idea that he could do anything he wanted to him, whenever he wanted. Ramón tolerated the violent thrashings. Whenever my friends visited and witnessed the merciless beatings, they asked me if they should intervene and separate José from Ramón. I would immediately respond, "Yes, do so if you are tired of living. José will definitely come after you too." I felt frustrated that I couldn't intervene in any way or could anyone else. Watching Ramón staggering away in defeat and humiliation when José was tired of beating on him made my heart break. He would quietly walk to the river and delicately reach for some water to wash off his bloody face.

By the end of junior high, at least some of my own needs were getting met. Suddenly, I found myself with more and more friends. It seemed the interpersonal skills of Maruca were readily contagious (though for every friend I made, she still made five). In terms of social status, we were in our glory. I knew that the single most important thing my new friends admired about me was my horse, Jackie, who I rode to school every day. Jackie was my mascot and best friend. Anyone who wanted to ride her could do so only with my special consent. This gave me admirable status, at least until Mom heard about it. She was concerned that Jackie would throw kids off her back and injure them. The compromise was tolerable: once a week, I could invite home a few buddies to play with Jackie. These buddies became lifelong friends: Joel, Richard, Junior, and my cousin Estela.

Jackie still got out and about on occasion. I took her on trips around the barrio to visit Joel and Estela when they weren't able to visit us. Joel's parents always greeted us with open arms, ready with an apple for Jackie and a meal for me. At Estela's house, we were equally welcomed. Estela's father was my uncle Juan, my dad's brother, and her mother was Aunt Carolina. Any morning that we stopped by, Aunt Carolina had a breakfast burrito for me and vegetables she had saved just for Jackie. Estela was the youngest of four daughters in the household, and for some reason, she welcomed herself into my life. Perhaps she was enthralled by my friend Jackie, or maybe she saw me as a brother figure she never had. Anyway, I didn't have a choice in the matter. She would advise me which girls to clear away from, which guys were bullies, and which places not to go to. If I ran into problems of any kind, Estela would usually be there to intervene. I never saw her physically beat up anyone on my behalf, but I knew she would go to any lengths to protect me if she felt I needed it.

These great friends were a highlight of my time in ninth grade. They knew me well, accepted me, and liked me. I didn't take this for granted. Mom always stressed that unless you were *una monedita de oro* (a gold coin), not everyone would necessarily like you. That was just how life went, and she was right. The same year that I made so many friends, I encountered my first real enemy: my math teacher Mrs. Tellez. I disliked her condescending demeanor toward me. She frequently made it clear to the rest of my classmates—in her vociferous, screeching voice—that I was late to class again. She did this only to embarrass me. She did not care for me, and I was determined to be trouble for her. I refused to learn from her and focused instead on making her teaching days a living hell. One of my favorite tactics was to excuse myself to the bathroom where I would proceed to eat colored chalk I had smuggled from the classroom, tainting my mouth blue like a monster's. I would time my reentrance for maximum effect. I always knew the perfect moment to jump back through the door baring my ghoulish fangs to the delight of my classmates and the terror of Mrs. Tellez. Because she shut out any hope I had of learning math, I shut down every opportunity for her to teach. She destroyed every ounce of respect I could have felt for her and damaged any appreciation I had for math for years to come. My reign of terror ceased when Mom caught wind of my misbehavior and applied her own disciplinary methods at home. That got the message across. She reminded me that I was not *una monedita de oro*, so I needed to learn to handle rejection and have tolerance for others. Though a harsh lesson to face at the time, I would remember it well as I got older and had to learn to cope with the demeaning realities of racial discrimination. In that sense, life had just begun. But for now, I focused on the many things that were wonderful in my life: my other teachers, my friends, and my horse.

In a flash, graduation from junior high had arrived. The theme of our eighth-grade graduation was "My Isle of Golden Dreams." In anticipation of this momentous occasion, I wore a new coat and tie for the entire last month of school. On the day of graduation, again donning my winning outfit, I was on top of the world. I had my first real girlfriend, Romelia, by my side: a beautiful and special person with whom I would go on to share my high school years. It had been a good year. With my family now receiving monthly funds from the government for Ramón's military service, some of the pressure on us had lifted. For now, everything was all right, and it was time to applaud and celebrate yet another powerful transition in my life.

Chapter Seven

I was now on to high school, with all the challenges that come with this stage of growing up. Academics became more complex, and romantic relationships were reconfigured every few months. First, Joel was going with Joelda, Arturo with Dalinda, Roberto with Enedina, Antero with Becky, Junior with Delma, and I with Romelia. Then in three months, most of these relationships had changed. This was the way it was. Undoubtedly, it's the way every high school in America was and still is. Promises of true love were abundant but tenuous. My relationship with Romelia was ongoing yet sporadic. Because of our work schedules, we didn't always have time to devote to each other. I had been hired at the drive-in theater where José worked and had to work evenings. My job was to pick up the food wrappers and bottles that people threw out of their car windows while watching the movie. Though it wasn't allowed, some people even drank beer in their cars. I guess Dad wasn't the only one who hid his beer. Anyway, despite my somewhat lowly position, I found my job lucrative. Besides picking up the awful mess people left, I found quarters and half dollars that made me almost rich.

Movies became my life. I often chose to stay late to watch the feature even if I'd seen it before. By this time, I was leaving Jackie at home in favor of transportation by vehicle: I now shared a car with Maruca. I would watch the movies from our car and wonder how these beautiful American actors and actresses had come to speak English so well. I memorized the lines they spoke. Through their stories, I also learned about love. There were so many idealized versions of it presented on the screen that I often wondered if I would ever find that one person with all the ingredients for a happy life. I thought perhaps having several partners to fulfill these challenging criteria was the way to go, and some movies didn't dissuade this strategy either. It occurred to me why in some cultures men are allowed to have multiple wives. In our lives, we want it all. We want sexual passion, we want earnest friendship and care, we want someone to take care of us, we want a companion in our struggle for financial security. We want someone to give us children and be a good parent to them. We want a person who listens when we talk, who cooks, who mows the lawn, who can dance and hopefully sing. Most of all, we expect to find a person who is in love with us and can't live a day in our absence. My goodness! Maybe it does take more than one partner to meet these incredible expectations.

My obsession with movies and the lofty questions they inspired had to be put on hold every morning when reality set in. Home and school responsibilities wouldn't wait, and all eyes were upon me to do what was expected. Our teachers knew about the economic disadvantages that my family and the families of my classmates faced, but maintained their academic and social expectations of us nonetheless. In fact, it often seemed as if they and our parents watched us like hawks, setting up stringent parameters that we dared not violate. They must have used their monthly parent-teacher conferences to develop strategies to shield us from our flaws. Despite this, the inevitable happened several times. Serious relationships eventuated in early pregnancies, early marriages, and discontinuance of school. It was difficult to maintain confidentiality and privacy in such a small group, and the gossip mill buzzed with stories of those who had fallen victim to their own bad decisions. In an effort to protect her own, Mom drove home the message of "Cuidanse" (Take care of yourselves). This meant being honest and alert, trusting minimally, and watching out for bad company. "El diablo nunca duerme ni toma siestas" (The devil never sleeps or takes naps), she would warn. She cautioned us about betrayal by friends and even people that we thought loved us. She emphasized the "sleeping with the enemy" concept over and over again. Sometimes I wondered if she was being too cynical and suspicious of people. I didn't like to live my life this way.

As the eldest daughter, I sometimes think Maruca got the worst of it. From as early as junior high, she was constantly warned by Mom of the long and torturous journey she would have to embark upon as a female.

Focusing specifically on Maruca's physical development—much more so than any of the boys—Mom's message about reaching maturity wasn't exactly comforting. "El pecado de Eva" (Eve's sin) was what Mom called the monthly bleeding and related pain that Maruca would have to endure for many years of her life. I remember being appalled that the ridiculous sin of eating that apple in the Garden of Eden would haunt Maruca forever. I admired my sister for her courage and acceptance of this unfathomable reality. Mom also described to Maruca the nature of childbirth and the extreme suffering that goes with it. If it was her goal to scare my sister away from the idea of getting pregnant, the plan was exquisitely executed.

Sometimes it is difficult to be grateful for circumstances in our lives. I had planned to spend my four years in high school enjoying the many social and academic pursuits I had thought were waiting for me there. But the social competition became brutally evident and the academic competition even worse. It was getting hard just to keep my head above water. Each day after school, I went to work at the theater or to one of my other jobs at a grocery store and a restaurant. But not before completing my duties at home. Since Mom was working until later, I had to be home when the rest of the kids arrived from school. Maruca too did her part to help out in Mom's absence. Not the best cook, my sister worked very hard to prepare dinner for all of us, which was nonetheless difficult to eat. One day, she proudly prepared a stew with onions, carrots, and anything else she could find. As she lifted the huge skillet off the stove, she lost her grip, and the entire contents went flying all over the kitchen floor. She gathered everything back up, rinsed it, and served us her watered-down meal. Mom enjoyed Maruca's attempts to please her. As for us kids, we'd go to the river after dinner to look for figs and berries to compensate for the meal we'd skipped.

With all that was going on, completing homework each evening was difficult, and not just for lack of time. Some weeks we had electricity in the house (if we paid the bill), and some weeks we lived in the dark. So whatever homework we wanted to complete needed to be done before nightfall. Winter evenings were the most difficult because we also battled the cold. All the heat we had came from a woodburning stove, which barely warmed the room where we congregated.

Though we all struggled to work and still stay afloat in school, José seemed to have found a way to have it all. His natural talent in sports was a huge asset. He was a boxer as well as the quarterback for the Mustangs, our high school football team. He had also become a manager at the drive-in theater. Typically, he worked from five to ten o'clock in the evening, but during football season, Mrs. Poag—angel unaware—would allow him to work fewer hours to accommodate his schedule. José was a star and everything I wanted to be. But who was I? High school years are demanding for everyone. Everyone desires to be a part of something: to belong to a club, play a sport, be recognized for academics, be in with the popular crowd, be the most handsome or beautiful, or most likely to succeed. Of course, the most honorable status is "best all around": that person who can win valedictorian *and* be the most popular kid in the class. But when a young person doesn't find himself to be a part of anything, the urge to escape from himself dominates his existence. When I realized I wouldn't be validated in any of these categories, I often wondered what would happen to me.

Usually, when you ask a question out of sincere fear and desperation, the answer slaps you in the face. Out of what seems like no choice, a new and unseen direction emerges. Having worked at the drive-in picking up trash and cleaning bathrooms almost every evening since I was thirteen, I was finally promoted to work in the concession stand. It was an elite privilege. I prepared popcorn and was eventually allowed to serve hot dogs. I even branched out and began making chili sauce of my own special recipe to smother on the dogs. It was such a big hit that it became a permanent concession-stand treat. Surely this was a sign that I was destined for great things.

A year later, I was promoted to assistant manager. I had to open the concession stand, prepare the food for the evening, then close and clean the stand after 10:00 p.m. It was also my job to hire and supervise the concession-stand workers, many of which were fellow students from my school. When my classmates learned of my prestigious position, the word spread like wildfire. Giving free movie passes and extra popcorn to all of them gave me a visibility at school I had never had before. Everyone knew me and appreciated my role. On Tuesday nights, it seemed as if the entire school made their way to the drive-in. A carload of people cost one dollar, so they piled in ten to a car. My name became synonymous with success and intelligence. Even my teachers referred to me when speaking of the importance of diligence and work ethic. I was invited to join the football team, the band, the drama club, and the Who's Who Among Students program. But I couldn't capitalize on my newfound popularity by joining any of these because of my commitment to work. And so even as I was admired, I still found myself outside of the social network formed through extracurriculars.

Nonetheless, I still had good friends, and together we came up with our own extracurriculars. Joel, Junior, and Richard often stayed with me at the drive-in while I completed my closing tasks as quickly as possible. We'd take the leftover hotdogs and popcorn and head off in my car, joined by some of the girls from school. We'd find a place to park and blast music from the car radio, dancing and having a good time until way past eleven.

The routine was fun, but soon it got boring. We needed something new and exciting to do. I suggested we drive to the cemetery and visit the graves in the dark of night. My dare would be scary fun. We all got out of the car and walked around long enough to get spooked. Then we ran back to the car like scared rabbits. We piled in and peeled away. However, in our excitement, we failed to notice we had left a very petrified friend behind. Delma was so determined to catch us that she grabbed hold of the back bumper for dear life, and we dragged her along screaming for a short distance. When my partners in crime saw what was going on, they yelled at me to stop. It was too late: there lay Delma, alive, but with a broken and badly mangled leg. The fear in each of us grew as we imagined explaining to our parents the awful mess we had created. For now, there was nothing to do but run to get Delma's family.

Though we hoped to keep the accident a secret from our parents, this was, of course, not to be. When I arrived home that very night right before midnight, Mom had already heard the news. She was waiting on the porch with a belt in her hand. The next morning, the whole cemetery crew was called in for a conference with the school principal. Our parents were also there, waiting to hear the lies. We had no choice but to tell the truth, the whole truth, and nothing but the truth—so help us God. God didn't help us much that day. Mom took my car keys from me, and each of us had to compensate Delma's family for her medical expenses. We were the talk of the school, and not in the way we had hoped.

Despite my transgressions with my friends, I remained a dutiful employee. Soon I was promoted to manager of the concession stand. Every night at closing time, after cleaning duties were done, it was my job to count the money made in concessions and take it to the downtown theater where it was collected. Though I had gained my driving privileges back, Maruca still had the car on some nights, so I performed my duty on foot. It was on just such a night that I set out on my walk with the sack of money securely in my hands. I actually enjoyed these late-night walks because they provided a solitary time to review new English words and songs I had learned from the movies. I also had a chance to recall the events of the day and think about what I had to do that night to prepare for my classes. I would even daydream about what the next year would bring. But on this quiet evening, after I left the money at the downtown office, I started walking across the bridge toward home. I sensed someone following me. I glanced behind me and saw a man: it was the same man I had noticed standing in front of the theater when I had left. I started walking faster, and so did he. Then I started to run, but it was too late. The man grabbed me, threw me to the river bank under the bridge, and again ran after me to the edge of the river. He finally caught up with me, grabbed me by the throat, and started strangling me. He wanted the keys to the office. He let go of my neck long enough for me to utter a response. I tried to scream but couldn't. He grabbed my head and started pounding it on the rocks. I felt blood gushing into my eye. I struggled free, took a rock, and hit him over the head. I had never been a marathon runner, but that night, I became one. I ran frantically back over the bridge and, through the night, my attacker right at my heels. Once we got to my territory, he became a clumsy runner, unfamiliar with the landscape. I ran to a neighbor's house, screaming with panic. From inside, I heard my neighbor's voice telling his wife to get the gun. The would-be thief heard too: he ran away just like that.

The next day and throughout the next week, my friends at school all congratulated me for my great escape. My assailant had been apprehended by the local police. He was a soldier stationed at a nearby military base who had been at the drive-in that evening, had seen me close the concession stand with the money, and had decided to make his move. After that episode, I had consent from Mom to buy my own car for safety's sake. But the sharp green convertible had the added benefit of giving me even more prestige with my friends, who I happily continued to card all over the neighborhood. Unfortunately, I still had to share it with Maruca, who now preferred my new car to the old one.

My adventures at the drive-in aside, I still walked through the halls of high school confused as to where I belonged. With no time for extracurriculars, I had given up on that dream, and academics—for the most part—didn't hold my interest at all. Geography was out of my reach. Math was out of the picture. History was boring. I couldn't care less about who discovered the New World: I never saw it and didn't have any interest in this fictitious land. John Smith and the rest of them were too far away from my reality to matter much. The only class that succeeded in sparking my curiosity was an English class taught by Mrs. Pasley. Through little fault of their own, most of my teachers just couldn't get through to me, but this individual touched a chord in my heart each time she read a poem. There was something poised and elegant about her—something dramatic about the way she looked at her students and held the book in her hands as if she were cradling a child. She caressed the story with her lovely voice, prancing delicately back and forth across the room as she read. One day, she read something that took hold of my entire heart and soul, stoking my love for literature. I know she looked straight at me as she read Wordsworth's poem:

> Though nothing can bring back the hour
> Of splendor in the grass, of glory in the flower;
> We will grieve not, rather find
> Strength in what remains behind.

This passage rattled my emotions so fiercely that it made me cry. The poem empowered me to focus not on the sadness and regrets of my childhood, but on the beauty of those days with my loved ones, by the river, and in my beloved placita. After class, I walked up to Mrs. Pasley's desk and glanced at the book from which she'd read. It was heavy and awkwardly huge. I felt her looking at me and slipped quickly out the door. The next day at the beginning of class, Mrs. Pasley collected our homework assignments. We were supposed to have written a single paragraph about the passage she had read us the previous day. I hadn't gotten the assignment done, so she asked me to stay after class to complete it. When class was over, I rushed out the door even more quickly than before. The following day, determined to get all her students to complete their missing homework assignments, Mrs. Pasley announced that she planned to arrange conferences with our parents to review in detail the various assignments we had missed. That afternoon, I messily scribbled out my paragraph and put it on her desk. The next day, she returned my paper marked with the largest A I had ever seen. I was confused and unsure, at first, how to interpret the grade especially since she wrote a note to see her after class. Again, I ran out. That Friday, Mrs. Pasley called my mom in for a conference. I knew I was in serious trouble. Talking to Mom but looking straight at me, she began to speak. She said I had a "rare love for literature" and was a "talented and smart young man" with "sensitive and mature insights." Wow! This was me? These were the highest compliments any teacher had ever given me. Mom stood up and hugged me until I felt oxygen deprived. This single meeting marked the beginning of a new and scholarly path for me.

I had finally found a passion for something academic. I began to read whatever stories and essays I could get my hands on at any opportunity I had. Most of what I read was complicated and unclear to me: the concepts far too intricate to understand. One day, Mrs. Pasley asked me if I was interested in entering an oratory contest organized by the Literary Club at school. Each contestant was to read a piece of literature of their choosing. I had been reading an essay by an American author who wrote during what Mrs. Pasley called the romantic period. I agreed to read this essay for the contest under the condition that I could leave by 2:30 p.m. to work at the drive-in. She promised I would be the second reader. The essay I had chosen was "Self-Reliance" by Ralph Waldo Emerson. Unlike some of the confusing readings I was struggling with, this essay spoke directly to my heart. It sent a clear message about the importance of maintaining one's individuality and not being preoccupied about what others think. My hands trembled as I read:

> What I must do is all that concerns me, not what the people think. This rule, equally arduous in actual and in intellectual life, may serve for the whole distinction between greatness and meanness.

All I could hear was my own voice. Within a few moments, I had the guts to look up to see my friends sitting in awe of my presentation. Romelia was beaming with pride. I smiled at them and continued:

> It is the harder because you will always find those who think they know what your duty is better than you know it. It is easy in the world to live after the world's opinion; it is easy in solitude to live after our own; but the great man is he who, in the midst of the crowd, keeps with perfect sweetness the independence of solitude.

When I had finished the last lines of the essay, the applause was so loud that my heart beat out of my chest. I don't even remember who won the contest—it wasn't important. Reading my essay had lifted me to a scholarly level that felt incredibly good. I felt fulfilled by the affirmations of my classmates, but more than this, I was deeply affected by my ability to understand and impart Emerson's important message. They were words I would take with me forever. Even then, I knew I would need them.

Chapter Eight

By junior year in high school, I was beginning to see the world around me in ways I'd never noticed before. My eyes were opening to the discrimination endured by Mexicans in the San Felipe District. It had always been there: a painful reality experienced in so many ways by our parents and their parents before them. For us as the younger generation, awakening to this fact happened slowly. As a kid, I had always wondered why we went to school separately from the Anglo kids across the bridge, but to me, it didn't really matter. I was perfectly content with my school, my barrio, and my family. As the proverb says, "Fish don't know they live in water." I didn't need or want anything other than what I had. Perhaps ignorance truly is bliss. I never thought in political or broader social terms: that was somebody else's war. However, all this changed one day when Maruca, a staunch realist, shared an event that made me privy to the insidious racism that had always been an inescapable part of our lives.

She had heard the story in her Texas government class taught by Mr. West, a talented Anglo teacher who won his students' respect with his ability to draw them into discussion about topics relevant to their lives. Mr. West had presented his class with a real occurrence. Johnny Paredes, Ramiro Reyes, Wow Lopez, and Frank Sanchez—all one grade ahead of Maruca—had gone to the Del Rio Municipal Public Swimming Pool, which, like many public facilities in the city of Del Rio in those days, was reserved for whites only. Banned from the pool despite paying taxes just like the Anglos, Mexicans were relegated to swim in the "pigpen," as some of the bigoted whites called my precious river. And so, no sooner had the three boys plunged into the pool than all the *gringos* got out like trained penguins. The lifeguard informed the boys that they were in violation of city regulations and ordered them to leave. "*Mes'kins,* go back to your pigpen!" some of the penguins yelled as the boys left.

Mr. West challenged the students to compare the federal laws that at that time protected segregation to the tenants of the U.S. Constitution, the standard by which all national law was to be measured. He encouraged the class to ponder how the current laws would have to change if they were found to be in violation of the Constitution, focusing on the concept of due process imbedded in the Bill of Rights. Mr. West reminded his class that whenever citizens pay taxes—in this case, city taxes—they have a legal right to use public facilities. By taking abstract concepts of legality and making them real, Mr. West drew Maruca and his other students into a dialogue about their own experiences and how they pertained to the subject of equal rights.

As for the boys from the pool, they had shared their experience firsthand with Mr. West, who, in turn, urged them to communicate the incident to their parents so that action could be taken. At the time I first heard the story, I wondered why these boys were making such a big deal about swimming where they were not welcome, especially since the river was cleaner, fresher, and healthier than the stupid swimming pool anyway. Later on, of course, I realized this was not the point. There was more at stake than just a dip in the pool. The boys' and their families' act of speaking out was an important step in paving the way toward racial integration. What they were fighting for was the very spirit of equal protection described in the Fourteenth Amendment. As fate would have it, the same year I graduated high school, Congress passed the Civil Rights Act of 1957. That year, San Felipe High School and the Anglo schools across the river were integrated into a single district known as Del Rio School District. At the time, both the Anglo and Mexican populations found this change difficult to accept. Change does not come easily for anyone. Only time would reveal how these developments would contribute to the economic and social enrichment of both cultures for generations to come.

But at the present moment, I still had my own high school career to complete. Now in my junior year, I was beginning to think about what lay beyond high school. Several of my friends who had graduated the year before had moved with their entire families to San Jose, California. Some were back briefly to wrap up loose ends, selling things they had left behind in Texas before returning to their new homes. They talked with the enthusiasm of early settlers about their discoveries in the West. They spoke of its glamour, beauty, and riches. They had returned from their gold rush in California with new cars, clothes, and money left over. Some of the families had even purchased their own houses there. Joel had gone to California but had come back to complete high school. He spoke of the many opportunities his family had found and urged me to take my family there too. Leaving my placita would not be easy: I knew that. But my entrepreneurial spirit—recognizing the potential of it all—was beginning to stir. As my returned friends described, the riches in California came from the many work opportunities available in fields that yielded the most prized produce in the country. You had only to choose the crop you wanted to harvest. Peaches, apricots, strawberries, cherries, plums, beans, lettuce, cabbage, oranges, and lemons all grew on this rich land. The list was endless, and you could eat to your heart's content, or at least until your stomach could no longer stand it. This was too much happiness. The larger the family, the better the opportunity to get rich. After hearing such incredible tales of success, my days and nights were spent wondering how we could get to this fantastic place. When I spoke to Mom about the stories my friends had shared, she told me that she too had heard about it.

That spring, José graduated from high school and immediately married his high school sweetheart. Within weeks, they too decided to venture west to begin their new life near San Jose. That summer, I asked Mom if I could go visit my brother and scout the situation in California. Incredibly, she agreed. I made the long road trip to San Jose with Joel and his brother. I worked for two months in the fields and returned with three new shirts, two pairs of jeans, a new pair of shoes, and presents for the entire family. I had also been able to save five hundred dollars that I hoped to invest in orchards to grow my own fruit and *really* get rich. With some of the money, Mom paid utility bills and bought groceries. She was shocked by the idea that there might be an alternative to the misery and poverty we would surely face for the rest of our lives in Del Rio. There was hope: the dream of making it elsewhere.

Although Mom was now convinced that leaving would be best for all of us, she made it very clear that my graduation from high school was not to be compromised. But with the seed of a new life planted in my head, I spent most of senior year dreaming of adventures to come. The entire year was agonizing. I kept my job at the drive-in, but now it was utterly secondary in my mind. I struggled with the thought of leaving my friends and saying good-bye to Romelia. I tried to grasp what it would be like to abandon our home, the river, and the placita with all the significant memories they held. Mom's reality was a bit different from mine. She kept herself focused on the practical aspects of preparation and wondered how we could accommodate the whole family in a two-door convertible with a malfunctioning roof. I silently wondered how we would get through a rain or hailstorm in this precarious vehicle. The answer was simple: we couldn't. We traded cars with a farmer—an old friend of my dad—who had a four-door Ford with eight thousand more miles on it than the convertible. To prevent the mileage from adding up anymore before the trip (should it become a reality), we drove the car only locally and for errands that were absolutely necessary.

Despite my preoccupation with the big changes that lay ahead, senior year also awakened in me a need to make my mark before I left. I became determined to campaign for one of the slots in the Who's Who club. To qualify, it was time for me to give extracurriculars a try. I had to make a lot of creative changes in my busy schedule at the drive-in, but I knew it was now or never to make something special of myself. I tried out for football. That effort lasted twenty minutes. I was too frail to even bear the weight of the shoulder pads. I volunteered for water boy; I was too skinny for that too. When the school band director Mr. Alaniz heard of my desperation to join a club, he recruited me to play in the band. My instrument was the clarinet. In my own head, I was the Benny Goodman of the era—the envy of all. In reality, I made second chair but was then demoted and eventually reassigned to play snare drum. I couldn't master the critical skill of this ridiculous instrument either. I finally got the message, left the band, and went to work my regular hours at the drive-in. Apparently, my untapped musical talents would go undiscovered for now.

Ignoring the limitations for my credentials, three of my most musically gifted friends and precious mentors—Dolores, Velma, and Leticia—managed to convince Mr. Alaniz to let me march with the band in the homecoming parade. But when I put on my uniform pants for the first time that day, they kept slipping off my scrawny frame. My mentors came to the rescue. They tactfully pinned my pants to my T-shirt to hold them up long enough to make it through the march down the main street of town. The only song we could play was "Cherry Pink and Apple Blossom White." As we marched down the long street, I felt like an emerging star. Suddenly, I felt the pins holding my pants slide right out. Mr. Alaniz, marching beside me, saw my pants going south and thought fast, reassigning me to hold a flag with one hand and my uniform bottoms with my other. It looked like my musical celebrity was to be short-lived after all.

The month of high school graduation finally arrived, and the news of who was slated for awards was out: Valedictorian, Salutatorian, Best Athlete, Most Handsome, Most Beautiful, Most Poetic, etc. I was not included in the cast of winners. My role was to applaud. I was proud of my friends for their achievements, but I also felt envious and isolated. I just wanted more of what I could not have. It was and had always been impossible. I could not be a scholar, a social butterfly, a surrogate parent, and a family provider all at the same time. I couldn't even manage to be me: whoever that was.

Nonetheless, I was grateful for all the support I had been given during my high school years. I realized how important my friends were to me. All of them, regardless of their important status in school, accepted and loved me for the person I was. My teachers were equally respectful and encouraging. They had consistently offered me affirmation and acknowledgment for my role as a student *and* family provider. They were extremely proud that I had managed to make it to graduation successfully. This combined regard for me ultimately seemed sufficient. In many ways, gathering up all the support from others during this time made me realize how fortunate I had been through the difficult years since I had lost my dad.

As graduation neared, I was also compelled to reflect on the unique things that had held significance for me throughout my years in high school. I had found joy and fulfillment in a million little things and discovered many opportunities to celebrate life. After years of literal hunger, these days I could eat all the popcorn and chili dogs I wanted. I could watch any movie I ever wanted to see and learn the powerful dialects spoken by Clark Gable, Olivia de Havilland, Peter O'Toole, Rock Hudson, Fred Astaire, Gene Kelley, and Lana Turner. They had become my pals. I researched everything I could about their personal affairs and intricate love lives. I watched some movies so many times that I had memorized the lines, practicing them to myself as I walked home from work. From these films, I had also learned the songs of Nat King Cole, Tony Bennett, The Platters, and Elvis. I sang them out loud on quiet, lonely evenings.

I often wondered about the movie industry and how writers could dream up the fascinating plots. What creative and brilliant minds they must have to bring forth a slice of life for a fictitious character and make it seem so real. Never was this observation so vivid for me than the day I walked to Mrs. Poag's downtown theater and saw the bright marquee blinking down at me: "Splendor in the Grass, starring Natalie Wood and Warren Beatty." For goodness sake! The title was taken from a line in Wordsworth's "Ode: Intimations of Immorality," the poem read by Mrs. Pasley that had touched me so deeply. I knew the entire thing by heart. "Thanks to the human heart by which we live. Thanks to its tenderness, its joys, and fears." I walked into the theater armed with a large popcorn, two chili dogs, and a jumbo soda.

The film addressed the illusions of love and explored themes like social status, parental control, attempted suicide, losing a loved one, and ultimately, accepting this loss and moving on. "We will grieve not, rather find strength in what remains behind." As I watched the story unfold on the screen, the words of the poem were newly powerful: true not just in my own life, but in the lives of so many people. I was touched again by this message and fell in love a thousand times with Natalie Wood. Years later, when she drowned in real life, my grief remained for many days. But at this particular moment, walking out of the theater, Wordsworth's lines were again fresh in my mind. And they would stay with me as I prepared for the day I would leave the placita and the people I had loved throughout my life forever.

My mother as a young girl entertaining in her parents' restaurant.
She loved music, costumes and audience acclaim from a very early age.

My mother Consuelo (foreground, younger) and her only sibling Amparo
(standing behind railing).
They had a close relationship when young girls which became strained
after the death of their parents.

Amparo, 'Payito', before and after

My mother and father on their wedding day—so very young and serious

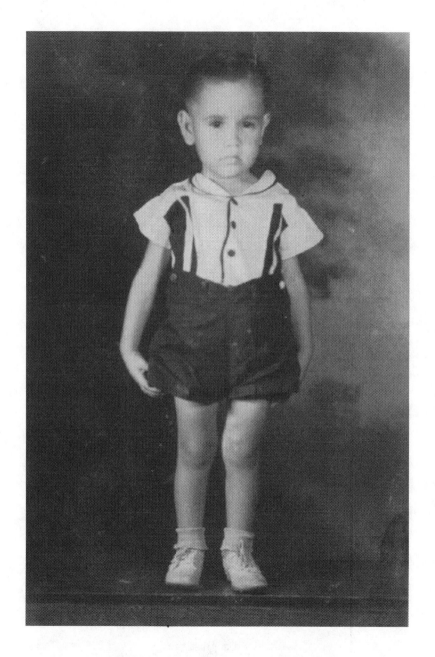

Me, even at three, a very serious lad

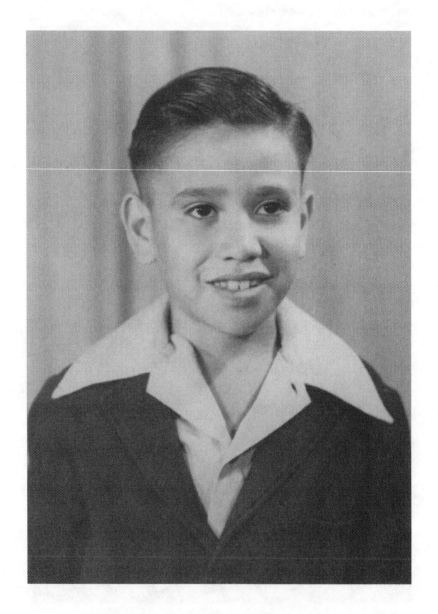

Tonito—an aspiring teacher

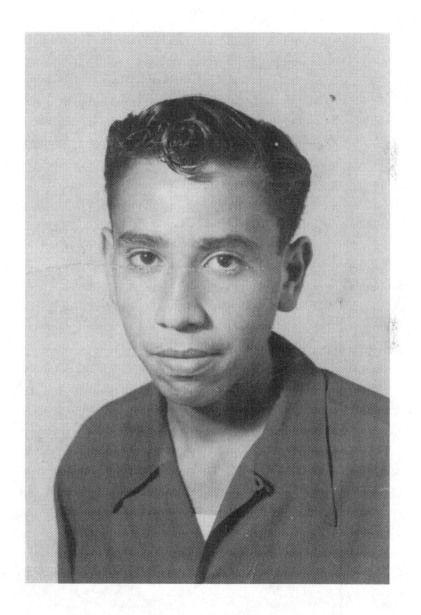

A skinny, serious and sensitive grade-schooler
after my father's death; a difficult time

Tony with horse and siblings

My older siblings—Joe, Maggie, Me and Raymond, 1941

Joe and Raymond, my two handsome brothers,
on their First Communion Day

My younger siblings, Raul, Payito, and Fransico

My cousins—Terry (later my high school English teacher), Berta, and Frenchy

Fun on our beloved river—our center of friendships,
imaginative play and bathing.
Frenchy, Berta, Tony, Terry, and Maggie

The Plaza—the center of social activity, courting, business,
and gossip in Del Rio

Celebration of neighbors

Part Two:
The Grapes of Wrath

In the evening a strange thing happened: the twenty families became one family, the children were the children of all. The loss of home became one loss, and the golden time in the West was one dream.

—John Steinbeck, *The Grapes of Wrath*

Chapter Nine

After my graduation and a month of solid preparation, it was time to go. We planned to leave at the crack of dawn on a Sunday morning. Our transportation, the old Ford, had to be reliable. I checked the oil, water, tires, and wipers. We had to be certain that all the luggage, which we'd packed mostly in cardboard boxes, could fit in the trunk. This was when the war started. Payito wanted to take one of our three cats. (I found myself thankful that her little lamb, Nicky Bunger Ray, was no longer a subject for argument as we had feasted on her one difficult Easter.) Mom wanted to take her box of records, her two dresses, and enough food for the nearly two-thousand-mile journey. Maruca wanted to take her dresses, shoes, and all the souvenirs and mementos she'd collected over the years. I wanted to take my guitar, Frank wanted to take his guitar, and *Raúl* wanted to take his bike. This is when the commander in chief in me took charge. I was the driver, so I would dictate who took what. After heated negotiations, we agreed to leave the bike and one guitar: mine. By this time, the cat, spooked and smarter than any of us, had scampered away never to be found again.

Dawn soon turned into midmorning and we still hadn't left. This was unfortunate since the day was already heating up, and we would be traveling without air-conditioning. One thing that was actually on our side was that the car had no glass over the windows so we could get maximum breeze and relief from the hundred-degree heat. Mom and I took financial inventory and concluded we had a total of $52.80. There was no way we would make it on this. It was time to get creative. Our elderly neighbor Señora Regina had been hoping to ride with us to the land of riches if we had enough room. She had offered twenty-five dollars for the fare, which we were able to negotiate up to thirty dollars. She wanted to take her five—and seven-year-old grandsons too and offered to pay an additional twenty-five dollars: two-for-one since they were so small. Mom thought this was sound business. Since she thought she could pull this, I decided to invite Richard along. Richard also wanted to see if the promises of the West were for real and paid a discounted rate of twenty dollars under the condition that he help me drive. I wasn't used to highway driving or really any driving outside of city limits. Now we definitely had a full load, or rather, a serious overload. I hated to face the fact that there had to be limits to our madness. I counted a crew of ten: Mom, Maruca, Frank, Raúl, Payito, Regina, the two nameless boys, Richard, and me—the captain of this unfortunate vessel.

The plan was that, on our way out of town, we would drive around and bid farewell to our old life: the placita, the school I had grown to love, the church, as well as all our friends and relatives. Instead, I insisted we get on the road destined to lead us toward our new life of opportunity and prosperity. I felt like crying when we finally departed, but was simply too tired for tears. I was driving twenty miles per hour and couldn't imagine wanting to go any faster. The rear of the car almost scraped the ground from all the weight. Maruca kept prodding me to go faster so we could at least get there in the next three months. After ten miles on the highway, I asked Richard to take the wheel. He pushed the pedal to the metal, and in seconds, we were going forty miles per hour. This is when we had our first flat tires: plural. There was one in front, one in back, and no spare. All eyes were upon me to solve the problem. We spent most of our travel money at a used-tire store back in town and off we went again.

The next day, we had another flat, this time in the desert. Richard laid it out bluntly. "We have too much fucking weight on this piece of shit. Why the hell did you invite all these damned people? That old lady was news to me. Why did you bring her and those damned kids? There's no room! Those little bastards are going to suffocate sitting under the vents like that. There are exhaust fumes coming in from the muffler."

"Listen, you lazy bastard," I shot back. "The old lady is a respectable woman and a well-paying customer. If anyone should get out of my car, it's you."

Right about then, we had our fourth flat tire. With no money left, we did the only thing we could: we rolled into the next little town and stole a tire off a car parked along the street. Luckily, Señora Regina still had some cash, so we started taking out small loans to pay for gas. It was at this point that Richard asserted his authority. He told everyone they had to discard any nonessential cargo or we wouldn't make it. With his help, we tossed several boxes and sacks of trinkets and toys. Richard even tried to get Mom to surrender her cosmetic box. Maruca warned him that he was asking for it: Mom would sooner beat him to a pulp than allow him to mess with her most precious possession. After the consolidation was complete, Richard took the remaining linens and clothing, wrapped them up, and neatly tied the bundles to the top of the car, giving everyone room to breathe. We were on our way once more.

Although Richard's efforts allowed us to carry on, nothing could eliminate the sheer misery of the journey. As we continued to drive straight through the next day, no one spoke. The car seemed like a stifling tomb. It was beginning to look as if we would die right there in our seats. The cruel desert sun depleted every drop of energy left in us. Francisco, sitting in the backseat next to Mom, finally broke the silence. "Flaco, Mom is dying . . . she's vomiting . . . she can't breathe! Stop the car! She's really dying!"

Well, she wasn't exactly dying, but she clearly *was* in a bad way: sweating, trembling, and gasping for breath. Suddenly, she forced her head out the window and expelled a rancid apple pie. She had bought the pie the day before and had been nibbling small chunks of it without anyone noticing. The smothering heat had, of course, spoiled the pie and given her food poisoning, accompanied by intense cramping, shaking, and vomiting. We pulled the car over and poured water on her face, propping her up against an abandoned truck until her breathing calmed down. Incredible to think that all because of a bad dessert, our usually stoic and unrelenting Amazon of a mother was finally left reliant on those who loved her.

As we sat there by the side of the road, it seemed our chances of reaching the promised land were fading. Looking up at the clear blue sky, I saw buzzards circling overheard. "You bastards aren't getting us yet!" I yelled. "Scram! Find your meal somewhere else! We're gonna make it!"

As we drove through most of the afternoon, at last it began to happen: out of the dusty brown desert emerged small green trees and bushes. A little while later, we came upon a fresh stream. We immediately pulled over and raced into the gushing water, screaming for joy. We bathed and drank as if we'd never seen water in our lifetimes, and it seemed as if we hadn't. All at once, the arguments, accusations, and insults of the past few days were forgotten, replaced with jubilation and true appreciation for each other. We had made it!

Well, almost. First, we had to cross through the city of Los Angeles so we could continue north, braving the jumble of freeways, horrific traffic, and impatient motorists honking at our overburdened boat the entire way. Maruca thought they were all waving welcome: "Bien Venidos!" Surely it couldn't have been the bird they were flipping us as our tattered clothes flew off the car roof and into the path of the early evening rush.

Chapter Ten

Our ultimate destination was José's house in Milpitas, California—just north of San Jose—where he now lived with his new bride. José had married the most exquisite woman I had ever known. Dora glittered with beauty both outside and in. Her kindness for others and thoughtfulness about life was immense. She was crowned Football Sweetheart by the football team during their senior year of high school. She and my brother, the football star, were destined to marry. It seemed like one of those marriages that would last a lifetime. After their high school graduation commencement, they eloped that very night, coming home afterward with their marriage certificate signed. After hearing the news, Mom quickly arranged a wedding ceremony at our home, which only our family would attend. I recall shining Mom's shoes for the grand occasion. Maruca prepared herself to be the one and only bridesmaid. As simple as the wedding was, it was a joyous and beautiful time, at least until Dora's furious father burst in after the ceremony and tried to take her away. He didn't succeed. She now belonged not only to José, but also to all of us. We adored this woman.

Driving through the outskirts of Milpitas, it was clear that the land was rich and fertile. Crop fields and orchards were everywhere. Anyone who took up residency there and liked to work hard was bound to do well financially. My brother and Dora certainly had. Though we drove around for nearly two hours looking for their place, we finally found the three-bedroom home nested in the foothills of a majestic mountain range. I now stood before José who was again at a very different place from me in his life. His and Dora's welcome embraces were sweet but awkward. All ten of us stayed for the first night. Fortunately, Señora Regina and the boys had family waiting the next morning, and Richard had an aunt to stay with in another nearby suburb. Our family stayed on with Dora and José. The plan was to stay there one week. One week turned into six months.

Eager to begin raking in money to ensure our financial security, we immediately started looking for work in and around San Jose. Upon arrival in the area, Raúl and Francisco literally ran to the plum orchards. Maruca chose the backbreaking job of picking strawberries, which required bending down to the earth constantly to carefully pick the berries that were ripe. With Richard as my guide, I decided to scout another option for myself. He drove me past the cherry orchards, which immediately evoked in me overwhelming excitement. The pay for cherry-picking was much more lucrative than for picking strawberries. However, it didn't take me long to realize that this monetary advantage was directly related to the skill needed at tree climbing: the higher the workers could climb, the better. My experiences as Tarzan in my younger days gave me a clear advantage: I was totally unafraid of heights. My brothers and Maruca, also part of the jungle crew, were also fearless climbers. I eventually recruited them to the cherry orchards. We approached our business venture as a family: taking on the task like an army takes on war. Mom served as plantation foreman but also contributed to the earnings by picking cherries from the lower branches. We were paid a dollar a crate for most of the fruit we picked, averaging about thirty crates a day between us. By the end of the week, we were buzzing with the sensation of wealth. We were flying high—higher than we ever had before.

My most cherished moments in those days came when we broke for lunch. I would climb my favorite cherry tree and survey the beauty of the land around me, allowing myself to indulge in my number one pastime of daydreaming. One day, my reverie was interrupted by a noise that reminded me of festivity preparations in the placita. It was the sound of construction: some enormous project was underway next to the orchard. The construction went on for weeks. If it was a home they were building, I wondered who would ever need one that big. Later on, I would discover what the project really was.

Each day when the family arrived home to José and Dora's, we barely had enough energy to walk through the door. After dinner and dessert generously prepared by Dora, each of us collapsed into bed, only to start all over again early the next morning. The longer we stayed with my brother, the more he seemed to withdraw from the family and from Dora too. By the time we were ready to rent a place of our own, their relationship was falling apart. At the time, I didn't realize what a strain our presence had put on my brother's new marriage and how terribly unfair our intrusion had really been. The whole situation had been too much for José. Gradually, he started to phase out of his home responsibilities and simply decided to check out. His marital problems would continue. Five years later and after the arrival of three babies, his marriage to Dora would be over.

After just weeks of arriving in San Jose, our family was undergoing major changes. I struggled to define our new identity. We were not from California, nor were we from the placita any longer. We were not immigrants to this country, but we did find ourselves in a brand-new world that was now our home. Though we were American born, we still, in many ways, felt new to this country: gradually learning the social conventions and expectations needed to assimilate. The very language we'd brought with us from Texas was slowly changing. We gave ourselves Anglo nicknames: José became Joe, Maruca became Maggie, Francisco became Frank, Raúl became Ralph, and I—Ony, Flaco, Toñito—became Tony. Each day, and with each new step forward, our past was fading. The placita, the river, Clara la India, the baker, and grocers of our little corner of the world were sorely missed, but they were no longer our reality. Without them as a frame of reference, the way we perceived even ourselves became vague and confusing.

When we finally left Dora and Joe's, we were able to move into a huge rental home big enough for us all. This was now our place—our refuge and sanctuary—as long as we could afford the monthly rent. This meant we needed to keep the income flowing all year round. We soon realized that our lucrative orchard jobs were only seasonal, ending in the early fall. We quickly had to find other alternatives. The network of friends around us that had moved to California earlier guided us to the canneries and packaging plants where they preserved and packaged all the fruits and vegetables families like ours had harvested. Work in these factories was always available for anyone who wanted to work any number of hours a day. Mom was the first to head for the canneries and did her work with pride. Her salary helped us maintain our financial security while we found our own employment. Maggie, as the eldest in the household at this point, was next to follow Mom's example, increasing our support to make it through the winter months. Payito, now known as Amy, had just begun the fourth grade and did not yet have to go to work. She remained the beloved babe of the family: our little princess.

For the next two summers, Frank, Ralph, and I returned to the same orchards that we had worked before. My tree was still there. Each year, it seemed to produce enough cherries to make hundreds of cherry pies: maybe its fruit was being enjoyed all over the world! During lunch, I continued to scramble to my treetop to resume my fantastical daydreams. Surveying the building that had been under construction for so long, I was surprised to see that it was now practically finished. One day, I saw an elderly lady waving at me from one of the rooms of this huge place. I waved back. The following week, she was there again, looking up at me and waving. A few weeks later, she waved again, this time shouting over to me to come and talk to her. I jumped down from the tree, told my brothers that I would be back in five, and before I knew it, I was climbing a temporary fence built to separate the orchards from the building. There she was: a lovely, intelligent-looking lady standing outside waiting for me. She had a box of books in her arms and asked me if I could help her unload boxes from her car. I complied. Her pleasant disposition and kindly demeanor encouraged me to speak to her in my broken English. I asked her when this house would be finished because the noise bothered the birds in my trees.

She giggled sweetly and said, "We will just have to complain to the builders and ask them to hurry up and finish." Just like that, we were both comfortably joking with each other. As we talked, the mystery of the building was revealed.

"We're building a college," said the friendly woman. "I'll be teaching here in the fall. Anyone who wants to attend must enroll by next month. If you're interested in being in my class, I'll bring you an application."

I felt a spark of something like excitement, but mostly, I felt sick. "I have no money or paper or books," I stammered. I felt like running back to my placita. "It's free," replied the woman. "No one pays to go to school here. All you have to do is complete the application, sign, and be here on September 15."

The next week, after finishing lunch, I descended from my tree and climbed the fence again. I went into the building and found the mysterious lady unpacking and preparing her classroom. She must have been a witch of some sort because she seemed to know I would be back: she had the application ready for me. It was then that I learned her name: Ms. Gibson. She was to be my first teacher at my new college: San Jose City College. When I had finally worked up the courage to visit the admissions office as I had promised Ms. Gibson I would, I was showered with support and advice from everyone I met. Loans for books, parking permits, part-time work, and bus schedules were all available. Many students are fortunate to find one strong and caring advisor and mentor in their journey through education. Amazingly, at San Jose City College, I found many. Most of the professors had a sincere and genuine concern for their students. My classes were fascinating. But my absolute favorite class turned out to be Ms. Gibson's. As luck would have it, she taught the basic course in speech and language that would become the anchor for my new life. I was required to make oral presentations in English—English only! In this class, I also met my first real Anglo friend: Gary Wright. The fact that I had to run off to help my brothers in the orchards after classes and even at lunchtime made it difficult for me to socialize with classmates. Nonetheless, Gary would often invite me to join him in the cafeteria where he worked part-time. I guess some part of me didn't want him to find out about my lowly status as a cherry picker, so I always had a made-up excuse ready for him. One day, however, Gary came looking for me during lunch hour to talk about a joint assignment we had to complete. Bigmouth Ms. Gibson told him where he could find me. Lost in my own world, singing to myself as I climbed a tree, I came face-to-face with Gary, sitting on a high branch and applauding my song. I wanted to murder him and Ms. Gibson for the embarrassment.

I was glad for all the support I was receiving at school, yet I found myself in a similar situation as in high school: trying to juggle financial and family responsibilities with my educational life. Things only became more difficult as the harvesting season finished up again.

Frank and Ralph started working at a car-detailing shop owned by a wonderful man named Frank Procello and fortunately made good money there. Paying rent and utilities in California was a lot more difficult than in our old barrio, and back then, we still struggled with it.

After my first year of junior college, it was getting impossible to meet the financial demands. Even though everyone in the family was doing their part to cover expenses, we still needed more. Unwilling to give up school, I continued to work when I wasn't in class. I joined my brothers at Frank Procello's shop and also applied for a job at Macy's department store.

Ms. Gibson wrote a letter of reference for me. In many ways, this felt like my first real step toward assimilating into the business practices and ambitions of the broader world. Soon after my initial interview, I was asked to return for a second one. Two weeks later, I was hired as a salesperson in Men's Furnishings. Macy's provided an excellent training in customer service that gave me the confidence I needed to express myself in English. My duty was to assist customers in selecting shirts, socks, and ties. I found my new role fascinating and artistic. Taking an art class at the city college had left me with an appreciation for color and texture. I used my newfound passion to match shirts to ties. The salespeople who sold suits and pants would send their customers my way to complete their looks. The job also required that I dress and groom impeccably each day I worked, and I loved doing so. I would step out of my filthy old car looking like a prince. I loved dressing up so much that I did so sometimes even for school, like when I had to make a two-minute oral presentation in Ms. Gibson's class. On such occasions, Ms. Gibson, Gary, and my other classmates usually complimented me on my professional style.

After completing two classes with Ms. Gibson with grades of A, I was beginning to feel like perhaps a college degree was not such a drastic and impossible idea. Her extremely positive affirmations of my work provided me with the impetus to pursue an associate of arts degree. Even though Ms. Gibson was not my academic program advisor, she continued to be a meaningful mentor and advocate for me. Her personal interest in each of her students was appreciated by us all. Though I loved Ms. Gibson's classes, they definitely presented me with plenty of challenges. The final exam in one class was a two-part assignment: a two-page essay on a quotation of our choosing and an oral presentation on the same topic. Both the essay and the presentation left me petrified. The oral portion was to last five deadly timed minutes. Our grade would be based on content, delivery, poise, articulation, and eye contact. I agonized about it day and night and even dreamed that I had been arrested for the audacity to speak English so awkwardly and unclearly in front of others. The dream probably came in part from the many conversations I had with Gary about his career plan to become a police officer. When I shared my nightmares with him, he told me to chill out and warned me that my neurotic worrying would probably lead me to an early death anyway, so who cared about the speech? Some friend! For as much as I agonized over the assignment, not much was getting done. One day at lunch, as I stewed in my doom and gloom, Gary insisted that I nail down some ideas. "Write your points on this paper and expand on each of them as if you and I were talking. Talk to yourself out loud and just address each of the points. Remember, you have to start with an introduction, then a main body, and then a conclusion—simple as that. Now get your ass moving!" I knew this guy would make a great cop someday.

I followed Gary's advice and got busy. After numerous trips to the library, the quotation I finally chose was a powerful statement I'd read somewhere years ago: "He who must rekindle the lives of others must himself shine." The paper ended up taking me three days. At a scant page and a half, I still felt it was a literary masterpiece. The preparation for the speech took every one of my free waking hours for thirteen days. My day of execution arrived before I knew it. I fumbled through the presentation and looked only at Gary and Ms. Gibson for the entire four minutes and one second. The excruciating mental torture prevented me from breathing up there for even one more second. I earned a grade of B.

As for Gary, he breezed through his presentation just as he aced every other assignment. The quote that drove his speech was "Don't rain on my parade." After sharing a list of "rainy day" episodes and grievances from his life, he concluded by telling us about the time a bird dropped a pile of shit right on his head. He dramatically recreated his reaction: "You too, bastard?" he yelled at the bird. "Didn't I tell you not to rain on my parade?" We the audience broke into laughter and applause. I couldn't believe that even Ms. Gibson laughed at his vulgarity. He was indeed one of those individuals who simply found a lot humor and laughter in life. He was also a terrific human being. I was very proud and honored that he chose me as a friend.

Another presentation for Ms. Gibson was to be on a topic she herself chose: What are the dangers of thinking of oneself as indispensable? "Indispensable" was a new word for me. I learned that it meant being absolutely necessary and important to others and to the things in which we are involved. Even though I knew I had a tendency to think of myself in this way, it got me wondering about whether I really was. Maybe I shouldn't continue considering myself an indispensable person: it would certainly make life lighter and more fun to not have the responsibility of this notion, which, when you thought about it, was actually kind of obsessive and ridiculous. The word, however, became one of my favorites. I would incorporate it into conversation at least twenty times a week, lording it ironically over anyone who seemed to think they were superspecial.

During my second year at the city college, Ms. Gibson arranged a field trip she defined as a "cultural experience." She made arrangements to take our entire class to the Berkley campus to see an adapted version of a Greek play. I immediately knew I would be very bored and looked forward to going only because of the opportunity this would give me to catch up on my sleep. The play was called "Orfeu Negro" (Black Orpheus) and was set in the tropical environment of Rio de Janeiro. The plot, which involved a love story, was powerful and intriguing. But as the tragedy unfolded and death inevitably caught up with the ill-fated lovers, I found the story so sad that it was extremely difficult for me to truly enjoy. All I knew was I was deeply moved. The sense of deep yearning and loss evoked in the play was heightened by its music: Brazilian bossa nova played softly on piano and guitar. I was transported back to my childhood, to the days when Dad and I used to listen to just this kind of music as it floated through the placita.

I had always wondered where such beautiful songs had come from—who had made them.

Eventually in the play, a song was played that ripped my soul to pieces: "Manhã de Carnaval" (Morning of Carnival). I had heard it several times before because it had already been adapted from Portuguese into both English and Spanish. The Spanish lyrics always spoke to my heart, making me recall the brief moments of endearment I had known with Dad.

> Despues, yo no se si hay despues
> Si el sol volverá a despertar . . .
> Es que te busco yo
> Aunque no habrás de estar.

> (I don't know if there is a hereafter
> Or if the sun will rise again . . .
> It's just that I look for you
> Even if you are no longer there.)

A week after we saw the play, Ms. Gibson required each of us to write a two-page paper on our experience at Berkley and share it with the class. I expressed to the group how the song "Manhã de Carnaval" in the play found its way to my heart and why it stayed there. I shared that I often wondered if the day my dad died had prepared me to withstand pain and learn how to grieve in silence. I recalled the days following his death when I kept waiting for him to come home and thinking how I would be the first to greet him and ask him for a nickel—even though I knew he would never again walk through the door.

After two years of hard work in junior college, another graduation day was approaching. The family began to plan for the celebration. But there was one problem. I still had to complete my astronomy class with a passing grade in order to satisfy my science requirement for graduation. This course was irrelevant to me, and it showed in my performance. I never planned to become an astronaut. Fear gripped me so tightly that I was nervous my family would catch on. The day the grades came back from the final exam, the professor signaled for me to see him. He asked me why I'd had such a difficult time with the course. He had awarded me a huge flat F for the whole thing and told me I had to repeat the entire course the following semester in order to graduate. Three days later, I received a letter outlining graduation details and procedures. With a ray of hope, I thought perhaps my teacher had made an error and decided to pass me after all.

The day of graduation, in front of all my family and friends, I received what I thought was my official diploma. I was so proud I had made it through and relieved that my fears of not graduating had been unfounded. But two weeks later, I received a letter from the school records office that my science credit was still missing. I had failed after all. I would have to return for the summer session to satisfactorily complete Introduction to Astronomy before my actual diploma was issued. This was not going to happen. Thus, I received no associate of arts degree from San Jose City College. I ignored the personal insult and applied to the four-year college close to where we lived: San Jose State. With my consistent grade point average of 3.0, I was admitted. San Jose State would be my next challenge, and forget about the rest. I was going to prove to these fools that a guy from the barrio doesn't stay on sinking ships. I would not allow anyone to rain on my parade.

Chapter Eleven

Another summer was here, and I continued to work in preparation for my first semester at San Jose State in the fall. By this time, the cherry orchards were being cleared to make room for new buildings. I was saddened by how quickly nature could be replaced by concrete. In addition to work at the detailing shop and Macy's, I applied for a job at Simple Simon's Pizza parlor, which was advertised in the college newspaper. The copy read, "An artful experience and great wages for college students that need money for fall: free meals!" The ad was very enticing. At the interview, the manager told me that employees were required to wear a uniform mandated by the company. I pleasantly agreed. I was offered the job and gallantly accepted. The first night I was scheduled to work, I was required to come in an hour early to be fitted with my uniform. An extremely officious seamstress took my measurements, muttering about how thin my legs were and how unbecoming the outfit would look on me. After she completed her task, she handed me a slip of paper and continued her automated routine on eight other new employees. I felt that I was being prepared for military duty. I was then given a large box containing a huge orange hat like a jester would wear. It had three long points, each ending in a tiny bell. Also in the box were purple tights, long matching socks, a long-sleeved red shirt, a yellow vest, and a yellow tie. A small case of cosmetics, meant to enhance the theatrics of the outfit, was included. I would be expected to wear this ridiculous ensemble every night to wait on customers. Morosely, I put on the uniform and applied a flash of rouge to each cheek. Then I reluctantly prepared myself to look in the mirror. I wondered if I would look stunningly cute or plain stupid. I was shocked at how absolutely stupid I looked. As a child, I had dreamed of being in the circus, but I don't think being a clown was ever one of my aspirations. Nonetheless, I needed the money from this job to meet my school expenses for the fall and was even willing to transform myself into a Simple Simon character for the cause.

For two weeks, I served my customers incognito. I made sure to wear my large black-rimmed glasses to better obscure my identity. Thank God no one I knew came in. However, I was then offered a promotion of sorts. For a little more money, I was asked to work in Santa Cruz about thirty miles away. I felt important. I also liked the idea of working where absolutely no one knew me. One night at my new position, however, my worst fear was realized. A group of soldiers from the nearby military base walked in rambling about the activities of their day. I immediately recognized three of them. Two of them pointed at me. I heard one of them laughing as he spoke, "Is that Ony from Del Rio? He used to live by the placita." I skipped out through the back door, took off my pointed hat, and imagined digging myself into the ground. Abe, the soldier who recognized me, quickly followed me out in back of the restaurant. He warmly said hello, asked me how I'd been, and invited me to come in and have a beer. When we went back in, I could see that none of the guys meant me any trouble—they were just glad to see a familiar face. I was impressed that not one of them made a crack about my stupid uniform. I apologized and told them that I could not drink beer while on duty. I embarrassedly told them that the uniform was a one-night deal for a special theatrical promotion. My last shred of dignity evaporated when the manager snapped at me in front of them, commanding me to get back on the floor to serve and entertain my customers. The next morning, I returned to the restaurant, collected my earnings, and told the greedy managers that I had a family emergency. I never returned to work, and I never looked back on that experience.

The following week, I took a job at the Del Monte food processing plant. They paid incredibly high wages, especially for working the night shift. I had never earned so much money in my life. The work, however, was not easy. From 10:00 p.m. to 7:00 a.m., my one and only job was to clean the fruit-cocktail machines with a huge hose that jerked my skinny body all over the floor. Fortunately, several of my buddies from Del Rio worked there with me and lent me a lot of support. I was determined to stick it out and quit one week before starting classes. When fall arrived, I started classes but did not quit work. The lucrative earnings helped us cover not just family expenses, but my tuition, books, and transportation to school. After my graveyard shift, I would have just enough time for breakfast at a nearby greasy spoon before driving to campus. Once there, I hurriedly found parking and ran to my 8:00 a.m. class.

My morning schedule was designed to fulfill the first requirements for my English teaching major, which was a move toward becoming an English teacher like Mrs. Pasley. I enrolled in the three introductory classes: Introduction to American Literature, Introduction to English Literature, and Structure and Origins of the English Language. At this new school, advisors were never available, so I had to plan my own schedule. I immediately felt the lack of advocacy and support. The campus was strange and lonely.

Nonetheless, my English curriculum became fascinating to me. In Dr. Shirley's American literature class, we read novels, essays, and poetry. Through her eloquent approach, the stirrings of emotion I had felt for literature in Mrs. Pasley's class began to resurface. I now found myself ready to process what I read on a deeper level. Rereading Emerson's "Self-Reliance," the words took on new and more profound meaning. Now I actually understood what I had read to my high school friends that trembling day six years before. I ultimately earned a C in Dr. Shirley's class, and I was proud of my success. I attributed it to perhaps the only professor I encountered there who respected and offered affirmation to her students. She had a gift for taking excerpts from our readings and applying them to situations in our daily lives. I still remember our discussion of Hemingway's *The Sun Also Rises*. One of the characters in the novel is an annoyance to the rest of the group because of his dependence on others. Dr. Shirley asked us if we knew anyone like that. "I do, and I won't talk about it," she added when no one spoke. "*You* know too, and you want to keep this to yourselves. Some things are better left unsaid, right? Let's move on to another character."

Dr. Shirley's dynamic style left us constantly on alert, waiting to hear her next magical example. She truly loved literature and passed this love on to us, contextualizing the work by describing each author and the period and place in which they had written. She was a convincing and extremely pleasant professor. On Valentine's Day, she asked the class if anyone was currently in love. I couldn't believe her gall. No one in class came forward, but it was enough to make us think about our own lives and loves, finding our own experiences within the poem she was about to read. It was from Elizabeth Barrett Browning's *Sonnets from the Portuguese*. "How do I love thee? Let me count the ways," Dr. Shirley began. The poignant message of love came alive as she continued:

> I love thee to the depth and breadth and height
> My soul can reach, when feeling out of sight
> For the ends of Being and ideal Grace.
> I love thee to the level of everyday's
> Most quiet need, by sun and candle-light.
> I love thee freely, as men strive for Right;
> I love thee purely, as they turn from Praise.
> I love thee with the passion put to use
> In my old griefs, and with my childhood's faith.
> I love thee with a love I seemed to lose
> With my lost saints,—I love thee with the breath,
> Smiles, tears, of all my life!—and, if God choose,
> I shall but love thee better after death.

When Dr. Shirley had finished, she looked up from her book and smiled at everyone with characteristic warmth. Because I always made it a point to be early to her class, I was occupying my usual seat in the front row. I removed my dark thick-framed glasses to wipe my perspiration. She looked at me directly and said, "Mr. Carvajal, young man, don't hide your expressive and handsome eyes behind those glasses." I almost passed out from the mixed emotions of embarrassment and pride. This was enough evidence for me to conclude that not all the professors at State were wet blankets.

My experience in Dr. Warren's Introduction to English Literature class was distinctly different. Dr. Warren was tall, skinny, and so cold it seemed as if he slept in a freezer. I had serious difficulties adapting to his impersonal and impassive style. Class with him consisted solely of him reading and teaching from his "bible," the thick *Anthology of English Literature* he carried with him each day when he walked in. No one spoke in class. Student interaction and class discussion were not welcomed. Under his instruction, the classroom—the one place where open intellectual exchange should happen—was transformed into a mortuary. It seemed as if any moment pallbearers would be hoisting a coffin to the front of the classroom. Dr. Water was no more engaging one-on-one. On various occasions when I approached him, needing desperately to clarify class assignments, I was met with the same icy demeanor. It was a tough place to be.

I learned more from my own interpretation of Dr. Warren's reading assignments than I did from his attempts to convince me of their intellectual power. And I had Josie to help me along. Josie Reyes was a brilliant classmate who navigated very well through Dr. Warren' class and who provided me with immense support. We would engage in long conversations about the readings. Her love for literature and her understanding of story and character in each novel astounded me. Comparing myself to her, I was becoming convinced that my problem was not that I couldn't read, but that I couldn't understand what I was reading. Classic English literature felt too complex and advanced for me, but Josie had a gift for making Shakespeare, Keats, and Longfellow come alive. I only wished that she were taking American lit with me as well. If Dr. Warren could match a tenth of a percent of the passion and genuine love Josie had for literature, I knew I would have tolerated the austere environment of class better and perhaps could have learned more.

Every week of class, Dr. Warren required us to read one entire English novel. It was an assignment I couldn't meet. The combination of this requirement plus the weekly novel from American literature was much more than I could handle. But what I dreaded even more was our term paper. Dr. Warren required the paper to be written using the guidelines from the Modern Language Association. Talk about adding insult to injury. We were required to adhere to the guidelines of the reference in every part of our paper. This required numerous hours of research I simply couldn't complete. Even though I carried the MLA manual with me everywhere I went, I had limited time to scrutinize the rules. Even after I completed my term paper at the end of the gruesome semester, I still had to take a written final that included questions about MLA protocol. I thought this was absurd. I froze in desperation and immediately skipped to the essay questions pertaining to the literature readings. I left the exam feeling small and inferior one more time. The grades were posted on a bulletin board two weeks later, and the term papers were piled in a plastic basket for us to retrieve. I had earned a D on my final and a grade of F on my term paper. It was the most violent F I had ever received: huge and bloody red. But Dr. Warren's comments on the back of the paper, although written in meticulous scholarly style, were the real killers:

> I have noticed your frustration in the preparation of this assignment each time you have made an appointment with me. I have admired your tenacity. However, not to criticize your efforts would be false kindness. 1.) The format of your paper is inadequate. 2.) Citations are incomplete throughout the manuscript. 3.) Syntax and spelling are atrocious and elementary; there are apparent hints of a certain level of illiteracy. 4.) Written expressions are infested with platitudes and triteness, and the entire format is awkward and difficult to follow. 5.) You struggle with footnotes without awareness of where they do and do not belong. I suggest that you return to San Jose City College and be advised of other professional directions you could pursue. Scholarly endeavors are not a direction you should contemplate.

The final two sentences were the ones that tore me apart. Dr. Warren had signed the note with a single pompous W. What ran through my mind at that moment was that I should invite him on a road trip from Texas to California in a broken-down car with nine cranky, smelly passengers and see how long he'd last. If raw intellect meant the ability to adapt and maneuver through our environment, Dr. Warren would be considered an imbecile. His precious *Anthology of English Literature* wouldn't be worth the paper it was printed on.

I ended up with a D in English lit, and I fared no better in Structure and Origins of Language, also taught by none other than Dr. Warren. Nonetheless, the course captured my interest. Here, Dr. Warren's exacting teaching style worked better. A technical examination of the roots of the English language, this course required him to be neither emotional nor personable. It gave me an excellent opportunity to learn how English was largely borrowed from the Latin and French roots I had been exposed to in Catholic school. It was fascinating to learn that Greek was also the foundation of so many words we use in English. I was astounded to discover that the meaning of a word could change completely simply by changing its prefix or suffix. This course not only provided me with appreciation for English—my still-unfamiliar language—but also gave me practical ways to expand my vocabulary for speaking and especially writing. I was finally able to understand where some of my writing deficiencies came from. I received a grade of C in the course and beamed with pride at my level of success. I believed I had crossed the first juncture in becoming an English teacher like Mrs. Pasley.

Despite my every effort and intention, I completed my first semester with only a 1.3 grade point average and was placed on academic probation. I was falling fast. My maddening schedule had left me emotionally and physically drained. Desperate for guidance and support, I sought out my first thoughtful college mentor Ms. Gibson. I learned that she had passed away two months previously, and I plunged deeper into sadness and despair. I then tried calling Gary, but his parents informed me that he had moved out of state. Yet another significant loss for me, but I knew that wherever he was, he would be content with his new life.

As for me, it was hard to be content. Conditions at home were getting worse. By this time, we had bought a home, but couldn't afford it. We were falling behind on our mortgage payments, and my part-time work at Macy's and the auto shop simply wasn't cutting it. Each member of the family also faced their individual struggles. Joe had briefly remarried only to divorce again. Frank and Ralph had joined the army and were now serving abroad. Maggie had married a lazy, useless liar. In the midst of all this, I continued to pursue whatever it was I was after at San Jose State: at times I could hardly remember.

One thing was clear: for my second semester, I had to make drastic academic improvements to raise my GPA. On my very own and under no advisement, I decided to begin pursuing a minor in speech and drama. I thought my exposure to so many movies would give me an advantage here. My fellow students pursuing this line of study immediately seemed more amicable than in my English classes. They actually talked to me and welcomed me into their world of theater where acting, singing, dancing, and oratory were treated earnestly, and fantasy and pretense were natural components. It was fascinating. My first two classes for the minor were Phonetics of the English Language and a class on stage design in which we learned about lighting and set construction. I really wondered if these skills would ultimately help me become a star or at least an ensemble actor in Hollywood.

For phonetics, one of the prerequisites was passing a language clearance test administered by a speech pathologist. This was not good. I went through three of these miserable screenings and failed each. They thought I was deaf. I was referred to a speech and hearing therapist from the school's speech-language audiology clinic. I was cleared for deafness: it was my speech that was the problem, they decided. The plan was to provide therapy to help me reduce my "significant foreign accent." But after my third failing mark on this test, which was also required for teaching certification, a well-reputed Harvard-educated professor advised me not to pursue a teaching major that led to certification but to continue on with a BA program only.

They were saying that my dream to become a teacher like Mrs. Pasley was at an end, but I couldn't let it go that easily. I wanted badly to learn how to properly execute this new form of speech so distinctly different from the language of the barrio. Everything about it fascinated me: the structure, lexicon, intonation, and articulation. It was the most difficult and unrealistic-seeming task I had ever encountered in my life. My therapist became gradually frustrated with me. "You have to alter the sounds of the language. You have to place your tongue at appropriate places when you articulate. You have to change the intonations of a sentence, the melodic patterns, and the rate of speech." She begged me to try harder. "Don't eat your consonants at the end of each word." She defined this awful tendency as "clipping." My dear Lord! As a boy, I sang when I talked. I thought that was part of who I was. Here, I talked too fast; I had to slow down. I thought to myself, "Ms. Speech Elegance, not only do I eat my consonants, I eat anything I can find to stop my tummy from growling." I could not continue. I was trying, but I began to find my therapist arrogant and compulsive. The science of linguistics dictating how one should speak was beginning to feel ridiculous and arbitrary. As for me, I simply felt inferior and hopeless. I felt derogated and filled with futility each time they suggested that I "spoke funny." I was throwing my hands up. To hell with them!

Though the speech part of my minor was off to a rocky start to say the least, my drama courses were overwhelmingly powerful. In my stage-design class, we learned about how to create backdrops, sets, lighting, and sound. It was stupendously exciting. What's more, we got to apply what we learned to the actual stage. We were divided into trios, each assigned to study an individual aspect of stage design. My trio was the construction team that would build backdrops and stairs. I was reluctant to get into this business because of the serious limitations I had always had when it came to carpentry. I was not raised to tell a hammer from a screwdriver. Nonetheless, I approached my assignment with a conscientious attitude. This was one of my last opportunities to do well, and I promised myself success. Each group would be helping in their own way with an upcoming college production of *Romeo and Juliet*. We began to attend the rehearsals, and I had never been so enthralled with anything in my life. I was reminded of my first exposure to these incredible tragedies through Mrs. Pasley when the literary brilliance of Shakespeare was first impressed on my memory. Right before me, I was seeing the wonder of this genius—a wonder I had longed to revisit—come to life. I found the actors in the play incredible: confident, articulate, convincing, and astoundingly glamorous. They walked across the stage with an elegance and poise that I would have liked to apply to my speeches in Ms. Gibson's classes. I knew Gary would have been impressed.

I would have been happy to watch the rehearsals for the rest of the course, but we were there to work. Our team was assigned to construct the balcony where that famous pledge of love between Romeo and Juliet was to occur, a scene that wrenched my guts with its supreme romantic poignancy.

Fortunately, one member of our team, Robert, had learned from his carpenter father. He became our leader and advisor. He was like a sculptor with his tools—hammer, nails, drill, electric saw, measuring tape, and level—creating something out of parts that seemed like nothing. He taught us how to use these things too, and I tried to emulate his confidence and do well to please him. I tried with all my resources to apply what he was teaching and avoid demonstrating ignorance. Chuck, our other partner, was as incompetent as I was. We felt secure in knowing that Robert would get us through our carpentry assignment with no problem.

The day of dress rehearsal was upon us, and it was time to put our work to the test. Only Chuck and I were there representing our group since Robert had been called out of state on a family emergency. I learned that this final rehearsal was to be conducted like an actual performance and used to correct minor odds and ends in the production. The actors and actresses were in full costume. Lighting and sound were both in place to impeccably complement the play. There was a full orchestra in a pit underneath the stage, which I was hearing for the first time. Our big scene—act 2, scene 2—was here at last. Romeo speaks to Juliet, who looks out from her window: "O, speak again, bright angel, for thou art as glorious to this night, being o'er my head, as is a winged messenger of heaven . . ." Chuck and I stared in anticipation at our artistically designed balcony, soon to be occupied by the lovely Juliet. Out she came right on cue, beginning to speak her famous lines: "O Romeo, Romeo! Wherefore art thou Romeo? . . . What's in a name? That which we call a rose by any other word would smell as sweet . . ." The scene unfolded at a flawless pace, the balcony bathed in the bright spotlight. Chuck and I beamed with pride and gave each other a congratulatory high five. Our celebration was premature. No sooner had we done this when one side of the balcony came crashing down, leaving Juliet grasping for dear life to the branch of an artificial tree. Dr. Timothy, the director, let out a bloodcurdling scream. I felt death calling. At least I would be killed alongside my partner. Dr. Timothy gave us five minutes to repair the mess. With hearts in hand, we walked timidly to him and explained that we couldn't undo the damage without our absent captain. We were flatly ordered out of the rehearsal and forbidden from going near the auditorium for the remainder of the semester.

The debacle earned us both a D in the course. We considered challenging our grade, but a gut feeling told us we had to let it be. Up until the fiasco of dress rehearsal, I had enjoyed myself in the class and gained some valuable lessons. However, my GPA had now sunk to a new low. At the end of the semester, I received a letter of suspension from San Jose State.

Around this time, the constant strain and pressure of my nonstop schedule finally took its toll. I had lived my days constantly unable to find sufficient amounts of food at home. Even on the rare occasions that food was available, I didn't give myself time to eat. I started noticing that my body felt unusually weak. One afternoon, while on my way home from returning books to the library, I fainted right on the bus. The next thing I knew, I was at home with Mom. She tried caring for me by fixing me a meal that I couldn't eat. Three hours later, I was taken to the hospital. The next day, just like that, I was diagnosed with chronic anemia because of malnutrition.

The severity of my situation was just too much for my already-struggling family at home to take on. The decision was made to fly me to Dallas, Texas, to stay with Ramón, who had made a home there with his wife and two young daughters. It was my cousin Berta—who lived close by in San Jose—who most encouraged the trip. As a nurse and a dear family member, she was extremely concerned about my well-being. She knew that my brother would take good care of me. Generously, she purchased my plane ticket to Dallas. As she took me to the airport, she assured me that all would be well and advised me not to return until Ramón agreed I was healthy enough.

As we drove along, I recalled the significant days that Berta and I had shared growing up. Berta was another daughter of my beloved aunt Manina. Like her sister Teresita, Berta was very special to me. The sisters had become like siblings to me in the time that I lived with their family during Dad's illness and death. Very similar in age, Berta—better known as Guera—and I had become especially close. We shared many a joyful day playing by the river and in the placita. However, Manina's family, better-off than we were financially, eventually moved to a better neighborhood of Del Rio. Naturally, Berta began to make friendships with those around her, and I was no longer in the same social league. However, I never stopped thinking that Berta was gifted with admirable genuineness and simple goodness. It was years later in San Jose that we reestablished our close friendship. Berta had moved there and now had a family of her own. I was so thankful when my mother informed me that Berta was going to finance my trip to Dallas. By this true act of kindness, Berta taught me a lot about the significance of extending myself to others without expecting anything in return. To date, she continues to be the best example I know of selflessness and enormous compassion.

Chapter Twelve

The jet flight to Dallas was my first experience on an airplane. It was so traumatic it made me want to die. Immediately upon landing, my stomach surrendered, expelling the snacks I had eaten on the way. Chilled and trembling, I relied on a kind stewardess to help me down the plank and into the terminal where four welcoming smiles awaited me. Ramón, his wife, Mary Ellen, and daughters—five-year-old Gigi and three-year-old Anna—had all come to greet me. Though I had met Ramón's beautiful wife on several occasions, this was the very first time I had seen his adorable little girls. The family could see I was not well and guided me to a chair to rest. After fifteen minutes and a few sips of iced water, I had regained enough energy to walk with them to baggage claim.

On the car ride to Ramón's, I felt so sick and drained that I slept in the front seat until we arrived. I was feeling worse than when I had left San Jose. The harrowing air travel and the uneasy excitement of being surrounded by a new family—on top of already being sick—was more than I could handle. I recall hearing all the well-meaning questions: "How was the flight? Are you thirsty? Would you like a snack?" But I could barely respond. Ramón chatted about his experience flying on jumbo jets overseas when he was in the air force, and Mary Ellen spoke of her promise never to travel by airplane. I was hardly able to utter a word. It was all I could do to thank them for meeting me and helping me home.

Since his days in the military, life seemed to have been kind to my brother. Soon after completing his service, he had moved to Dallas, gone to engineering school, met his wife, and settled down to begin a family. Ramón's home looked just like the house I used to admire in the Dick and

Jane readers. Father, Mother, Jane, Sally—even Spot the dog and Puff the cat—were there. When I got out of the car, the warm, clear air felt healing and refreshing. The lawn was the greenest I had ever seen: even Mrs. Poag's couldn't have compared. Tall magnolia trees, rose bushes, and daffodil beds surrounded the house. The home itself, with its beautiful architecture, reflected the skill and precision of a true engineer: my brother had done it himself. It was a showcase to behold.

As we walked through the back door into the house, two small hands wrapped their tiny fingers around each of my thumbs in loving welcome. Gigi and Anna were extremely pleased to be meeting Uncle Tony. I felt a wave of endearment for my delightful new friends. Inside the house, more perfection awaited. Every detail of décor and cleanliness had been attended to with pride and meticulous care. Ramón walked me to my guest bedroom and bathroom. I was stunned to see that I had my own sink and bathtub—scrubbed so clean I could see my own reflection—along with lots of clean, fluffy towels carefully arranged on a rack. Bars of soap in a rainbow of colors and a box of Kleenex were reserved for my own private use. I was cautious not to touch anything.

On the door to my bedroom was a crayon drawing of two little girls and a cat, saying, "Welcome, Uncle Tony!" I felt my heart leap and thanked my nieces profusely for the gorgeous artwork. "My girls, this is the most beautiful picture I have ever seen. It's special because you made it for me and you have your names on it." They beamed with pride. "And who is this horse on the picture?" I asked. They laughed and said it was the cat. I knew this cat was destined to make my life miserable during my stay: cats always do.

In preparation for dinner, we followed a ritual new to me. We had to wash our hands and "freshen up." I washed my hands but could not bring myself to use the pristine towels. Instead, I brushed my hands across my pants and wiped the sink dry with my handkerchief. I dreaded the next step. Dinner was uncomfortable. Mary Ellen, a devout Catholic, had instilled in her family the essentiality of beginning the evening meal with a prayer. My own family had been religious, no doubt, but prayer before meals had never been a tradition. What's more, we only ever used one utensil to scoop up our food: a fork or a spoon. Mary Ellen's table, on the other hand, had four or five pieces of silverware per setting as well as an exactingly placed napkin and glass. A small vase with a single elegant rose from the garden graced the center of the exquisite table. As beautiful as everything was, it felt strange. I knew I would have trouble adapting to this. That evening, we had broiled chicken, baked potatoes, a salad prepared exclusively from vegetables fresh from the garden, and homemade rolls by Mary Ellen. I learned that we passed the large serving platter around the table only once. The girls were told that dessert was contingent on how well they ate their dinner. Hearing this, I made an attempt at conversation, saying that I often confused the word "dessert" with "desert," the hot and dry land we had crossed on our trip to California. Everyone, including little Gigi and Anna, was confused. Despite my best attempts to please, my social ineptness was evident. The moment I started on my plate, Mary Ellen graciously suggested that I not use the serving spoon from the chicken platter to eat. I learned to watch every move Ramón seemed to have so tactfully mastered. He would be my model. "When in Rome . . . ," I thought. It took me two weeks to get the hang of this new way of eating at the table.

After dinner that first night, each of us got on with our evening activities. The girls helped Mary Ellen clean up the kitchen, and Ramón—as was apparently typical—returned to the office to work. I knew it would be a difficult night for me. The more I struggled to find sleep, the less I could. Instead of lying there between the crisp sheets, I sat on the floor in the dark to dream with my eyes open. Staring blankly at the wall, my thoughts turned to memories of Ramón from years ago. He had always been a person of few words who navigated cautiously through life. Of course, he had always tried to avoid confrontation with the bullying José. Ramón was not much of a fighter, and any time he tried to retaliate, José would easily kick him back down again. We were all frustrated and distressed to witness Ramón's unwillingness or inability to defend himself.

After his departure to the air force, Ramón would seldom write. However, we received a monthly government stipend for his service, which for us was a godsend. Each month, the check was spent before we even got it on grocery bills and utilities. Other expenses had to wait until our own meager paychecks trickled in. Now six years later, I was learning about my brother all over again. Witnessing and admiring his surprising prosperity made me realize how things in life can, indeed, change if and when we define and pursue our goals as vigorously as he did.

The first three weeks of my stay in Dallas, I rested, recuperated, and was cared for by Mary Ellen and the clan. Her conscientious focus on proper nutrition and consistency of meals was healing me. My skinny frame, devastated by chronic anemia and severe malnutrition, was transforming into a healthy and resilient body. Once this time had gone by and some of my strength had returned, Mary Ellen outlined the clinical agenda she felt appropriate for my recovery. She had scheduled an exam for me with both a physician and a dentist. She cleverly kept these appointments in close proximity to home so there was little excuse not to go. At the dentist, I discovered I had severe infection of the gums and would have to have my two front teeth removed. This was devastating and embarrassing for me. Fortunately, thanks to modern dentistry, I was soon sporting handsome temporary teeth. Gigi and Anna were big fans. They thrilled when I removed my teeth with a magical flourish, replacing them just as quickly with a hocus-pocus touch. I became a sensation among their little neighborhood friends. Two weeks later, the show was over. I received a permanent dental bridge. Even though I missed my family back home, my precious little nurses—Gigi and Anna—were a delightful gift to me. They would wake me up with the sweetest morning-bell calls of "Ding-dong!" Their unconditional love more than compensated for the lack of emotional support I had endured in school. They were indeed my special angels without wings. To them, Uncle Ding Dong was perfect just as he was.

As time went on and my physical body recovered from my nutritionally abusive habits in San Jose, I started sensing a mood from my brother that was difficult to define. The dinner hour was quiet and somber. After dinner, I would take the girls outside to play pretend games. I started to wonder if my stay was becoming a burden to the family. I recalled the famous proverb "El muerto y el arrimado al tercer día apestan" (The corpse and the houseguest both start to smell by the third day). I didn't know quite what to do. I wanted to ask about it, but was also afraid of the response. One Saturday morning, as Ramón and I worked in the yard, I could hold it in no longer. "I wonder if it's time for me to go back to San Jose," I carefully began. "I feel quite strong and need to get back to help Mom with house payments. I should be there for Payito too." After a dead silence, Ramón laid down his shovel and responded with uncharacteristic firmness. "This is your home," he said. "You are part of this family, and the girls adore you. You came to us when I needed someone to keep me company. I know the day will come when you have to leave. I also know that it will be soon. When the doctors give you a clean bill of health—that is when you should go. Not before." His statement left me relieved, yet puzzled as well. Didn't he wish to get back to regular life with his family? The following Saturday, Ramón and I went fishing. It was a terrific day. As we sat in the sun drinking beer, he asked me to keep the subject of drinking between us. Mary Ellen did not tolerate this type of "sin" in her husband.

As time passed, Ramón became even more shut off during our nightly dinners. He gobbled his meal without raising his head, then immediately excused himself, saying he needed to get back to the office to complete some unfinished project. Before his quick departure, he would say good night to the sweet daughters he adored. He would return after ten and go immediately to his bedroom. From there, I could hear Mary Ellen arguing and weeping. Ramón would emerge from the bedroom quietly and sit outside for the longest time.

In the midst of her apparent strife with her husband, Mary Ellen was becoming my best friend. After Ramón left for the day, we would talk incessantly about my upbringing. In return, she would share with me the pain and suffering she had experienced after her mother died when she was young. She spoke of her mother with a deep sense of love, respect, and admiration. She felt this love so strongly that even now, in front of me, she would openly weep at her loss. She spoke of her sisters with equal devotion.

Mary Ellen's genuine goodness shone through when I had to have oral surgery to remove infected tissue from my gums. The surgeon operated on the upper gums first and, two weeks later, on the lower gums. The bleeding both times was profuse. The pain was unbearable, even with medication. Between my sorry state and the all-liquid diet I had to consume, there was little reason for me to come down for dinner. Ramón used my absence from the table to excuse himself from coming home for dinner at all. Mary Ellen spent her days in the kitchen preparing soft meals I would hopefully be able eat. I could hear her humming or belting out tunes from *The Sound of Music*. She could sing any song from any musical I had seen during my years at the drive-in. I marveled at her unique musical talent and wondered why she had never gone to Hollywood or Broadway.

My nurse around the clock, Mary Ellen prepared chicken broth and soft vegetable soup that was the best I've ever had. Gigi and Anna would come to lie down next to me with washcloths or Kleenex on their mouths to demonstrate their empathy for poor Uncle Ding Dong. I was once again filled with love and gratitude, moved by them to silent tears. I promised myself that I would always be there for these girls—always. Ramón too did his part to cheer me. Each morning as I healed, he would stop by my room to see how I was progressing. His reassurance was a tremendous comfort. With little way to really give back, I felt the need to at least make record of their selfless acts of kindness. I expressed my gratitude for everything they did in short labored sentences written in a notebook. The journal would be a keepsake to remind me always of their generosity.

Ramón continued to leave in the evenings and return home late. To help fill the void of his absence, I would sometimes force myself to leave my room and come to the dinner table, quietly drinking my soup or a glass of water. Then I'd uneasily return to my room. I could not understand why my brother would create this wall between himself and his wife and daughters. I once again called to mind memories of Ramón as a younger man. I remembered many times when he would isolate himself with a small radio, listening over and over again to songs that I thought were extremely sad.

As I healed from my surgeries, I spent much of my time reading. I'd brought with me from San Jose a stack of books on my must-read list. Among them was *The Labyrinth of Solitude* by Octavio Paz. One of the essays in the book immediately jarred me because the language seemed to speak of Ramón. It compelled me to define and understand his deep loneliness, which I saw and would continue to see in the months to come.

He passes through life like a man who has been flayed; everything can hurt him, including words and the very suspicion of words. His language is full of reticences, of metaphors and allusions of unfinished phrases . . . . Even in a quarrel he prefers veiled expressions to outright insults.

This is just how my brother seemed to quarrel with his wife. Everything was under the surface. I often wondered if Ramón felt somehow inferior to Mary Ellen in the face of her rigorous religiosity, piousness, and stringent expectations of etiquette. Maybe his emotional distance was a strategy to avoid competing with and comparing himself to her. I remembered the days before their marriage, when we were still in Del Rio, but Ramón had established himself in Dallas. He would send us pictures clipped from the Sunday newspaper: photos of Mary Ellen posing alongside other elegant women. The newspaper article indicated that she had been a debutant in Dallas's high social circles. When I had met her for the first time two years later, she and Ramón were dating. I was astonished by the precision of her speech. I wondered if this was the ultimate goal my speech therapist at San Jose State had envisioned for me. I was in constant awe whenever she spoke. No matter what she said, her soft voice was bathed in elegance and glamour. Only the purest articulation and intonation left her mouth. Where in the world had my barrio brother found this delicate human being—this precious and lovely woman? I was so proud of him and delighted that he would marry a princess more beautiful than anyone I had ever seen on or off the silver screen. When she walked down the aisle, her beauty was so astounding that she made Natalie Wood and Elizabeth Taylor look like nothing. I had to restrain myself from breaking into applause.

I guess no one ever fully knows all the factors that contribute to the denouement of a relationship. Unresolved resentments, whatever the source, often creep in. Differing ideas about finances, children, religion, class, education, respect, and communication can all cause partnerships to break down. We know that often the single force that takes two people to the altar in the first place is the genuine love they've found for each other. But when this love disappears, what is to blame? Perhaps it doesn't matter how it happens: what the reasons, where it goes, or who took it away. Just like time, this love is simply squandered and disappears into nothing but memory.

Ramón's somberness deepened as the months went by. Likewise, my discomfort and preoccupation for him and Mary Ellen grew. The Dick-and-Jane spotlessness of their home was beginning to feel cloying, making me wish I could leave at a moment's notice back to my chaotic life in San Jose. If only I could take my precious Gigi and Anna, who I had grown to love so much.

In the meantime, Ramón and I were developing a more comfortable relationship and becoming closer than we'd ever been before. We spent many hours talking about our days back in the barrio. He shared with me the experiences he'd had with bigotry and racism while growing up and during his years in the service. He also spoke of the loneliness and disappointment he'd felt when many of his friends in the air force received packages and letters from their families while he received nothing. He bluntly expressed his anger and resentment of José as he recalled all the times our brother had given him violent, bloody thrashings. I had hoped he had forgotten, but how could he? Despite this, it hadn't been all unhappiness for Ramón in those days. His face lit up as he recalled his dear high school girlfriend Alicia. He also spoke with conviction and confidence about his current investment strategies and the portfolios he'd prepared for himself and his family. He coached me on the importance of investing in land and stocks—especially oil. His business knowledge was amazing. My only reaction, due to my ignorance, was a simple acknowledgment that I was listening. He stressed to me the importance of a good education, talking proudly of how, after returning from the service, he had enrolled in the engineering program at Southern Methodist University, graduating with a BA in just four years. This last note made me squirm with embarrassment and regret at my academic failure at San Jose State. He paused and asked me how school was going for me. I grieved internally. Then suddenly, it all came rushing out. I rambled idiotically about the family's harvesting endeavors, meeting Ms. Gibson and my dear friend Gary—who had accepted me unconditionally, accent and all. Finally, I had the nerve to share with Ramón the horrors of my failures at San Jose State. I told him about my dismal experience at the speech clinic. I took the time to give him a play-by-play description of the catastrophe involving Juliet's balcony. Ramón laughed so hard he cried. It was the first time I'd ever seen him do this: I thought he would faint. He couldn't believe what a clown I had been all these years, he said, as he put his arm around me. At least something had come out of me almost murdering Juliet before she'd even had a chance to kill herself: I had finally found my brother.

On weekends, Ramón and Mary Ellen would sometimes invite friends over to barbecue in the yard. He would grill the most humongous T-bone steaks I had ever seen. We'd drink beer and, at some point, begin to sing. The wife of one of Ramón's friends was one of the most joyful and delightful people I'd ever met. She'd ask me to join her in singing songs Ramón and I remembered from our days in the placita. My brother was impressed that I knew all the words and told me that I had missed my calling. I felt honored. He said that I should be a mariachi with a silver-studded suit and a huge sombrero. He would buy a band to accompany me for my recordings and travel engagements. I was thrilled and delighted by the way Ramón made his guests laugh at the thought of my ridiculous future image. Shortly after his joke, I snuck to the garage, grabbed a small sombrero I had seen hanging from a hook, and came out bowing in front of everyone. I was given a standing ovation for my entrance. My brother's lonely soul was slowly healing. We cherished the beautiful moments of that evening for months after. He yearned to replicate the good times.

A few weeks after my musical debut in front of my brother and his friends, Ramón asked me to join him on a shopping trip. We went in and out of several music stores, looking at trumpets, guitars, drums, and clarinets. My heart was pounding. I wondered if he had lost his mind and was actually going to send me somewhere to become a mariachi. I knew for sure he had a generous heart, but this would be pretty insane. After visiting four stores, we went back to the second. There, he purchased a stereo system he had always wanted to use in his library. We looked for recordings of music that Mom used to play on the piano. His favorites had been the zandungas and a particular song called "Farolito" composed by Agustin Lara. We never

found it, but after he hummed it for me and remembered some of the lyrics,
I could slowly sing the song for him as we drove home.

Farolito que alumbras apenas
Mi calle desierta
Cuantas noches me has visto llorando
A llamar a tu puerta

(Guiding light that softly illuminates
My lonely street
Many nights you have seen me crying
As I call at your door)

When we arrived at the house with the four huge boxes, Mary Ellen
went berserk. Shocked to the core, she wept uncontrollably, telling Ramón
how ridiculous and irresponsible he had been to buy such unnecessary
and foolish items. To her, splurging was another sin. He simply stared
at her and then went about setting up the stereo he had always wanted.
Even though in that moment I wished I could sink into the floor or at
least be a traveling mariachi far, far away, I was also proud of Ramón for
his courage. He was standing up for himself, even if there was a tinge of
"getting even" attached. If Ramón was trying to assert his control, he had
scored a home run.

That same afternoon, after setting up the stereo, Ramón left for the office
without uttering a sound. I went back to my room and sat, wondering how
he and Mary Ellen could have navigated so completely toward two separate
and distant worlds. I loved them both so much. Their unhappiness made
me terribly sad. I was honored that, on his good days and when we were
alone, my brother confided in me about his plans, passions, and memories
of life long ago. Yet even when he spoke of those times, a tone of regret and
deep loneliness came through. I wondered if a doctor far away, where no
one knew of his family or profession, could give Ramón medicine or therapy
for loneliness. Evidently, having money to buy stuff wasn't the answer to
everything.

As my caregivers suffered through their own brand of war, my health continued to improve. I was gaining weight and exercising. Mary Ellen's nutritious meals were promptly served at 5:15 p.m. She wore a starched apron and set the table with a crisp tablecloth that matched the flowers she placed as a centerpiece. Ramón was not impressed. He would arrive between 7:00 and 8:00 p.m. without calling to let her know he would be late. The weeping would start again. I finally stepped in myself, urging Ramón to simply make a quick call to let his wife know when he'd be home. My idea was met with thick indifference. It was obvious to me that indifference itself had become Ramón's weapon of choice against his wife. He was getting even, showing her that he too could be perfectly obnoxious.

I had now been in Dallas for five months and was fully healed. The date of my departure back to San Jose was at last agreed upon. The month leading up to it was busy. Ramón's friends returned to bid me a proper farewell party with steak, beer, and music. They could make any occasion happy. I kept occupied with painting and landscaping projects around the neighborhood to earn money for my fare home. In three weeks, I had enough for a one-way ticket.

Good-byes are never easy, and this one was no exception. How was I to express the depth of my appreciation and gratitude to this family? It felt cheap to simply say, "Thanks for everything, it was great. Take care and I'll see you guys later. Give me a big hug." No way! No words could express the love I felt for both Ramón and Mary Ellen. They had taken care of me with the dedication and skill nurses have for their patients. They had loved me as if I was their own child. They had given me strength to pursue a new direction of wellness. There was so much I now had to do with my life to show them that their loving efforts had not been in vain.

The evening before my departure, Mary Ellen prepared a meal fit for a king. On the table were all my favorites: Spanish rice, beans, and enchiladas as only she could prepare. A pineapple pie like no one else on earth could make topped off the evening. We listened to songs on the stereo and promised each other many happy returns. That night when I retired to my room, I wrote a letter to both of them. I promised that I would always pray that they never let go of the love and respect they had for each other. With a thankful and very sorrowful heart, I started packing and cried until my vision was blurred.

Thankfully, I was better prepared to say good-bye to my precious little ones: Gigi and Anna. We had practiced our good-byes for days to make the leaving easier. We talked about how we would always visit each other for holidays when I would make sure the Easter Bunny and Santa Claus made them first on their list. After dinner that final night, I added an act to my magic show, making coins disappear and reappear as carrots. We paraded around the house singing "Doe, a Deer" over and over again with me strumming the chords on the guitar. Then they cuddled in my arms, praising me for my talents. There was absolutely nothing Ding Dong couldn't do. The two precious princesses had carved their way very deep into my heart and soul. I knew that the next day would be devastating: far more so than the day I had left San Jose. When morning finally came, the biggest torture was seeing the tears in my brother's eyes.

Chapter Thirteen

When I returned to San Jose, the city had changed. The buildings seemed taller and the streets wider. New developments were springing up all over. The entire area was more populated with people and automobiles. The bountiful orchards—which had blossomed each spring and borne fruit for our summer work—had disappeared, replaced by banks, office buildings, and shopping centers.

On a positive note, it was nice to come back to a house that was our own. Though we continued to struggle with mortgage payments, they were no worse than our rent had been. In fact, the house we had bought was the same one we'd rented. Mom had somehow made a deal with the owner, purchasing the home directly from him and bypassing the outrageous processing fees charged by the banks. The house on McKee Avenue was perfect for us and in a great location too: just a few blocks away from the school Ralph, Frank, and Amy attended.

After arriving home, my first visit was to Frank Procello's shop, which looked exactly as it had on my last day of work there. Frank and his wife, Viola, were still keeping the business going. They were happy to see me again and thought I looked terrific. They asked if I was working. My reply was an immediate "No, when do I start?" I made sure to leave room in my schedule in case Macy's still had an opening for me, which they did. They rehired me to work once more in Men's Furnishings. The same manager was still there. I had learned valuable sales approaches from him the last time around and was glad to be back in his department, which I found pleasant and professionally fulfilling. Two months into my rehire, I was offered a transfer to the Men's Wardrobe department. Mr. Dave was the manager of

Men's Wardrobe, and though I'd worked congenially with him for years previously, he apparently now saw me as a threat. The commission he earned was lucrative, and now I had a chance to take some of it away. He threatened to quit if my reassignment went through. So I returned without malice to my cozy corner of shirts and ties where I worked forty hours a week, including every other weekend. Two months later, I was asked to attend a workshop to train as a buyer for the department. After three days of excruciating lessons, I surrendered and honestly confessed that this role was certainly not for me. Instead, I continued working my regular evening hours at Macy's, and when I had extra time on the weekends, I chose to work with Frank Procello at the detail shop. I liked seeing the old used cars transformed into nice-looking vehicles through our artistic and hard work. Besides, Frank had been a family support for all of us through the years. In no time, my status in the shop improved. My job of cleaning the interior of cars was upgraded to delivering newly detailed vehicles to be sold at used-car lots. The owners of the lots complimented us on our vehicles, saying they were the first to be sold, thanks to the beautiful luster and glitter treatments we had given them. We were proud.

My brothers Frank and Ralph were also helping to deliver cars under my guidance and supervision. When we had several cars to take to the same place, my brothers each drove one while I drove ahead of them in another. While I served as liaison with the lot management, my brothers would wait in the vehicles as they were inspected and approved. Frank and Viola were thrilled that we had designed such a professional system. All went well until Friday in September when we had to deliver three vehicles to a lot 120 miles away. Mr. Procello was reluctant to entrust this task to us since none of us had seasoned experience driving on the Interstate. The cars had to be delivered on time: the lot managers were waiting to place theme sale for the weekend. Procello gave me a map, specifically instructing me to go east on the freeway and drive to the town of Watsonville. We would take the first exit, and the car lot would be on the right: piece of cake. The first part of the trip went smoothly. Frank and Ralph followed me cautiously onto the freeway, watching for my hand signals to slow down or proceed—I had designed my own code as the leader. But an hour into our trip, I felt a barrage of traffic whizzing by us like bullets. I kept looking back to see if Frank and Ralph were following as directed. They were both safe drivers and respected the state speed limit, which other drivers seemed to ignore. As for me, I was maintaining a safe speed of seventy miles an hour when I saw an aqua-colored car abruptly pull onto the highway right in front of me. There was no time: I slammed on the brakes to avoid collision. Frank, who was following right behind me, suddenly rear-ended my vehicle, which went careening over the median into westbound traffic, rolling over several times before landing upright. I felt the horror of impact with metal exploding all over my body. I thought I was dead until I saw Frank's face peering down on me. "My dear, dear guardian angel," I said, "I am alive." Strangely, my vain brother's only worry was that one of my shoes had come off during the accident, exposing my dirty sock full of holes. He quickly and efficiently placed a torn piece of my shirt over my foot to avoid embarrassment.

I was rushed to the hospital in an ambulance, examined from head to toe, and miraculously released to go home. I thanked God one more time for the gift of life. Frank, Ralph, and I were offered a free ride home in the ambulance, but were disappointed that this time the sirens were not used. On the way home, I thought to myself that if cats had nine lives, well, so must I.

A month later, after a complete investigation of the accident, it was disclosed that the driver of the aqua car had definitely been at fault. Unfortunately, she had died instantly. She and her unborn baby had never had a chance. As the months after the accident went by, I lived in a trance of sorrow for the death of the other driver. I had difficulty sleeping and concentrating at work. I learned that alcohol provided immediate relief from the ugly pain I was living with. On weekends, I'd take off with my hometown friends Richard and Joel to the beach in Santa Cruz to sun and drink beer. On Saturdays, after the beach, we would head back to San Jose to a place called the Rainbow Ballroom. This was an actual ballroom with colored lights circling all over the walls and ceiling. There, we met the loveliest girls in town. Later, we learned that the ballroom attracted professional dancers to entertain the weekend crowds. This was indeed the place to party and forget the horror that haunted me. I lived for the weekend. My purchases from Macy's always included new shirts and ties to show off for the girls. I was the best-dressed *pachanga* dancer in the city of San Jose, or so I thought. After the ballroom closed at one in the morning, we would find a place to party until three or four. I had a system of sneaking into the house through a back window, then sleeping until noon, only to return to the ballroom that afternoon. These afternoon dances were known as *tardeadas* (afternoon parties), and they went from 2:00 to 9:00 p.m. They were a clever way to get people home early on Sunday night to start the workweek semisober. During the rest of the week, I had time to think of Ramón and his family. I remembered the promises I had made to myself to make something valuable of my life. This would last three or four days until the weekend rolled around again. Week after week held the same agenda: work, drink booze, party, and sleep. The Rainbow Ballroom became my wonderland of drinking, smoking, singing, and dancing. It was both a sanctuary and an addiction.

For a special celebration at the ballroom, the popular singer Vicki Carr, liked by us all, was scheduled to perform. Tickets went on sale early and sold out quickly. Because I wasn't too busy during the day, I bought three tickets during the first two hours they were on sale. Joel and Richard were pleased to benefit from my gumption, and each promised to buy me a drink. That night, I wore the best shirt and tie I could find with a brand-new pair of dark slacks to match. I applied the Macy's wardrobe rules carefully to myself. We were among the first people in line. When we looked back, we could see a line of people as long as the entire block waiting to enter the fabulous and enticing venue. We found seats right near the orchestra and as close to the stage as we could get to where Vicki Carr would entertain her admiring fans. She spoke to my heart when she sang my favorite song "Te Extraño." This song reminded me of my Dallas family each time I heard it.

Te extraño
Como se extañan
Las noches sin estrellas
Como se extrañan las mañanas bellas,
No estar contigo, por Dios
Que me hace daño.

(I miss you,
Like one misses
The nights without stars,
Like one misses beautiful mornings,
Being without you, God knows
How it is anguish for me.)

During the first intermission of Vicki's show, various other musicians filled the gap with their talents. Joel and Richard went outside for a break, and I stayed to continue drinking my beer and smoking by the bar. I always seemed to have a cigarette lit to make myself look more awesome. It was definitely the macho thing to do in those days. Standing in front of me was a guy dressed in an army uniform with a short-sleeved shirt. Suddenly, he stepped backward and accidentally brushed his elbow against my cigarette. He jumped at the burn and, when he saw where it had come from, started yelling that he would kill me. He sure had learned a lot of vulgar stuff in the army: words I'd never heard. He used every single one of them to define me. I apologized profusely and, being totally scared of this monster, quickly rushed outside to find Joel and Richard. They had probably gone back in because the only person I found out there was the army madman who had followed me outside to beat the living pulp out of me. He grabbed me by my tie and shirt and dragged me to the back of the building where he planned to offer my body to the army gods. As he was getting ready for round one with the intention of destroying my face, a security officer intervened and broke up the fight. I trembled and shook and vomited from total fear. No one had been so personally threatening, offensive, or rude to me before. I had always considered myself a nice guy. The security officer waited until I composed myself and, with the voice of an angel, said, "Hi, Tony. Don't you remember me? I'm Gary Wright, your friend from city college? Remember Ms. Gibson?" Right before my very eyes was my old pal! "Welcome to the nightlife of San Jose," he said. "This is a dangerous place." He embraced me so hard I wished the army guy would intervene.

Gary and I visited for the rest of the evening. He suggested that I go home early in case the military man was not done with me. I said I would, but only if he promised to meet me for breakfast the next day. We met for breakfast at 2:30 a.m. He remembered every detail of our friendship at the city college and asked me if I still owned the cherry tree. We laughed. He asked if I had completed my degree at San Jose State. He wanted to know the details of my experiences there. After I shared my dreadful, though admittedly sometimes funny ordeal, I told him that I was proud of him for achieving his dream of becoming a policeman. He had been a successful officer for over three years. Even more importantly, he had a family now. He'd married a girl he'd met at the police academy, and they had son. They were now getting ready to move from California. He had been offered a promotion in Oregon that would benefit him professionally in many ways. We said good-bye and promised to stay in contact, but as often happens even with good friends, that was not to be. I never saw Gary again.

My days in San Jose were empty. It seemed as if the good times were gone. Procello closed shop, Gary moved, and my yearning for another chance at school evoked sadness and regret as I had never known. Maggie was having a dreadful time with her chronically unemployed husband, and I could offer little help. I felt like a dismal failure. My salary at Macy's was barely enough to help Mom with the monthly essentials. Weekends were all the same: party after party after party.

To get to Macy's for my shift, I took the bus, which stopped numerous times along the way. Sometimes I left before noon to have time to stop somewhere and read the paper, go to a matinee movie, or shop around before going in at 3:00 p.m. One day, as I was browsing in a mall before catching the bus, I noticed a familiar-looking person walking out of one of the shops. Had I met him before? He walked past me and, five seconds later, made an about-face and caught up with me again. He stood right in front of me. I had seen this face. As I froze in place, he stretched out his hand, grabbed mine, and shook it. "You probably don't remember me," he said. "I'm the jerk that scared the living hell out of you at the Rainbow Ballroom way back. Don't you remember? You were scared shitless!"

I felt like passing out. My first inclination was to run away and hide in the nearby movie theater or to thank him for sparing my life. He laughed at his stupid behavior that night and apologized for being an "asshole." I also apologized for almost cremating him with a cigarette in a public place. We laughed again, this time without fear. He asked what I was doing in this part of the city. I told him I worked at Macy's and that if I didn't hurry, I would miss my bus to work. "Bus? My car is on the next block parked in a no-parking zone. I have to move the damn thing or I'll get another ticket. I get one every week. Why don't you ride with me?"

We walked to his car talking about the Rainbow Ballroom, and I told him that the security officer who had saved my life that night was my friend Gary. He thought I was lucky to have such a neat guy as a friend. When we got to his car, sure enough, there was a ticket on the windshield. I admired his brand-new Pontiac unabashedly. We drove to Macy's, and he decided to get out with me, walking with me through the store. He asked if I had a ride back home. I said, "Yes, one of my brothers, who has several cars, will pick me up." I lied.

Two weeks later, the same guy came into Macy's to buy two shirts. I helped him out, and he said he had forgotten to introduce himself the day we met in the mall. "My name is Dale Garza. I know your name is Tony Carvajal. I asked that man that sells men's suits—that ugly dude. He doesn't seem to like you. I think we should take him on." That evening, Dale gave me a ride home. From a very unlikely start, we were becoming friends. Little did I know that this man was destined to be the one person who would change my course in life from a dead end to a road that would lead me to ultimate success.

As the weeks went by, Dale and I continued to hang out together. On weekends, he would meet one more member of my family and make himself available when we needed a ride somewhere. We all started to develop admiration for him and gratitude for his friendship. The family gushed about his spotless car with the gas tank always on full. On Saturdays, when I was working at Macy's, Dale often drove Mom to the packing plants where she worked eight months out of the year. He was our all-around Johnny on the spot. Several times, when Dale joined us for dinner, my family would ask him where his own family was. "Mom died a long time ago," was his short reply. He had told me his brothers and dad lived away from San Jose and that he rarely had time to see them. Dale preferred to talk about his experiences in Vietnam and avoided making reference to his family.

One Saturday afternoon, on a weekend I didn't have to work, Dale invited me to his aunt's house forty miles away. He wanted me to meet Aunt Stefena, who had been the one to raise him. He spoke of her loving devotion. His dad, who lived with Aunt Stefena and had been ill for some time, had apparently played a minimal parental role. The home was not what I expected: it was dilapidated and old. The paint was decaying and peeling, and the wooden fence around the yard, warped. This was where Dale had lived throughout his life until he left for the army. As he showed me around the house, he spoke of his childhood dream of becoming a professional baseball pitcher. He displayed to me the trophies he had earned for Player of the Year and other significant achievements: every single one of them in baseball. Our visit with Aunt Stefena and Dale's dad was brief, courteous, and pleasant. His aunt had prepared a delicious lunch for the four of us, and even though mealtime seemed to lack much in the way of meaningful conversation, the family's appreciation and respect for Dale was clearly evident. Before we left, Dale placed money in an envelope for his aunt. This must have been his way of continuing to look out for her needs. Dale's endearing manner and obvious affection for his aunt reminded me of the way he treated my own family and others he met. Who knew that a man who once strung me up by the neck on a very off night actually had such an ingratiating and generous spirit after all?

When Dale and I arrived back in San Jose, my own family was waiting for us. As was usual on weekends, Mom prepared the most delicious meal for us all. At our house, these dinners were the highlight of the week. We shared with each other the current news about all the incredible things that had happened to us. Dinner was usually interrupted by a phone call from Maggie, who lived with her husband elsewhere in San Jose. Usually, she would complain that she hadn't seen a paycheck from her husband in three weeks. After dinner, Dale would drive Mom and me over to Maggie's house so we could babysit while she ran errands. By now, my sister had three kids—ages four, six, and eight. I would watch them for two or three hours while Mom took a rest; then, she would take over nanny duty.

My family was everything to me, and my life was just as caught up with them as ever. It was now early November. Over a year had passed since I had last attended school, and despite my silent promise to Ramón, I had nothing to show for it. I told Dale that my plan had been to return to the city college to seek career advice. That never happened. I had planned to look for a job with a salary that could meet our monthly expenses. That hadn't happened either. Dale could see the cycle of discontentment that was entrapping me. "You can't continue this, Tony, your family will devour you." I dreamed sometimes of abandoning the endless turmoil of San Jose, but I had nowhere to run and nowhere to hide. The rainy, gloomy days of autumn contributed to my sense of disappointment and loss. The glitter and gentility of San Jose were gone. We were once again failing to meet our house payments. Mom's health was slowly eroding. Diabetes was setting in. My brothers and sisters too were infected with the awful sense of hopelessness. Even Dale seemed caught up in his own melancholy: his pleasant and enlightening disposition was beginning to fade. It was frightening to see despair creep into the hearts of every single one of us. Our lives, just like the rainstorms, grew worse with each passing day.

Then on the morning of one more rainy day, a ray of sunshine broke through the gloom of my life. I received a phone call from a very old friend: Arturo, my buddy from junior high. He was calling to check on my whereabouts, see how I was doing, and discover my progress in school. We met for coffee and talked for two hours. The conversation lifted and revitalized my very soul. Arturo shared that he had experienced similar obstacles at San Jose State. Even though mine had been worse, I still felt better. The place, we realized, was simply not prepared to meet the challenges of students with the limited educational backgrounds we had. We talked and talked until we had each come to the conclusion for ourselves that we had to leave San Jose. Arturo had learned from several of our friends in Del Rio that there was a state university in Alpine, Texas, that welcomed and embraced diversity. The administration at Sul Ross State College had always recruited academically talented students of diverse backgrounds and retained them through the completion of their programs. As Arturo talked, I felt a surge of hope. This was absolutely incredible. Like many times when I was emotionally overcome, I responded by rushing to the bathroom to vomit. Arturo and I promised to reconvene the following week to continue discussing the potentially favorable implications of such a big move.

Over the weekend, Dale spent time at our house as usual. He had embraced his surrogate family so wholeheartedly that he actually contributed to our mortgage payments and generously assisted us with the expenses we continued to incur. He earned an excellent salary as an automotive repairman, but was bored and unfulfilled by the work, which he felt led nowhere. It was certainly not what he had dreamed of doing once he got out of Vietnam. Dale shared his dreams with me of becoming "somebody" through education. So far, this goal had been unattainable, especially now that he had become a part of my crazy, needy family.

That Saturday, Arturo joined Dale and me for a concert. I asked him to describe for Dale the bright possibilities he had shared with me. Arturo, set on going to school, had already begun to prepare his application. His enthusiasm ignited a fire under Dale who, after that night, insisted that I contact the school. "You should go. You have what it takes," he urged. "I'll be okay here once I change jobs. I'll help your mom for three months before I leave to work in the San Joaquin Valley—there are a lot of good jobs there. You should go to Sul Ross. Talk to your mom. You have to go. I'll be okay."

But the thought of leaving my family was inconceivable. I told the army madman that he was being totally unrealistic.

Dale retorted with something I didn't see coming: "Your problem is that you want and need to be in charge. They will do fine or even better without you. Let's call Art . . . I'll go there with you guys."

"What? Are you insane?!" I exclaimed. I couldn't believe what I was hearing.

"I think so," replied Dale. "Yes, let's get the hell out of here before you die. Let's get the paperwork done to start in January. Wow, me in college? It will be one awesome journey. My aunt will be proud."

As it turned out, his family was confused by his decision and his several girlfriends shocked. My family, on the other hand, was ecstatic for me. Mom cried with joy. Maggie and Amy were stunned with happiness. I was glad for their support, but caught off guard by the extent and passion of their approval. How could they let me go that easily? I felt suddenly unwanted.

However, with my new dream on its way to becoming a reality, I let the momentum of the plan carry me forward. Art, Dale, and I wrote our admission papers and forwarded our transcripts to Sul Ross. Within two weeks, we had all received letters of acceptance. This was a legitimate opportunity to celebrate. Dale would matriculate as a freshman with a preengineering major. As for me, the admissions office had accepted the transfer of fifty-seven hours from San Jose City College and twelve hours from San Jose State, making me a bonafide junior in good academic standing at Sul Ross. I chose English as a major and speech and drama as a minor. If all went well, I could complete my bachelor's degree, along with my high school teaching certification, in less than two years.

I'll always be grateful to Arturo for introducing the option that would get me back on track with my college education. And though we remained friends at Sul Ross and beyond, it was Dale who I would rely on most as we finally left San Jose to discover whatever was awaiting us back in my home state of Texas.

Part Three: Háblame

Cuando te haga falta una illusion
Háblame.
Cuando sienta frío tu corazón
Háblame
Que no habrá distancia en todo el mundo
Que no alcance por ti
Ni tendrá un rincón el mar profundo
Que yo no encuentre por ti.

(When you need an illusion
Call me
When your heart feels cold
Call me
Because there is no distance in all the world
That I wouldn't reach for you
Nor is there a corner in the deep sea
That I wouldn't reach for you.)

—From the song "Y Háblame,"
lyrics by Paco Michel

Chapter Fourteen

It was the day before Christmas when Dale and I departed for Texas. My heart and soul felt an anguish I had never known before. My precious Amy, particularly, gave me the strength to withstand the guilt I felt about leaving the family by supporting my decision. After we'd loaded everything in the car, we turned to say good-bye. Mom blessed us. Amy presented me with a tumbler stuffed with candy for our trip and a drawing she'd made of a Christmas tree, which I promised myself I would keep as a reminder of her love. Maggie, Frank, and Ralph showered us with sarcastic advice. They told Dale not to let me drive even one mile. If he did, they said, we would never make it. We laughed, hopped in the car, and drove away. We avoided looking back. In no time, we were on the freeway, on our way toward our magnificent goal. I left wondering how my family would make it without me. I vowed that, should they need me, they had only to call and I'd always be there for them.

Our road trip from San Jose to Alpine, Texas, provided Dale and me with time to chat endlessly and reevaluate—or more accurately, evaluate for the first time—exactly what it was we were doing. We had left so much behind. What *was* this new venture anyway? We discussed the financial commitments I'd left behind and the whole new set of expenses we were about to incur. I told Dale that I'd been notified that I was only eligible for a stipend that would cover the cost of books and administrative fees. Aside from that, I had just $120 saved from the last two months I'd worked in San Jose. Dale was doing much better. His tuition, books, fees, and housing were covered by a federal GI student grant. On top of that, I was impressed to learn that he'd saved over eight thousand dollars since returning from Vietnam. He was a disciplined financial planner and could account for every dollar he spent. He had tallied expenses using the school catalog and now had a budget for the first year at Sul Ross already outlined. In this budget, Dale had included my school expenses as well. I was incredibly impressed and relieved. For the first time ever, I felt unworried about money: financially secure. I had a safety net. I promised Dale that I would get a part-time job at a department store to cover my rent and our utilities and groceries. He was pleased at how serious I was and proud of the both of us for our cautiousness and foresight. Through our cooperation and compatibility, we would certainly cover the financial demands of the first year.

Sul Ross State College (now known as Sul Ross State University) sat on a hill overlooking the city of Alpine, Texas. Alpine was known as the Alps of Texas. It was truly where the deer and the antelope played: beautiful mountainous country with alpine forests and wildlife galore. The city itself was quite small, but pleasant: indeed, seldom was heard a discouraging word there. It was a beautiful natural setting to address the educational goals we had so firmly set for ourselves. We approached it with the devotion of pilgrims reaching a sacred land. It was the sanctuary where our new lives were about to begin.

Upon arrival, Dale and I were eager to select our classes for the first semester. Along with our letters of acceptance, we had also been given the names of our academic advisors. What we hadn't considered when we'd eagerly departed California was that our arrival would fall during the Christmas holidays when all the professors were gone. We took a shot at building a tentative schedule ourselves. My experience with planning my course work at the city college and San Jose State helped us. Dale's schedule was easy to make: as a freshman, he would need to include only general education requirements. He had some twenty classes to choose from. We decided he should take a class in American history, one in geography, one in biology, and one in math. Twelve semester hours would be enough for his first attempt at college. My choices had to be more specific since my transferred credits had put me much farther along in my studies. My academic misadventures in California, I realized, had not been completely in vain. I had already fulfilled many of the requirements for my English major and some for my speech and drama minor, transferring credit even from classes in which I'd earned a D. All considered, I still needed three full semesters of eighteen credit hours each to complete the requirements for a BA with a teaching certification. This would be splendid timing. In just a year and a half, I could complete my program and begin teaching, thus supporting Dale in his efforts to obtain a degree. This would be the deal: a dream in the making for us both.

After the holiday break, the university opened for enrollment. Our advisors were now available to review our academic plans. This was new for me: I would actually have the privilege of talking to a real person who would guide my program to completion. The advisors, one from my major area and one from my minor area, were professors who taught undergraduate courses. They showed personal and genuine interest in each student. I met with each of them and shared, for their approval, the classes I had selected: three classes in English and three in speech and drama. They made some minor revisions, shook my hand, welcomed me, and sent me off with tears in my eyes. How could professors be so kind? Dale shared similar experiences. His advisors were impressed with his achievements in baseball during high school and with his military service in Vietnam. When the first day of classes rolled around, we were well prepared.

The Alps of Texas turned out to be an appropriate moniker for Alpine in another way: the snow. In the winter, it came down by the foot. We had never seen snow in California and were in for a rude awakening. Though we were almost the only students with a car, it did us little good those first weeks. Due to the heavy snowfall, we could drive it no more than five feet up the hill to campus. So we began walking all the way up the hill to class and back down afterward, day in and day out. We were unprepared for the cold. Our California Windbreakers and tennis shoes were ill suited to the cold fronts that ravaged the area. And though I was much healthier than I'd once been, I was certainly not prepared to hike up the hill without several rest stops. To me, the ordeal was like climbing Mt. Everest. Many times, I wondered if I would die of a heart attack on the way up. Buried in the snow, my remains wouldn't be found until spring. Since Dale and I had resolved to approach our new experience with unconditionally positive attitudes, this was not a good thought.

I met the first day of classes at Sul Ross with the same blend of excitement and anxiety as on my first day at the yellow school. I found my classes with no problem, having taken a "dry run" through the buildings earlier in preparation for the day. All the required textbooks were in my bag. I was used to being a nameless face in my classes, fighting to grasp what was expected of me. But when I entered each of my classes that first day at Sul Ross, I—along with all the other students—was given a syllabus that explained the nature of the course, requirements, and expectations and a list of office hours when each professor would be available specifically to address questions and concerns. Most professors even prescheduled a thirty-minute meeting with each of us to allow us to share our career plans and talk about timelines for graduation. I trembled with excitement. For each class on that first day, the professor had us introduce ourselves to the others and, in two minutes, share where we'd come from, our major, and anything else we wanted to let people know. I spoke for forty seconds. This was totally unreal. I was so impressed that I called Mom that night to tell her that I had, indeed, found heaven. Maggie wondered if I'd been drinking. Finally, I found not just a few but an entire institution full of individuals in an educational setting who were real human beings.

In exuberance, I devoured class readings and lectures and then redigested them after class. I was gobbling up literature, writing essays, and staying at the library until closing time. My new scholarly world was becoming addictive. Dale was not connecting in the same way to college academics. He missed a girlfriend he'd left behind in San Jose and talked to her often by phone. It seemed to sadden his days. As we walked to the library together in the afternoon, he'd express his lack of interest in classes, saying that he was doing okay but that his excitement was fading.

My first semester at Sul Ross, I earned five As and one B. My GPA soared to 3.9. Hooked on the feeling this gave me, I felt I could have done even better. I knew exactly where I'd faltered and would strive to complete my next semester with a perfect 4.0. I don't know when ambition becomes addictive, when dedication to a goal becomes compulsion, or when success becomes its own reward. All I knew was that accomplishment felt good. In American history, I read that people who survived the Great Depression tended to value above all else whatever they'd missed out during their difficult times. In this way, significant deprivation can create a different monster in later years. College was what I now valued almost to obsession. I was not going back to where I'd been. My world was now the library; my textbooks were my weekend companions. As I insistently submerged myself deeper into the isolation of academia, I left Dale at the edge of the water. Whatever problems invaded his spirit, he bore the agony alone. The carefree, pleasant, and loveable guy I'd known was fading day by day.

As my second semester at Sul Ross began, two professors gave me the inspiration I needed to move forward with my course work: Dr. Ramey and Dr. Prude. Dr. Ramey was my teaching certification advisor and my professor for Educational Foundations. She was my definition of superiority in teaching. Her high caliber of instruction and ability to hook students into a love of teaching drove a sense of urgency in me to pursue the field immediately. When the time came, she discussed with me the places that I might apply for my student teaching. Of course, I still had to pass another awful speech clearance first, for which we were awaiting the results. One day, Dr. Ramey called me in to complete the paperwork for my student teaching placement: I had finally conquered the godforsaken, ridiculous, clinical barrier that had almost killed my aspirations to become a teacher once before. I had passed!

Then there was Dr. Prude, a professor in the Professional Education department. A month after my triumph over the speech clearance test, he raised my spirits through the roof, calling me in to congratulate me for an Excellence in Academics award, a recognition given by the dean of the college. It carried a stipend of two hundred dollars as well as a voucher for a delicious meal at the college cafeteria. I ran out of Prude's office and immediately called Mom, assuring her that I would be sending a copy of the award certificate. With it, I sent a check for one hundred dollars. I told her this was the first step of many to come in my professional life.

Nights and days began to blur together without my awareness. I would go to bed around one in the morning and get up at six. I'd peek into Dale's room to make sure he'd come home from his night out, grab whatever I could find to eat from the kitchen, then make my way panting up the hill to the library. The back entrance usually opened for library staff at sixty thirty, and I was allowed to enter this way since I worked there part-time. But on one particular Monday morning, I waited at the door until almost seventy thirty with no sign of anyone. A campus security truck drove by, and the officer stopped to ask if I needed help. "No, sir, I'm a student and an employee here. I'm waiting for the place to open." The officer responded with loud laughter. "Tony, today is a holiday. It's Labor Day. Don't you keep track of your life? Go party, man." I was furious with myself for my stupidity, but thankful to the guy for letting me know. It turned out to be Mike, a guy in my educational psychology class. He promised not to mention this to anyone.

I walked down the hill and into a diner to treat myself to breakfast. I scattered my books on the table and ordered. A wave of depression overwhelmed me. I thought how empty my life had become. I'd become obsessed with my academic agenda. I missed having a normal social life. I missed the company of a special girl. Since starting at Sul Ross, my romantic life had been pretty much put on hold. I had dated a girl on campus that Dale and his new girlfriend had introduced me to, but the whole thing had been absurd. I dated her about three times in one month, and the whole time, she was also seeing someone from her hometown. In fact, she finally told me that she was three months pregnant with his child, and that after he'd found out, he'd left the state. She told me how important I'd become in her life and how much she admired a man like me who was kind, responsible, and respectful. I was as tactful and caring as I could be and explained to her that I could not continue seeing her. I wished her well and assured her that she would find a good man to be a father to her baby. There was nothing else I could do for her: I had to stay focused on myself. After my solitary breakfast and the thoughts that came with it, I walked back home. Practically everyone had left campus for the long weekend break. Dale continued to snore through the afternoon. I was lost without my routine. I realized I had to make some changes in my life. I had to find someone to share my days with. This was too lonely an existence.

After classes resumed, Dr. Boyd, a professor in Shakespeare literature, called me in to review the clinical requirements for the minor in speech and drama. She shared that she had met with Dr. Clark, my advisor in both English and drama. They had agreed I should complete my minor by acting in a school production of Tennessee Williams's *The Glass Menagerie*, a play that led to what Williams called "the catastrophe of success." I wasn't interested in any more catastrophes. Yet the play was appealing in its simplicity: it only required four actors. I read it and immediately knew this one was for me. Tennessee Williams describes the mother, Amanda, as "a little woman of great but confused vitality," who also exhibits "endurance" and "a kind of heroism." This immediately brought forth memories of Mom. Laura, Amanda's daughter, is an extremely shy individual who walks with a slight limp, a residual defect from a childhood illness. This apparently minor problem affected her so seriously that it resulted in a significant lack of self-esteem and a tendency to withdraw from people. Laura's only escape from her lonely existence is her collection of glass figurine animals. Tom is Laura's brother and the narrator of the play. He is a sensitive poet with a job in a common warehouse. Devastatingly, he is the target of his mother's constant nagging. The fourth character, Jim, is the "gentleman caller." He is a nice, ordinary young man who is invited to dinner to meet Laura.

I was cast in the role of Jim, and soon all four of us actors began meeting to study our characters. I was elated, yet nervous. I was assured that this was a typical nervousness most actors feel. Without this rush, the performances would remain flat. But I was in a constant state of "rush," and it wasn't all due to the acting. The part of Laura was to be played by a young lady named Carol. Since we had important scenes together, Carol and I began to meet afternoons and evenings to rehearse alone together. Her sweet, loving manner slowly began to make its way into my needy heart, sparking ideas of love at a time when I really needed them. As the story of the play unfolded on stage, another was unfolding in my heart. Carol sent me to the moon and back, and I wondered if she too was falling crazy in love with me. She seemed to be. She was a good actress, but people can't fake love: no way. However, she did happen to have a boyfriend already, so we kept our passions relegated to the realm of rehearsal kisses and our confessions to the words on the printed page.

The drama of the production swept me up in the romance even more. When showtime finally rolled around, I couldn't wait to take the stage. Since Jim doesn't appear until later in the play, I was frustrated by how long I had to wait for the cue to make my entrance. But at last, I was on stage for a long, intricate, and intense scene with Laura. The music and lighting only enhanced my passion and emotion. As Carol and I spoke our lines to each other, the exchange felt personal—natural:

> Jim: You know I have a sense that I have seen you before. I had that idea as soon as you opened the door. It seemed that I was about ready to remember your name. But the name that I started to call you wasn't really a name—so I stopped myself before I said it.
>
> Laura: Wasn't it Blue Roses?
>
> Jim: My gosh yes, it was Blue Roses. How was it that I started calling you that?
>
> Laura: I was out of school with Pleurisies. When I came back you asked me what was the matter. I said I had Pleurisies, you thought I said Blue Roses. That's what you called me after that.

After this revealing dialogue about how they met and Laura's confession about her shy encounters at school, Jim speaks again. These words emerged from a very deep part of my own soul. My voice almost cracked as I approached Carol and looked her straight in the eyes:

> People are not so dreadful when you know them. That's what you have to remember! And everybody has problems, not just you, but practically everybody has got some problems. You think of yourself as having the only problems, as being the only one that is disappointed. But just look around you and you will see lots

of people as disappointed as you are. For instance, when I was going to high school, I hoped that I would be further along at this time, six years later, than I am now.

As I heard the words my own voice was expressing, I let myself, for the first time, fully identify with the message. That evening, on that stage, I realized a truth I had long denied: I was a lonely and empty man. Struggles and setbacks had been part of who I was for so long that I was beginning to believe that this is just the way life would be. I was not so unlike my brother Ramón: plagued by pain and regret. I had missed so much in my life, I realized now. And just as this admission came to me, I began to feel a sense of tranquility and peace—long searched for—wash over me. In confronting the negative feelings I had denied and shoved away for so long, I was already getting ready to let them go. I wondered if acting was a form of personal catharsis for other actors. It had certainly become a healing experience for me. As I spoke my next lines, I felt Tennessee Williams had written them for me. They are words I will never forget:

> You know what I judge to be the trouble with you? Inferiority complex! Know what that is? That's what they call it when someone low rates himself. I understand it because I had it too. Although my case was not so aggravated as yours seems to be. I had it until I took up public speaking, developed my voice, and learned that I had an aptitude for science . . . Yep, that's what I judge to be your principal trouble, a lack of confidence in you as a person. You don't have the proper amount of faith in yourself.

Jim's words, spoken through me, prepared me for a long journey of learning to appreciate who I was and who I'd been. The assignment had become a turning point in my life in which I had discovered the capacity for love—for others and for myself—that had been hidden in the corners of my heart. I had to let go of the awful memories of failure at San Jose State. Being here with Carol helped me look within myself and continue forward through self-affirmation and personal growth. We spoke our final lines:

Jim: You know—you're different—very different—surprisingly different from anyone else I know. I mean it in a nice way—you make me feel sort of—I don't know how to say it, I'm usually pretty good at expressing things, but—this time it is something that I don't know how to say! Has anyone ever told you that you are pretty? Well you are. In a very different way than anyone else. The different people are not like other people, but different is nothing to be ashamed of. Because other people are not such wonderful people. They're one hundred times one thousand. You are one times one! They walk all over the earth. You just stay here. They're common as—weeds, but—you—well. You're Blue Roses!

Laura: "But Blue is wrong for—roses."

Jim: It's right for you, your eyes—your hair—they're pretty. Your hands are pretty. I am talking to you sincerely. Somebody needs to build up your confidence. And make you proud instead of shy and turning away—and blushing—somebody—ought to, ought to—kiss you, Laura.

When I kissed Carol on her warm and beautiful lips, it was not a stage kiss by any means. I promised myself that I would remember her loveliness and tenderness forever. The combination of the powerful script, the music, and the fact that when I'd met Carol I hadn't had a tender relationship with a girl in months combined to ingrain the memory permanently into my brain. At curtain call, we received immense applause from the audience, mostly made up of fellow students and faculty. Dale was in attendance along with some of our other friends. Dale complimented me and said I should marry Laura immediately and in real life. He knew I'd fallen in love with Carol after so many rehearsed kisses. Of course, her boyfriend had always been there to take her home, just as he was tonight. Selfish idiot. Carol and I thanked each other and went our separate ways. I never saw her again, and neither did I ever get a call from Hollywood.

Chapter Fifteen

The magnificent literary gift of Tennessee Williams made an indelible impression on me that year. The complex characters in *The Glass Menagerie*, in whom I could recognize traits of myself and others, left me with an inclination to further study human psychology and the fascinating concept of self-image. The character of Laura in the play also brought up insights into what it meant to be different and the importance of how one regards oneself because of this difference. With the help of Jim, Laura comes to realize that her uniqueness is not a curse, but something actually admired by others. I realized now that I had started out with an innate appreciation for myself long ago during my days in the placita. Back then, I had considered the uniqueness of my culture to be a gift. I was not an Anglo, and I did talk differently, but this made me something that wasn't as common as weeds. So much had happened since then that had made me forget that my differentness was something in which I should take pride. Perhaps it was time to return to that unconditional love for myself once again.

In the midst of these realizations, the fall semester was quickly passing. Our funds were also rapidly depleting. My wages from working part-time at the library and cafeteria were so minimal that Dale and I could hardly make utility payments. Dale continued to work part-time also, but we both worried we would not meet expenses for the last two months of the semester. This is when my noble and kind brother Ramón came back into my life. I borrowed five hundred dollars from him with the promise that I'd pay him when I started teaching the following year. Mom had written two weeks earlier with an urgent need for money to pay the family's utilities. I sent her two hundred dollars from Ramón's loan. I wrote and thanked my brother profusely and reiterated my pledge to pay him back. This would be top priority when I got rich. Two months later, I found myself writing him for another loan. His kindness and trust in me was once again exemplified. This was, however, getting very worrisome. I couldn't continue traveling down this road into dependence and debt.

Finally, the last few weeks of the semester were here, and it looked as if at last my academic efforts had paid off. There was a strong possibility that I would complete the term with five grades of A. My GPA would be 4.0. I wrote to Ramón to share the good news, and I sent him a copy of my academic excellence certificate from the previous semester. In response, he sent a congratulatory card with signatures from Mary Ellen and my little angels. As I studied the card carefully, I allowed myself to reminisce for the longest time about the emotional day I had departed Dallas.

The library was packed with students preparing for finals. A state of panic swept over the procrastinators, who all clamored for my assistance in finding resources. I ran up and down the stairs for hours, trying to respond to all the requests. Though the current chaos sent me into a state of annoyance, I enjoyed my job at the library. The staff was outstanding. We worked as a family to support each other and the student body. Professors knew that their students would get sound guidance from us to complete required assignments. Yes, I was the one giving the advice now. I thought of Dr. Warren and how far I'd come since the days I'd earned his merciless evaluation. He would be shocked at how well I now knew the ins and outs of grammar, spelling, and proper form for citations. I remembered clearly what he had written: that not to criticize would be false kindness. Perhaps there had been a kernel of truth to this after all, considering how much I'd taken the criticism to heart and how hard I'd worked to dig myself out from under it.

Generally, after I finished my five-hour shift at the library in the early evening, I would stay for just as long—until the library closed—to complete my own assignments. This last month of the term was no exception. One evening, as I sat in the reading room highlighting passages from *King Lear*, I noticed an attractive young lady sitting nearby. I had, in fact, seen her many times before in this section of the library. She also read from a copy of *King Lear*. I immediately asked her if she was in Dr. Bosley's class, and she replied, "Yes, my name is Rosie. I sit in the back. And you, Tony, sit in the second row, and you run out when class is over." She reached out her hand and shook mine lightly. I found it uncommon for a girl to do this and thought maybe she was flirting with me. My hunch was right on. We started dating, seeing each other almost every night for three solid weeks. Rosie was brilliant and serious about her work. She too was an English major getting ready to graduate the following spring. To me, it was rare to find an ardently scholarly person who was so funny at the same time. She had seen our production of *The Glass Menagerie* and cracked me up with her imitation of Laura's mother. She thought I had made a perfect "gentleman caller," handsome and debonair. She said "Laura" was stupid not to hit on me. Rosie and I enjoyed each other's company immensely. Even though she lived in the dormitory and had to make curfew, we found ways to see each other in the evenings. She lived on the third floor and designed an ingenious way for me to crawl up the side of the brick building using the climbing vines that grew there. My kinesthetic talents impressed even me. Tarzan had returned.

The week of finals was a nightmare. Students plodded around like zombies from so many late hours of study. The library was suddenly quiet and somber. For some reason, Rosie had stopped calling, and I couldn't find her anywhere. She had been absent from class for over a week. After several attempts at contacting her without success, I decided to call the receptionist at the dorm. I became dreadfully concerned and started to look for her. I first went to her dorm room with the receptionist. There was no answer when I knocked at her door. She was nowhere to be found at the cafeteria or at a nearby park where we liked to go. Finally, I got a dorm attendant to try calling her room. When there was no answer, the attendant checked Rosie's file. She said that Rosie had gone home on a family emergency. I got Rosie's family's number and called. Her sister informed me that Rosie was very sick and would not be returning to school until the following semester. I felt empty. Why hadn't Rosie called to tell me? I thought we were important to each other. We had spoken of traveling together at some point after our first year of teaching: we would blow our earnings at some exotic resort since teachers didn't have to work summers. Maybe the relationship was not as honest and romantic as I'd thought. Perhaps she had another boyfriend somewhere.

The following day, I drove to Rosie's family's home eighty miles away. I listened to our favorite song "Blue Velvet" over and over again. When I arrived, I knocked at the front door and waited. There was no answer. I tried again: still nothing. I returned to my car and sat for over forty minutes. Finally, I noticed a car approaching. It pulled up next to me. "Can I help you?" the woman at the wheel asked. "Who are you looking for? This is my house." I responded carefully, "I am Tony, a friend of Rosie. I was worried because she wasn't in school. I just came to talk to her. You see, she has some of my books." The woman turned out to be Rosie's sister. Hesitantly, she invited me into the house. It felt like a hospital: austere and sterile. I was breathing hard. The sister disappeared briefly and then came back, saying that Rosie was too tired to see anybody and to come back another day. I told her how important it was for me to see Rosie. "I love your sister very much," I confessed. "I need to talk to her. Please take me to her." Noting my urgency and sincerity, Rosie's sister kindly relented, "Okay, come with me." We walked down the hall past three rooms before reaching a room with a Do Not Disturb sign on the door. The sister knocked, giving Rosie a ten-second notice before she opened the door. There was Rosie in bed, covered with a white sheet. Her face was deathly pale and moist with perspiration. Her sunken appearance was startling. She looked as if she had lost twenty pounds since our last date. I told her I missed her and needed her to be with me. She said she was not going back. "Why? What happened?" I asked. "Ask that fucking bastard, Bosley," Rosie angrily responded. "He accused me of plagiarizing. I was suspended from school. I'm finished. What I want from you, if you love me as I think you do, is to leave and never look for me again. Tony, please go!" I reached for Rosie's skeletal arm and kissed her forehead. Then I walked out of the house without even saying good-bye to her sister.

Evidently, the day Dr. Bosley had called Rosie in with the accusation and reviewed its dire implication of permanent suspension from the university, Rosie had suffered a major emotional collapse and had attempted suicide.

This was when her family intervened to rush her home. Even if Rosie didn't want to see me, I still had to do something on her behalf. I went to see Dr. Bosley and asked him if there was any way Rosie could be pardoned. Perhaps there had been some kind of misunderstanding. Even if there was any shred of merit to the charges, which I doubted, this punishment seemed far too severe and brutal. I pleaded with Bosley to find a way to allow Rosie to come back and finish her program. "Sir, literature has been Rosie's life since she was in the third grade. Her aspirations have been sincere and unyielding, she's always wanted to become an English teacher. Please!" Dr. Bosley merely turned his back and asked me to leave his office. I hated him with a deadly passion I had never before felt for anyone. As far as I was concerned, his rigidness and condescension had destroyed a brilliant, promising life. I hoped Rosie's suicide attempt would haunt him for the rest of his miserable days. Yet I could see that Bosley seemed startlingly unmoved by the chain of events his accusations had caused. It was my first true lesson in scholarly arrogance and hypocrisy.

For Rosie's terrible situation and the sudden end of our special relationship, my heart broke into many pieces. It was a wonder I got through finals week, but my diligence carried me through. I had completed all my written assignments before learning the devastating news about Rosie. I had prepared tirelessly for finals. As a result, my grades ended up ranking at the very top of each of my classes. But after the grades were in, I got an unexpected message to see my English advisor Dr. Taylor for a conference. I felt a chill of doom run through me. Dr. Prude, as another of my advisors for the teaching certification program, would also be at the meeting.

I wondered what this conference was all about. Was I to be the next victim of the senseless and inhumane system that had crushed Rosie? I wished I was going anywhere but to this meeting. I dreamed of being back at the very top of my cherry tree with Ms. Gibson and Gary holding my hands. I arrived at Dr. Taylor's office out of breath and perspiring. The conference seemed to have started without me. My advisors both stood up and came over to shake my hand. Dr. Prude, my faithful advocate up until this point, embraced me. "Et tu, Brute?" I thought, recalling the famous line from *Julius Caesar*. They asked me to sit down.

Dr. Prude began, "First of all, young man, I want to congratulate you for your admirable efforts and ultimate success in your work here at Sul Ross. Evelyn is proud of you and sends congratulations. I know you are puzzled. Do you remember Mrs. Poag, the owner and manager of the theaters in Del Rio?"

I excitedly responded, "Yes, I do—quite a wonderful lady. She helped me and my family a lot while I was going through high school in Del Rio."

Dr. Prude went on, "Her husband, Paul Poag, died sometime ago. I had known Evelyn for a few years before that. I found her to be quite wonderful just as you do. After she lost her husband, we fell in love and married. We've been married now for ten years. We've often talked about you, and she remembers you as a very hard worker and an honest individual."

In my surprise, somehow, all I could think was *She probably didn't find out about all the admission tickets and popcorn we gave away free to our friends.*

"Anyway, congratulations again," Dr. Prude said. He shook my hand, and I stood up to leave. "Wait, wait, one more thing," he said. "Last month, I returned from Eagle Pass where I place student teachers. Mr. Ford, the superintendent there, is in desperate need of three English teachers. I spoke to him about you, and he is eager to consider you for one of the positions. He was impressed and very pleased to learn about you."

I turned to Dr. Taylor, who agreed that I should consider the opportunity. "You're as ready as you will ever be," Taylor remarked. "You have a talent for writing and enormous appreciation for literature. You are one of the best students I have known. Besides, Eagle Pass, being a border town, enrolls many students who only speak Spanish or are bilingual. Your background makes you a double asset to the district."

I was ready to teach *now*? I didn't know how to respond.

Dr. Taylor continued to explain, "You've completed 123 semester hours toward your bachelor's degree, you're required to have 120. You've completed all courses required for the English major and the minor in speech and drama. You will graduate this fall with a BA degree. In addition, you have completed the twelve hours of course work required for your teaching certification. The only requirement you still have to meet is for student teaching. The superintendent of the school district Mr. Ford and Dr. Prude will work with you on this. You will earn student teaching credit while you teach. At the end of this semester, we'll recommend you to the state for Texas teaching certification. While that goes through, Eagle Pass will request permission from the state to hire you provisionally with a full salary."

I gulped and asked, "So what's the next step?"

Mr. Taylor responded, "Let me stress again. You will be completing your program here in just three weeks. You should set an appointment with Mr. Ford at the Eagle Pass School District to review your contract. Are you willing to take this on? If you do, you should now consider yourself a professional teacher. Think about it and let me know by tomorrow at this time."

I thanked Dr. Taylor and Dr. Prude both and rushed out of the office. As I was passing the library, I stopped and turned back around. Was there really any question about what I would choose? I raced back, hoping my advisors were still in the office. When I saw them, I went inside and blurted, "Yes, I'll take it."

All three of us were pleased and proud of the remarkable and expedient results of our discussion. I was starting to utter words of appreciation when Dr. Clark, the director of the teacher education program, interrupted. He came into the office and asked me to sit down. "Mr. Carvajal," he began, "I want you to know that my regrets and heartfelt sorrow are with you over Rosie's plagiarism mess. We all feel terrible about it. She should have never plagiarized your work. I know you feel betrayed."

I felt suddenly sick. "What?" I asked in shock. "She didn't plagiarize my work! We always worked together . . . we were a team."

"No, she copied three paragraphs verbatim from one of your papers," Dr. Clark responded. "It was your work, and the evidence is clear. Dr. Bosley knows your writing style very well. You write in short sentences, and her writing style is very wordy. It was very obvious."

I began to shake. "No, no!" I stammered. "Rosie always had my permission to see my work just as I always had her permission to see hers. We were a team. We were respectful of each other's work. No, she did not steal from me. That is ridiculous. No wonder she was so embarrassed to talk to me. Please, can I appeal? Can she appeal?"

Clark responded, "No, the damage is done. Like the saying goes, 'You can't unring a bell.' God be with you, young man."

This time, I left the office feeling regretful and disgusted. Whether Rosie had copied some of my work or not was now irrelevant to me. What I wanted to know was how a system—any system—could tear away a person's dignity and end their endeavors so mercilessly. It was one thing to be rigorous in maintaining academic standards; it was another to treat a person so contemptuously—like a criminal. I promised myself that after the semester ended, I would never again set foot on the Sul Ross campus. And I never did.

Chapter Sixteen

When I got home, I shared with Dale the dismal news about Rosie and the exciting news about the teaching offer. This was the first time I'd seen him in days. He was almost always gone lately, busy dating a girl who lived in a nearby town. He was barely finishing the semester with a GPA of 2.0. I told him that the job in Eagle Pass was a full-time teaching position and that I had already accepted. He seemed uneasy. "It's your turn to focus on your program," I encouraged him. "Have you considered a major? We should meet with an advisor. We should get some advice from anyone willing to spend time with us." He ignored my ideas. Instead, he wanted to know more about Rosie. He was genuinely concerned about her. I assured him that I had done all I could to correct the mess. He interrupted abruptly, "I have to make a quick trip back to San Jose. This is one I have to make by myself." I was confused and asked, "Why do you have to go back? I'm sorry I haven't been as supportive as I should've been lately. I've been busy with my own program. Now that I've completed my degree, I'm ready to help you in any way I can. Come on, let's get with it!" Without another word, he walked away.

Within days, I wrote to Mom and Ramón the first letters of totally good news they'd ever received from me. I told them not to write back until I contacted them with an Eagle Pass address. Being too busy preparing to leave for Eagle Pass, I skipped commencement. My paperwork validating eligibility for graduation was still in the works, but the director of records assured me that my name would be on the list of graduates. Not walking in commencement that day made little difference to me. The only person I cared to have seen me do so would have been Dale. My family didn't even know I was graduating yet.

Despite the restlessness I was sensing from Dale, he seemed relieved to have finished the semester and was ready to accompany me on my trip to Eagle Pass. Soon, everything was in order for our departure. As we drove away from campus, I glanced back and thanked God for the gift of endurance and strength he had given me throughout my entire educational journey: from the city college, to San Jose State, to the past eighteen months at Sul Ross. I also turned to Dale and thanked him for his part in my success. He had been there for me when I needed to be rescued from the trap I had fallen into. There could have been many other outcomes at that point in my life, and his tenacious inspiration compelled me to choose the option that led me toward my true goals. As we drove away from Sul Ross, Dale inserted a tape into the tape deck and played a song that he dedicated to me: "Que Seas Feliz" (I Wish You Happiness). It had always been a favorite of mine: a song that spoke of the ways unselfish and good friendships give us the strength and tenacity to let go and move forward, simply in the name of love.

When we finally arrived in Eagle Pass that evening, the entire town was already asleep. We drove around starved and tired. We asked a cab driver where we could find a restaurant. He pointed to a bridge and responded in Spanish, "All the restaurants and bars are closed on this side, you have to go into Mexico across the bridge. Everything is open there. You have to be approved by immigration before you're allowed to drive across, but I can take you. You have a lot of luggage, so it would be best if you left your car on this side where someone can take care of it." Dale's Spanish was limited, so I translated and asked him what he wanted to do. He said we should go across to Mexico.

We got a motel room in town, left the car there, and went to Mexico to eat. When we returned, I thanked Dale again for everything he'd done for me. We were indeed two tough guys, and we kept our promises to ourselves and to each other. Then Dale said something I didn't expect. "Please don't be angry about what I have to say," he began. "I have to leave tomorrow for San Jose."

In shock, I responded, "I thought you were staying a few days to plan a budget for next semester."

Dale replied, "Tony, I have to go, and I don't know if I want to come back to Texas next term. School is not for me. I've been miserable and miss my life back in San Jose. I'm happy for you and glad you accomplished what you wanted to. You are one intelligent and strong dude. I can't do this—I know I can't."

I felt all the energy drain out of me. I wanted to vomit. "You lied to me," I responded. "I left San Jose because you wanted to leave. It was a plan we set for both of us. I feel like you're betraying me. I'm going to get stuck in this godforsaken place because of you. I never wanted to stay here in Texas. I had hoped that eventually I'd return to San Jose and get a teaching job there near my family. It feels like you're dumping me here without anyone!"

I've never been a violent person, but that night, I threw anything I could find at Dale: boxes, shoes, and beer bottles. I picked up a huge rock and threw it right at his face, but instead broke one of the car windows. I was sick with disgust and fear, ranting and raving until I finally passed out, exhausted, at three in the morning.

When I awoke later that morning, Dale was gone. He left a note of thanks and appreciation for everything my family and I had done for him when he needed it most. The pain and anguish I felt lasted for days. The friend and advocate who had not left my side through years of struggle and searching was now gone—simply gone. Yet even as I stewed in my hurt and loneliness, I realized that once again I would have to move forward and forge ahead as I had always done.

I never heard from Dale again. Years later, through my friends in San Jose, I learned that he had died in a car accident. I was paralyzed with sorrow. The thoughts of his goodness came flooding back to me: all he had done for me and for my family in crucial and difficult times. I would be eternally grateful to him for everything I had become and for everything I would later accomplish in my life. Even today, I often say a prayer for him.

After I read Dale's note that morning, I left the motel and walked through town. The morning was quiet and the streets damp with rain from the night before. I soon realized that what was considered the town center was only six blocks long. I walked into a twenty-four-hour diner and ordered my version of a farmer's breakfast: eggs, chorizo, and flour tortillas, along with all the coffee I could drink. After breakfast, I immediately felt a sense of well-being and was thankful to be in the place that would be my home at least for the next year.

I realized I had a rare weekend on my hands: two days completely free to do whatever I wanted. My appointment with Mr. Ford was not until Monday morning at nine. Dr. Prude had made the appointment for me and had reminded me to bring my letter of graduation with its official signature and seal, verifying the completion of my BA. I had read the letter over and over again before making five copies. Mom and Ramón would certainly each get one. I extended my stay at the motel for three more days. After Monday, I would know for sure what my housing options would be. Without a car, I also had to consider transportation. But for now, all I could do was collapse again into bed, sleeping my day away. I must have slept uninterrupted for twelve hours because when I awoke, it was almost ten at night. I returned to the diner for a full-course dinner and dessert. That night, I worried I would not sleep a wink. Instead, I slept for eleven more hours *seguiditas*, as Mom would have said "eleven hours straight." She always said this with an air of pride: she considered someone who could sleep at least eight uninterrupted hours to be truly mentally healthy indeed. In many ways, she was absolutely right.

Sunday, I went to the laundromat and washed three loads of clothes, went to a movie, walked the streets, and called Mom and Ramón. When I called both homes, everyone raved with pride at my incredible success. I humbly responded, "No big deal. Piece of cake." That night, my worry caught up with me, and I probably slept three hours at the most. At eight thirty Monday morning, I called the district office to reconfirm my appointment. An extremely friendly voice verified my appointment and said I could come earlier if I wished. I couldn't, of course: I had to throw up first.

The district office was an easy walk: just five blocks from the motel. When I arrived, three lovely ladies were in the main office responding to telephone calls and greeting visitors. One of them was Mr. Ford's secretary. She stood up from her chair and, for some reason, blushed as she approached me. She reached for my hand and introduced herself as Felicia Degracia. I responded,

"You have a cheery name, for sure—*es muy feliz*. My name is Antonio." She blushed again. I worried that she might pass out.

I sat and waited less than five minutes before Felicia announced, "Mr. Antonio Carvajal, Mr. Ford will see you now."

The meeting with the superintendent was delightful and productive, but extremely confusing. "Mr. Carvajal," began Mr. Ford, "your letters of recommendation are simply outstanding. Your professors think the world of you. They have a lot of respect for you. You must be very proud of yourself." I thanked him and assured him that it was the quality of the professors that had inspired me to do well. After a long conversation that focused on my resume, Mr. Ford paused and said, "We have a slight problem. Not serious, and you can tell me honestly what you think. The position at the high school in teaching English is no longer open. However, we desperately need to fill a position for a speech therapist. It pays much more than a regular teaching position because of federal funding we will receive if we find a qualified person. Your minor in speech unquestionably qualifies you." He stared at me and must have known I was getting sick.

This had to be a nightmare, a joke, an impossible error, a brutal mistake. Mr. Ford offered me a glass of iced water. After taking two gulps, I gathered my wits and was able to respond, "That sounds like a terrific challenge and a fantastic opportunity to apply my expertise in language so early in my professional career."

Ford was elated, shook my hand, and said that my contract would be ready by two that afternoon. "In the meantime," he said, "you can apply for a loan for incidental expenses at the school district credit union if you need to."

That day, I returned to Mr. Ford's office by one thirty, signed my hire paperwork, thanked him again, thanked the secretaries—who seemed to watch me with admiration—and walked to the credit union three blocks away. The walk took all three minutes, and when I got there, the same cordial welcome was extended to me. It felt as if they were expecting me and were ready to lay down the red carpet. I filled out the papers required to become a member, opened a checking account, and withdrew cash. My cash withdrawal limit was $1,500. I withdrew the full amount and marched immediately to the bank next door where I purchased two money orders: one of five hundred dollars for Ramón and another of five hundred for Mom. Time was passing in a blur, but the one thing I'll never forget about my first days in Eagle Pass was that every person I met addressed me as "Mister." That gesture of respect was an awesome feeling. Another feeling that overwhelmed me was confusion. I felt that signing a contract to serve as a speech pathologist was way off of my professional competencies. I did it anyway.

On the walk back to the motel, I noticed a church steeple two blocks away from the main street. In a pensive daze, I walked toward the building, went in the door, and sat down in a back pew hardly aware of what I was doing. I thanked God, Ramón, Mom, Payito, Maggie, and Dale for believing in me and for all the love and staunch support they had continued to give me since that dreadful morning in December when I left San Jose.

School didn't start for another month, which meant I had four more weeks of free time to do as I wished. Now that I was rich from the loan—with the promise of my own salary coming in soon—it was time to rent an apartment, buy or rent a car, and get some new clothes. I thought the purchase of a vehicle should be the first item on the agenda. The feeling was exhilarating. This was the first time in my life I had ever had money to buy whatever I needed. And I did need transportation: without a car, it would be virtually impossible to look for an apartment or do anything that required traveling more than a mile. Besides, the weather was getting cooler and hints of winter were quickly approaching: walking just wouldn't work all year round.

Over the next few days, I bought a used vehicle, two complete suits with shirts and ties, and two pairs of shoes. Next on the agenda was finding housing. As it happened, I found it without even having to look. A few of the secretaries at the credit union, aware that I was looking for housing, suggested to me a boarding house where I could pay by the week. They said rent was reasonable and that it was clean and close to town. The meals there, they said, were exceptional. When I pulled up in front of the house, I was impressed by its massive colonial facade. I rang the doorbell and was greeted by a lady with an official disposition. She introduced herself as

Señora Degracia. She seemed to sneakily look me over as if assessing the general acceptability of my appearance. I found this uncomfortable. With a certain degree of sternness, she walked me to the only room available and gave me the details of the rental agreement: ten dollars a week to be paid each Monday morning by seven. Rent included three meals a day, seven days a week. Take it or leave it. If I accepted, she warned, I had to notify her a day in advance if I was not going to be present for a meal: she prepared and served them all herself. I felt as if I was a kindergartener being scolded. I started to explain to her that I was a new teacher in town, and she quickly interrupted, "I know who you are. My daughter is Felicia Degracia. She is the special secretary to the superintendent." Well, what a perfect setup. Now it was becoming clear how I had gotten here to Señora Degracia's boarding house. Eagle Pass was a small world.

Eager to have a place to live, I accepted the terms of the rental. The first time we gathered for dinner, I realized that, in addition to her secretarial job, Felicia helped her mother quite a bit at the boarding house. Her responsibilities included setting the table for meals and clearing the dishes. She also served dessert. During the first evening at dinner, she smiled and quietly asked me if I had survived her mother's litany of rules and regulations. I responded quickly and even more quietly, "Yes! I'm a fast learner. Would you please pass the rolls?" I already sensed that one of the rules her mother had was that Felicia was not allowed to fraternize with the tenants. The next day, Señora Degracia felt it necessary to review every single rule with me again. For whatever reason, she seemed to enjoy nothing more than having total control over her kitchen and dining room. I got the impression that she expected to have control over all her tenants too. Reluctantly, I reiterated that I would comply. The second night at the boarding house was a sleepless one. In the morning, I left the room early, went to my favorite diner for my farmer's breakfast, and stayed until eleven that morning. Later, I drove around town to get acquainted with the school sites. By the time I returned to the house, it was after two in the afternoon. I had missed breakfast and lunch. This time, instead of a warning, I got a true scolding. I promised Mrs. Degracia that I would not break the rules again.

The next day, sitting on my bed and staring at the wall, I felt like a monk in some faraway monastery. After an hour, I realized that I had no business moping around the somber room. I had a checkbook for the first time ever, a wallet full of money, a vehicle, free time, and—despite what Señora Degracia would have me believe—no one to answer to, at least not for four weeks. I'd have to deal with my claustrophobic housing situation when school started in January, but it was still early December, and there was no reason to stick around. The next day, I notified Señora Degracia that I would be leaving for the next three weeks. I purposely didn't tell her where I was going or with whom or when I would return to stay in her suffocating home with her bland meals. It was my life, and no one could tell me how to live it. I pretended that I was on my way to travel the world.

In reality, I decided to make a visit to Ramón's in Dallas, a solid day's drive away. My brother and his family were thrilled to learn I was on my way. I could almost hear Gigi and Anna screaming with joy, "Ding Dong is coming back!" That morning, I woke up at five and packed the car with gifts I had bought for my precious angels. I would keep my promise to make them the first on Santa's list. I left Eagle Pass feeling very proud of myself.

When I arrived with my car full of presents, Mary Ellen, even though appreciative of my thoughtful generosity, was a bit concerned that I was spending too much money too quickly. I sort of agreed, but told her that for the rest of my life, for as long as I lived, I would give back all I had received from so many people. That was simply going to be my modus operandi. I would cling to life with this philosophy.

It seemed that Ramón and Mary Ellen were experiencing better times. I still believe that my overstayed welcome must have caused more discomfort and frustration for them than they were willing to admit. My girls were as dear and loving as always. I walked around the neighborhood with them each of the three days I was there. They wanted to pretend that Ding Dong was sick again and that they were still my nurses. They wanted me to stay forever. I told them that I had to go on a plane to see my other family in San Jose. They were astounded that I was going to fly a huge airplane up in the sky. I said good-bye to them with my heart filled with love and gratitude for making me part of their lives. When I left, all of us cried. Again, my brother said good-bye with tears in his eyes.

My next stop was to San Jose. When I stepped off the plane, I was prepared to receive my welcoming committee. I had purposely worn a coat and tie that day to accentuate my new status. I carried a professional-looking satchel. I had an armful of presents for everyone. I was now a Mr. Somebody. I looked around expectantly for colored balloons and signs reading, "Welcome home, Tony! We love you!" I would be extremely embarrassed if my family had gone to the expense of hiring a marching band. I looked around, feigning nonchalance so as not to ruin their surprise. I walked and I walked until I realized that no one was there. There were no welcome signs or balloons. I felt empty and desolate. After waiting for over an hour, I called home. The phone was disconnected. This was a standard situation with my family: they were always behind in making payments.

On the taxi drive to the house, I was filled with regret. I regretted I had left Dallas to come here. I regretted I had left Sul Ross so abruptly. I felt somehow very sad that I was returning to the place where Dale had found me. This was like returning to a nightmare of bad memories. When I finally arrived to the situation at home, everything was in turmoil. Maggie had divorced, José had married and divorced again for a third time, and my two younger brothers, Ralph and Frank, were in total disarray. The only one who seemed to maintain any sense of wellness was Payito. She simply had the gift of surviving difficult times. Nothing and no one could put a damper on her beautiful soul. Her radiant and ever-positive disposition in any situation was admirable. Mom, on the other hand, didn't seem well. She'd gained an enormous amount of weight and seemed to have lost the exuberance, tenacity, and strength that had always been her gift. She had been a fighter all her life, meeting hardship with hopefulness and determination. But this seemed to be dwindling away.

Nonetheless, Christmas remained a happy occasion. We invited cousins, friends, and neighbors. Mom made my favorite meal of hers: tamales, chili con carne, rice, refried beans, and *buñuelos* for dessert. Alcoholic beverages were never allowed in her home: memories of my dad's drinking remained ever-present in her mind. She despised booze. She sang Christmas carols and played the piano for us for over two hours. After everyone but the main family had left, we opened presents. No one interrupted the celebration with talk of going to mass. That made me happy. Instead, we said a prayer of Thanksgiving for my success.

When I left San Jose after Christmas, I knew I would not return. The place held an eerie feeling for me. I knew I simply had to slam shut that chapter of my life forever. And I did. I returned to Texas through Dallas again where I'd left my car at the airport. From there, I called Ramón. He asked how Mom and the family were doing. I struggled to be honest. "Not well. Mom seems tired and has gained a lot of weight. Ramón, family problems never seem to end, do they? They just go on and on. Oh, and by the way, everyone is thinking of you. They send their love." It was the kind thing to say, but it was not true.

Part Four:
To Sweep a Room

The simplest thing we learn to do well—even if it is only to sweep a room in a beautiful spirit of service—makes life infinitely worthwhile, and is true education.

—Helen Keller

Chapter Seventeen

When I arrived back in Eagle Pass, the old year was gone. I returned to the boarding house and prepared for a series of in-services for new teachers, all scheduled for the second week in January. I reviewed what I had learned in my language and speech classes and wondered what relevance, if any, my Tennessee Williams's stage debut would have to my new job. After reading the job description for the hundredth time, I was certain that someone had made a dreadful error in assigning the role of speech therapist to me.

At each meeting I attended, Mr. Ford introduced me as one of two speech therapists for the elementary schools. While I came from Sul Ross, the other speech therapist was from the University of Texas's School of Speech-Language Pathology. Next to these impressive credentials, I felt awkward. I was definitely in the wrong place. I had done many things in my life: sometimes I'd been dishonest or unfair to people. However, a charlatan I was not. I'd never pretended to be someone I wasn't. I'd been true blue during my days in the placita: that's how I was brought up. But a fraud was exactly what I felt like now.

When I finally talked with the other speech therapist, however, I realized she was in the same boat as I. Ms. Monroe and I decided to meet to discuss and divide our assignments, and I confessed to her that I was simply petrified. She laughed and said she was beyond scared. She had received the entire list of students we would be asked to serve. The sheer number of these referrals was unmanageable. We split up our work by grades: I took first, second, and third grades at all the schools, while Ms. Monroe took fourth and fifth grades. When I read through the names of the students in my caseload, 80 percent had Latino last names. These children were either born in Texas or across the border in Mexico. Many were from migrant families who still lived in Mexico and traveled across the border to find work in the fields each year. Very few of the children were Anglo. The kids on the list had severe articulation and fluency issues as well as other language and speech problems. Looking over their files, I knew they would give me a run for my money. I didn't know where I'd start.

After three days of in-services, however, I started feeling more comfortable with myself. I met many outstanding professionals who were eager to make a difference to kids. I was very impressed by their enthusiasm and dedication. I did not want these meetings to end. For once in my life, I was truly part of something. I knew teaching was going to be my life for many years to come. What a fantastic and honorable system. At the end of that week, I was invited to have dinner across the border. Forgetting to warn Mrs. Commander in Chief that I'd be absent from the boarding house's evening meal, I counted on Felicia to cover for me. She was kind to share with me how glad Mr. Ford was that I'd joined the ranks. She told me he thought I was a remarkable young man that fit very well within the system. I totally agreed. I could attend parties for the entire year with so many friendly and gregarious people.

The last day of in-services, the teaching staff for the entire district was required to attend the meeting, which addressed a single topic: new federal regulations. Mr. Ford and his assistants bored us for three hours. I wondered how anyone could sit and listen to this discussion for so long. It would be too long even for an otherwise entertaining movie, and that was something I knew well. I looked around and saw a lot of teachers reading novels and writing letters. I slept. When Mr. Ford finally finished, everyone woke up and applauded.

The handouts we received that day, however—which we could read on our own—were surprisingly relevant. They pertained to special education law, outlining the fact that each district in the state was mandated to identify, assess, place, and provide appropriate education for children with handicaps. The financial benefits to the schools were enormous. I was unable to interpret the amount of money allocated to our district. All I knew was there were a whole lot of zeros trailing at the end of the numerals on the page. This amazing amount of money came to the district—through the state—from the federal government.

The following day, Mr. Ford called another "final" meeting. By this time, we were all wiped out. "I have an extremely positive mandate for all of you," he began. "I know you've been frustrated with the limited resources available in the district to provide services for kids in your classrooms who are difficult, if not impossible, to teach." I started to detect pompousness in Mr. Ford's words that I'd never noticed before. "Most of you know which kids I'm speaking about, a certain population that cannot learn because of cultural and familial retardation. Let's call a spade a spade. These are kids who can't get close to the average scores in the district. Well, now we have the resources—and plenty of them—your task now will be to identify those kids you know very well are not meeting the academic standards of the district and recommend them for testing by our competent school psychologists. We will hire six new psychometricians—I guess that's what we'll call them—for this important task. They'll be our testers." After emphatic applause, Mr. Ford described the new special education staff that was to work with this population. The procedure would be simple: The regular classroom teachers would refer those students who met the criteria of mental retardation established by the district to the school psychologists. After these students were evaluated, the special education team would provide their education. Mr. Ford declined to describe the nature of this learning setting.

I was introduced as a speech pathologist that would provide therapy sessions for the elementary grades. I was provided with the results of individual language assessments that were administered by previous language clinicians. My responsibility was to design individual language plans based on these assessments. Mr. Ford went on and on, talking about building educational leaders for each grade. He introduced new English, history, and physical education teachers. Then came a glowing introduction for the new special education teachers.

"They will be our lifesavers. They are truly the cream of the crop because of their kind hearts, these individuals have already earned a special place in heaven," Mr. Ford continued to gush with admiration for the apparent saints. "Many of you have probably seen some of the movies out there that show severely mentally retarded children. Well, folks, I am here to tell you that we'll be getting those kids in our schools. These are children who've spent their lives trapped in institutions. We will make sure they are no longer locked up in those awful places. We'll welcome these retardates into our schools and embrace them as real human beings." I could have sworn I saw tears in Ford's eyes. "Will those teachers who will be their angels please stand up. We want to recognize you and applaud you for your undying dedication and devotion." Six bewildered-looking women stood, a couple of them laying down knitting projects to do so. I wondered if anyone had informed them that some of the children they'd work with would be transferred from the Texas State Institution for the Mentally Retarded. One could hear the applause blocks away. I did admire these teachers. I was also thankful that I wasn't one of this chosen few.

The following week, school began, and so did the pandemonium. I was shocked at the ocean of students immediately referred to me. I gave speech assessments to thirty kids a day. By the end of the week, 120 first graders had met the guidelines for speech and language services. I dreaded starting on the second and third grades. At this rate, I would have a caseload of 360 students to serve. This was simply inconceivable, unmanageable, and impossible. After a few weeks of knowing the students, however, I realized how linguistically capable they seemed to be in their own Spanish language. Clearly, most did not have problems with speech itself, but merely with articulating themselves in a still-unfamiliar language.

Ms. Monroe, my closest professional confidant by default, suggested that I maximize my time by teaching the monolingual and bilingual students from Spanish-speaking homes through group instruction. The advice was brilliant: Monroe seemed to know the name of the game. However, she also sought advice from me. Able to speak only English, she was at a total loss as to how to help the 80 percent of her caseload who were native Spanish speakers—be they monolingual or bilingual. She was desperate to set up some kind of helpful intervention system for them. The incredible stress of the job was taking its toll. Each time we met, she looked thinner—she was turning into a skeleton of a lady. Her addiction to nicotine, coffee, and alcohol was taking its toll. She confided to me her worst fears. "Tony, each day is a living hell. I'm angry that my clinical training in speech pathology didn't include information on this population. Sometimes in the morning, I just sit in my car trying to work up the courage to walk into the building." Feeling how unfair it was for the district to have put her in this situation, I told Ms. Monroe honestly that if I were in her shoes, I would resign. She understood that I was also trapped, but knew that at least I was fluent in the students' predominant language. I didn't want to see Ms. Monroe go, but she followed my advice. One month into the semester, she vanished. One of the teachers jokingly told me that, after her ordeal, she had joined a convent.

At the end of each day, I was exhausted. I'd return to the boarding house, beg Mrs. Degracia's pardon for skipping dinner, and retire to my prison cell of a room to fall fast asleep. Felicia continued to be a good advocate for me, explaining to her mother how hard I worked and how impossible it was for me to make my appearance at the dinner table.

After the first arduous months at my new position, spring break finally rolled around. Unsurprisingly, teachers tend to live for the month of March. It seems like if we make it until spring break, we'll survive the rest of the year. That year, I successfully made it to March, which meant I only had to stick it out for a few more months as a speech pathologist. I knew that if I returned to teach in the district the following year, it would not be in my current role. Yes, the position had paid more than I'd expected and came with a prestigious-sounding title. However, the role left me somehow on the surface of teaching. It was not me—it was too clinical for me. There was no way I could go through this charade a second year around. Not only was this job not right for me: I believed the system itself was flawed. The paradigm was wrong. The resources and support that had been touted by the district and promised to the students were not apparent. This was not how I'd imagined education to be. That compulsive part of me that strove for perfection seemed to insist there was a better way—a way to provide the right programs for these students and put their needs first. The only path on which I knew I could make a difference was teaching English: I had to do this or leave.

After spring break, I continued to evaluate my plans for the coming year. Aside from my discontent with work, I had to admit that I was not comfortable living at the boarding house. My living arrangements had to change. One afternoon before I left my office, I received a phone call from a teacher at a junior high school across town. Paul Palacios and his cousin and coteacher Robert had seen me at the January in-services and recognized me from two years before. I couldn't remember who they were. They told me that we'd met in San Jose at the Rainbow Ballroom. With this unexpected mention of my old stomping grounds, I was sure they did know me. However, since I couldn't recall exactly who they were, they asked me if I'd like to meet them for dinner across the border. The minute I walked into the restaurant, I knew them. Dale and I had enjoyed talking with them one evening when the Rainbow Ballroom was having a dance marathon and had never seen them after that.

Paul, Robert, and I visited for two hours over dinner and beers and then walked around the nearby plaza for two more hours. I finally confessed that I had broken curfew and was already in violation of other rules at my boarding house. They laughed at the absurdity of it all. They wondered whether my landlady would put me on time-out or spank me. They were absolutely right to chide me: it was ridiculous. The next day, Paul and Robert again wanted to meet for dinner. Over our meal, they asked me if I'd like to share a house with them. The idea was the answer to my prayers. The very next morning, I notified the Degracia family that I was moving. Mrs. Degracia seemed unabashedly disgusted with me.

After meeting Paul and Robert, the remaining weeks of the spring semester breezed by. I could not remember ever having such a fantastic time. We made up a trio of elegant and intelligent dudes. I had discovered freedom for the first time ever. I knew this was the way heaven would be. We dated the most glamorous and delightful girls in Eagle Pass. As our professional lives began to take off, our social lives were abundant with generous and thoughtful friends. Life was good—very, very good. It was virtually impossible to deny ourselves the life we had found as a group, so we made a pact to return to teaching in the district the following year: they at their same positions and I at another position in the district. I simply had to find my way out of my job.

Robert became my agent. He would read the current listings of openings in the district and encourage me to apply. Most of these jobs were in special education. I recalled what Mr. Ford had said that the field would be wide open because of the new federal funding. Mr. Ford had also, Robert added, stressed that special educators would receive an additional signing bonus of three hundred dollars on top of their salary. Robert kept reminding me of what a terrific deal this was. Another positive factor was that one of the positions was a block away from our house.

I submitted my application for this job. Three days later, I was called in for an interview. Shortly after, I was offered the position, contingent on my admission to a graduate program for certification in special education. I gratefully accepted. Then I returned home to punch Robert in the face. If I were accepted into the graduate program, I would be in school for the entire summer. That would certainly thwart my plans to travel the world just yet.

Chapter Eighteen

Graduate school was the last place in the entire world I wanted to be for the summer. I'd thought I was done with school. Yet despite my resistance, the reality was simple: the only way to keep this new job that paid so well for the next school year was to suffer through ten weeks of classes to be properly credentialed for the position. That was the deal: not fair, totally ugly, but completely real. I had complied and compromised many times before, and good outcomes had resulted. Perhaps this time the outcome would be the same: positive and to my advantage.

My only consolation was that Paul and Robert would also be in school at other graduate universities that summer. We examined the Texas map and realized that we would not be too far from each other. I would be going to East Texas State University in Commerce. When I located it on the map, I was pleasantly surprised to realize that Dallas was only eighty miles away. This time around, I did not plan on hibernating at my brother's, but I was pleased to know I'd be close and could pay a visit every few weeks. It seemed as if destiny was again stepping in to support me. It kept happening.

Commerce, Texas, was just two hours from the Arkansas border. I could not believe I'd landed here. It certainly was not a place where deer and antelope played: it was mostly flat plains where cattle grazed. The city population seemed to be about 99.9 percent Anglo. The remainder was made up mostly of Mexican migrant workers or farmhands who seldom ventured to the central part of town. The student population was about three thousand, and of those students, about 99 percent again seemed to be white. Students like me made up the other 1 percent.

Tuition at East Texas State was expensive, the price of textbooks outrageous, and the rental rates sky-high. Since I'd been saving up for travel that was not to be, I had funds to sink into summer school expenses. In order to comply with state certification regulations for special educators, I was required to complete at least nine semester hours in the field. I felt an overwhelming impulse to cry every time I thought of where I'd rather be that summer. If I couldn't travel, I would have at least liked to be at home in Eagle Pass with its culture, friendly people, and beautiful ladies. As usual, however, I did what I had to do rather than what I wanted to do.

Though I thought I'd get to see Robert and Paul that summer, they suddenly disappeared, swept up in their own studies. They too were struggling to complete the minimum nine hours required to renew their certificates. We were all part of a multitude of teachers enrolled in classes to meet certification requirements, improve our skills, or simply meet the criteria for salary increases. This seemed terribly unhealthy to me. I thought summer was supposed to be a time to rest, reflect, and explore the world.

My classes were boring. I enrolled in Foundations of Special Education I, Foundations of Special Education II, and Introduction to Special Education. Though the titles were different, the classes were the same. Literally, they all contained the same information, impressing upon us the history of special education, the nature of the population we would serve, and the ins and outs of federal law and finances as they pertained to our field. To me, they were just redundant. I missed the spark of my classes in literature at Sul Ross. Thinking of my time there immediately brought back endearing memories of Rosie. It seemed so long ago, yet still the memories were strong. I had to let go of those times. Now I had a new life and new academic responsibilities. I had to make the best of my days at East Texas State.

There was, however, some content in my classes that intrigued me. It came from lectures on the nature of mental retardation: the various conditions falling under this definition, their degree of severity, their underlying causes, as well as current educational interventions. (The role of parents in educating children with mental retardation was never discussed.) I learned that mental retardation resulted from "cultural and familial" influences. According to the theory of the day, culture and heredity were always the culprits of retardation. This was an uneasy concept for me, and though my gut reaction was to reject it, it was overwhelmingly supported by both sociological and medical professional literature and reemphasized in all our textbooks.

With nothing else to go on, I had to accept what I was taught. My knowledge of mental disorders was extremely limited—my only insight into them coming from characters I'd encountered in my literature studies. William Faulkner's novels usually included some atypical "village idiot" sort who was in some way central to the story. In *Of Mice and Men*, Steinbeck thoughtfully and quite tenderly describes an adult whose odd behaviors reflect the immaturity, innocence, and poor social skills of someone afflicted by mental retardation. These characters had intrigued me, and now I was struck with the desire to know more—much more. I had to learn what in the world I had gotten myself into with this population. At this point, my knowledge of their medical and social challenges was superficial at best.

At first glance, however, I felt that the role of genetics in causing mental retardation seemed more valid than the idea of culture being the primary determinant. If culture created retardation, how did you account for my family? My mind kept wandering back to life in the placita. Though we kids had lacked advantages in our youth, our intelligent decisions had allowed us to survive. There was no doubt we'd had the gift of resiliency. Cognitively, no one could argue that we'd been extremely strong. In the face of the events we'd endured, one might even say we'd been brilliant. So how had our culture hindered us? We'd drawn strength from each other; from our friends and neighbors; from our food, music, and celebrations. Ultimately, with or without accents, we'd turned out okay.

Much of my confusion came from the use of the word "culture" to determine retardation. At this point in my life, I had encountered people who looked at me as "less than" because of my accent and racial background. I naturally positioned myself against this. However, as I struggled with the class readings and lectures, I finally realized that the term "cultural" in this context meant "environmental." Though this did include an examination of economic factors, it was not really about speaking a different language, practicing a certain religion, or dressing differently. These things did not make you mentally retarded. However, I did realize that this was perhaps where so much confusion and bias came from. I had the urge to call the speech-therapy folks at the clinic in San Jose to clarify for them that even though I was linguistically different, I was not handicapped.

As I sat through my lectures on legislation and funding, my mind wandered back again and again to my days in Del Rio. Self-hypnosis really worked for me. Against the backdrop of my beautiful placita and river, I remembered all the scenes of our lives and how my family—through resiliency and creative brilliance—maneuvered through each new hardship that came our way. I became obsessed with the way people were misled to believe that cultural otherness somehow meant cognitive inferiority. It became a personal scholarly challenge, at least for the summer, to think about how this assumption might be changed. This new awareness, at any rate, moved me beyond the boredom of the lecture hall and on to imagining a new purpose for myself.

That summer, Ramón's home again became a sanctuary. I visited the family every three weeks. In fact, I had arranged for all my mail to be forwarded from the Degracia residence to Ramón's. On one of my weekend visits, he gave me a stack of mail that had accumulated for me. He thought I should open the two envelopes marked Special Delivery first. They seemed urgent. He told Gigi and Anna to give me some privacy so I could read my mail undisturbed. As I read the letters, my heart fell to my feet. They were each from the superintendent's office and held the same information. Each came with a note from Felicia saying, "Take care of this immediately. Mr. Ford is very upset. Please call me if I can do anything. I'm shocked and concerned. Please call me anyway."

The notices were typed on official Texas government stationary that scared the living hell out of me. I knew I was going to be locked up for life for some stupid thing I'd probably done during my earlier days in the placita. I instantly recalled a time when I'd taken a beer away from a napping drunk. I remembered how I'd curiously taken a tiny sip of beer—just one! I also remembered how awful it had tasted and how I'd cautiously and thoughtfully placed the bottle back in his hand. I wondered if someone had taken a picture of me. I could explain.

But when I read the notice, I realized this was a bigger problem entirely. It said that Eagle Pass School District had submitted their application for my provisional teaching certificate to the Texas Vital Statistics office in Austin. That office had sent a notice back to the school district, saying that, after searching for three days, they could not find any documentation of my birth or any documented proof, for that matter, of my existence. I told Ramón and Mary Ellen that the problem was simple: these people were saying that I was never born. "I think you were born," Ramón joked. "I remember what a terrible and ugly baby you were. Let me call them." Mary Ellen, however, didn't think this was funny, and neither did I. The state had said it would allow fifteen days for the school district to resolve the problem, or they could not hire me for the fall. I broke out in a cold sweat. I wished my cherry tree hadn't been demolished by greedy Corporate America. At least *it* had always been a safe place to earn money and find peace.

That Monday morning, I called for an appointment at the Texas Vital Statistics office. When I returned to campus that day, I notified each of my professors that I had a family emergency and had to be gone for three days. At least this explanation would excuse me from classes so I could drive to Austin.

Once at the office, my anxiety only increased. What sent it skyrocketing was a woman there who looked just like Ms. Quack Quack. It's astounding how biases, formed so early in our minds as children, stay with us throughout our lives. I took one look at the receptionist at the office, noted her resemblance to my odious former teacher, and immediately knew she would hassle me, interrogate me, and demand that I apologize for the audacity to pretend I was of this earth. I knew she would rake the hell out of me for being an alien from some planet far from earth. I knew she would spit when she talked. The closer she walked toward me, the more she looked like Ms. Quack Quack. Her thick glasses covered half her face. She had huge teeth and cracked her gum incessantly. It had to be her. I instantly had a flashback to a day in preschool when Ms. Quack Quack had threatened to report me to Mom for eating the stupid artificial grapes from her table. Now snapping out of my memories, I nervously cleared my throat and stated, "I am Antonio Carvajal, and I have an appointment to discuss the content of this letter. I know I'm a few minutes early. I'm actually an hour early. You see, I drove from Commerce where I am attending summer school. I can wait. Sorry. Well, I'm here."

The receptionist's face lit up like a neon light. "Honey, that's my school! I'm from Commerce! I went to East Texas!" I loved her Southern accent. She sang just like me when she spoke. Suddenly, I loved this woman. "Is the drive-in theater still there?" she asked. "Ray's Restaurant? The farmer's market? I spent many a lonely hour at the school library."

Tell me about it, I thought to myself. *I consider the place a morgue.* What I said was "Oh yes, yes! I go there all the time. And also there are a lot of cows all over the place."

I don't know why I'd said that: I felt like a total idiot. The receptionist just patted my hand and told me how thankful she was for my visit.

"I just brewed a pot of coffee, and there are some fresh rolls," she said. "I'll be right back. You just consider yourself right at home, hon."

I felt so guilty about my prejudgment that I was close to apologizing to her. What a stupid, bigoted jerk I'd been. The receptionist sat right down and had refreshments with me before returning to her desk to greet other guests in her cordial and beautiful drawl. What a kind and fantastic human being, and what a lesson in humility for me. Ten minutes later, she came back to tell me that Mrs. Cassed was ready to see me. She winked and told me not to worry. She whispered that Mrs. Cassed's bark was worse than her bite. "You'll be all right, honey," she encouraged. "Just tell her the truth."

I didn't even know the nature of the problem yet, so whether I knew the truth remained to be seen. What I did have was a Social Security card, a driver's license, and a copy of my BA diploma. I also had letters of recommendation, a letter from the superintendent verifying my professional probationary assignment, and my heart in my hand.

Mrs. Cassed's first question seemed simple enough. "What is your date of birth?" I told her and confidently reached for my driver's license as proof. "I need an official certificate of birth," she sternly replied. "A driver's license is not an acceptable document, nor is a Social Security card." She looked up and stared at me with the eyes of a killer. "Antonio, this is a problem. It is serious, and you need to listen to me."

I wanted to vomit. *My dear Lord,* I thought to myself, *here we go again. This woman is going to have me for lunch.* I almost told her that if I didn't think it was serious, I wouldn't be here to listen to what was coming out of her stupid mouth. I held my tongue.

She cut to the chase. "We cannot find any trace whatsoever that you were born in the United States. Were you born in Mexico?"

"No, I was born in Del Rio, Texas, right near the river by my placita. My mother is from Mexico, and my dad is from the United States of America. My mother came to the United States when she was five years old during the Mexican Revolution. Then they were married."

I hoped my interrogator would be impressed. Instead, I saw that she was getting exasperated with my explanation. She was obviously not interested in history.

"I have four brothers and two sisters," I continued, "who were also born there near the same river. My older brother Ramón married a debutant from Dallas. He is a graduate of SMU in Dallas. He served in the air force of America." *Oh hell,* I thought, *I didn't have to say "of America." That was so lame.*

Mrs. Cassed wanted to know where I'd gone to school, the colleges I'd attended, the places I'd worked, and how I was able to get a teaching job without proper certification. I was really getting livid. I sternly explained that I had proper credentials, and the problem had to do with her office—with processing the certification. That's all. I didn't see a major problem. I was getting proud of myself for applying the lessons of assertiveness I'd learned in my speech classes.

Now Mrs. Cassed was getting furious. She blasted back at me, "No, young man, you have a much bigger problem. You are not a documented citizen of this country, and we need to either get to the bottom of this, or you'll go back to . . . wherever you're from."

Witch! I could sense the Carvajal fury I'd witnessed more than a few times in Mom begin to boil over. I decided against that route and chose to compose myself. The truth was, this woman had the power. I had learned to bow down to people in charge during many other tough times. Mom had not only shown me what fury was but had taught me how to check that emotion when the occasion called for it. But I'd already been through so many of those times—when would they end? This one was a new test of tolerance and humility. No anger, no tears: I had to submit.

This woman was not a friend—like the kind, reassuring secretary in the front office. She was out to make me squirm and suffer. She could not only bark but could bite, and bite viciously. She could do both at the same time. She pushed her chair back and left for more ammunition. I thought she was calling the feds. Instead, she came back with a list of items I had to provide to her, personally, within fifteen days. When she completed her task, she stared at me and walked away with an air of superiority and self-importance. I had always doubted the existence of hell. Heaven I was sure existed. But if there was truly a hell, I knew this woman would end up in the deepest place in Dante's inferno.

When I came out of Mrs. Cassed's office, I was so relieved that I wanted to kiss the woman that looked like Ms. Quack Quack and thank her for her wonderful Texas hospitality. I actually kissed her hand as she beamed through her very thick glasses. The next week, I wrote her a thank-you note for her kindness and generosity.

I called Ramón to share my dreadful experience and tell him that my birth was still not certifiable. He joked again. "I always wondered if someone had just left you in front of a church somewhere." I was beginning to wonder the same.

When I called Mom, she was furious and wondered who was this *pendeja* (idiot) I had dealt with. I didn't go into details. I didn't want to play the blame game: I just wanted to get to the bottom of this. I asked Mom where my birth certificate was. She got mad again. Mom was a person who, when she got angry, could lose all control of herself and awareness of her surrounding reality. I knew she was foaming at the mouth as she spoke. "All of you were born at home. Your aunt Manina delivered each of you. I was not a modern woman: weak and wimpy. I was strong and didn't need any of these modern male doctors that don't know anything about childbirth to help me. None of you have papers of birth." This was news to me. I felt my profession melting away before my eyes.

So much for the first item on Mrs. Cassed's list. Without it, I would need to find as much other documentation as I could: a baptismal certificate (I wrote a request for it to our old church and hoped that Father Santos, who had hated me and excommunicated us, had finally died), a notarized signature from a person present when I was born, and two more signatures from individuals who would testify that I was born at 302 Guillen Street in the United States of America. I had fifteen days to complete my homework. On the eleventh day, a notarized letter arrived at Ramón's from Aunt Manina. That day, I ranked her on the very upper tier of angels. By the fifteenth day, I had received all the official evidence I needed to prove that I was born on December 8. However, quite oddly, I didn't know the exact year I was born. It isn't as if I had a birthday party every year and kept careful count. When anyone asked, I always approximated. What's more, Mom and Manina couldn't seem to agree either. Anyway, I could ballpark the date within a few years. For the documents, I settled on 1936 since the Dallas Cowboys had just won their preseason game, 36-6. What a genius!

I drove to Dallas, collected the documents, went to the post office, and mailed—First Class—all the documents to the superintendent's office. Just a few days later, Felicia called to inform me that the forms had been filed and that my contract would be sent within ten days.

With that catastrophe averted, I had little time to recover from the emotional trauma. I had to shift my energies immediately back to my studies. There were readings, term papers, and final exams to study for. Nothing else mattered. A week before finals, my advisor Dr. Armfield called me in to review my academic plan. "You should be very proud of your academic work here at East Texas," he began. "Two other professors who've had you in class are impressed with the quality of your scholarly performance. What are your plans for completing the master of science degree? Do you intend to return to Eagle Pass, or will you return to school here this fall?"

"I'm returning to Eagle Pass," I responded definitively. "I'm signing my contract next week. Beyond that, I really haven't planned much."

Dr. Armfield responded with incredible news, "You know, all you need for your MS degree is to complete thirty academic hours. You're completing nine hours this summer. If you enroll for nine hours next summer and complete your practice teaching in special education for nine additional hours, you can complete all program requirements for your degree by the end of next summer."

I had become an expert at counting credits and scrutinizing degree requirements. It seemed that my entire adult life had been about adding and subtracting semester hours. I interrupted, "Dr. Armfield, I'm sorry, but I can't afford to quit my teaching job to complete the practice teaching requirement. I still have a lot of financial obligations for myself and to my family. That's a priority." I knew Dr. Armfield didn't have a clue what had gone into getting me to this point.

This time, it was Dr. Armfield who spoke definitively, "This is the plan: you will enroll for the nine hours of practice teaching and complete them in your own classroom. I will assign a mentor to evaluate your performance each month. This person will submit progress reports to me, and we'll arrange a conference for the final evaluation."

Having a paid job and getting school credit for it? This was awesome! So grateful for Dr. Armfield's thoughtful and caring advice, I still had a few doubts. "But I would still need an additional course for three semester hours," I reminded him.

"Have you decided on a topic for your master's thesis?" Dr. Armfield asked.

I really hadn't given it a thought. "No, I have not," I admitted. "I've had some pressing situations in my life that have distracted my attention from my thesis."

Right then and there, Dr. Armfield helped me enroll in six semester hours for my thesis, which would take care of the additional hours needed for the MS. He also helped me choose a topic: Maria Montessori's educational paradigms. I would incorporate her teaching theories into my classroom plans for the coming year and present my findings to a committee of three professors when I returned to campus the following summer. My advisor was not only insightful, he was also a gifted professor. He was knowledgeable of the field and definitely student centered, just like Montessori. I knew these were rare qualities in professors in higher education.

Before I left the East Texas campus, I called Ramón to share the good news about my graduate plan. He immediately called for a dinner celebration in Dallas. Everyone was surprised that I would be completing my graduate program so soon. I gushed about my advisor and dared anyone to find another person like him.

It was finally time to return to Eagle Pass and the new job that awaited me. Robert was already back from his summer term, and I called him the night before I left Commerce to let him know I'd be arriving early the next evening. He planned a party to reunite with all the friends we'd left at the beginning of the summer. We gathered at one of the most beautiful nightclubs across the border known as Campestre. It had an exotic tropical theme and stayed open until 4:00 a.m. That night, we danced, sang, and shared stories of our summer adventures. Mine was the story of never being born and the credential-gathering nightmare that had ensued. It was the best, funniest, and most incredible story of them all.

The following week, I received my contract in the mail. An additional bonus of four hundred dollars was added to my base salary. It was a great feeling to be earning money again. The letter also indicated that I was supposed to make an appointment within the week with the director of special education. Mr. Lopez was responsible for anything regarding special education services within the district. As such, he was also the principal of the special-needs school where I would teach. He would review with me the nature of my teaching assignment, the school setting, and the times when parents would come to meet me. I was eager to finally have my own classroom and office. Maybe they'd even throw in my own parking space.

Chapter Nineteen

The day of my meeting, as I drove to my new school to meet the director, I realized that the address was not included in the informational letter. I stopped for directions at three different gas stations with no luck until I finally ran into a young kid who knew where the school was. "Es la escuela de los loquitos. Allí está" (It's the school for crazy kids. Right over there), he said. It turned out to be the right school. When I arrived, I was shocked. The school grounds were overgrown with weeds as if they hadn't been attended to all summer. The building looked like an old army barracks: the peeling paint was a dirty military brown. This certainly didn't look like a place I would choose to teach. I started to wonder why the kid had referred to this as "the school for crazy kids." Somebody should have known by now that I was a graduate student soon to complete his program of study. This was certainly not the way to treat a professional educator. How could anyone have the gall to think that I would teach in this ugly shack? Some idiot sure made a mistake. When I got out of the car, I realized I could see our rental house from where I was standing. I could so easily just leave and go home. I felt disgusted and embarrassed that this was to be my new post. Suddenly, out of nowhere, a man in an old pickup truck pulled up next to me in a cloud of dust. The man yelled, "I bet you're Tony!" I hesitated and said, "Yes, sir. I'm looking for Mr. Leo Lopez, the principal of the school." He proudly yelled, "That's me in living color!"

Leo Lopez invited me into the dreadful school building, which was only uglier and filthier inside. He apologized for the mess in a personally detached sort of way. "The janitors will eventually come around and clean this place after they finish with the school for the normal kids." I felt sad and repulsed by the entire scene. The building consisted of three units. The first included the office, conference room, testing room, kitchen, and nurse's room. The second consisted of a classroom. This room was designated for a class of severe yet "educable" mentally retarded kids. Unit 3 had its own entrance and was the classroom for the "trainable" mentally retarded boys and girls. These were the most severe cases of mental retardation that the school took on. "This will be your classroom," said Mr. Lopez. I was shocked: I'd had no idea.

Leo seemed proud at how swiftly and efficiently they categorized kids at his school and how the facility served as the end of the line in many cases. "Other regular public schools in the district have the same system of separating the retarded," he explained. "But when kids can't make it there, they come here." Mr. Lopez's casual tone made me extremely uneasy.

"So," I asked, "is this what would be considered a 'small institution' in Eagle Pass? Mr. Ford said that kids with severe cases are no longer being kept in large institutions. Are they closing larger facilities and opening smaller ones like this?"

Leo's response was matter-of-fact, just like everything he'd said up until now. "I'm a farmer, a bus driver, the director of special education, and a family man. I'll tell you right now, Tony, one thing I'm not is a bureaucrat. I have one of the best jobs in Eagle Pass. Many people would die to have my status. Asking too many questions only gets you into trouble. You just roll with the punches. That's how I survive. That's why everybody respects me. I roll with the punches."

I almost admired Leo's realistic outlook but also felt uncomfortable with the idea of "rolling with the punches." I thought the role of educators was to be agents of social change when it was needed, not to simply survive or unquestionably accept the status quo, especially if it was unjust or unfair.

After I left the school, I went directly home to my mentors: Robert and Paul. I paced around the room, ranting about the horror of my situation. They were waiting for me to settle down and start making dinner for all of us. Paul was the realist. "Hey, welcome to America," he said wryly. "Enjoy what you do, do what you can, and survive."

Robert was more philosophical. "You need to read Thomas Wolfe's book *You Can't Go Home Again*, Dostoevsky's book *The Idiot,* and Proust's book *The Sweet Cheat Gone* to get a sneak preview of the ugly and sordid side of life. Forget what you learned in college: that was mostly bullshit—mostly fantasy. They know how to fool simpleminded folks like us. College is about paying your entire life for student loans. The degree was a ticket to nowhere. Teachers are the servants—the peons—of the educational system. Administrators don't give a shit about us or about kids. Ultimately, no one does. I'm beginning to question if parents even care for their own kids."

I hated his pessimism. But Paul supported Robert, concluding, "Get a grip, Carvajal. Let's plan for the weekend. And feed us now!"

All there was to do was laugh at the irony of our days. But in my heart of hearts, I refused to agree with Robert. Perhaps much of what he said was true. However, at least for me, education had been my ticket out of poverty—to where I was today. I had to believe it was important.

Three days before classes started for the entire district, each school held teacher in-services. I showed up at my new school as scheduled at 8:00 a.m. There were only two other staff members there: another special education teacher and the school nurse. No one came to tell us what we were supposed to be doing. We waited for forty-five minutes and then decided to get coffee and pastries at a nearby restaurant. We used the opportunity to get to know each other and discuss our roles at the school. The other special education teacher, Sue, was also new to the district. The school nurse, Pam, had already been there for years and seemed to know the system well. She let us know this. She reminded me that the kids I'd been assigned to work with were severely mentally retarded, confirming what Leo had already said: unit 3 would be my designated dungeon. I wanted to know more. "I'm in total confusion. I'm absolutely clueless as to who these kids are," I admitted.

Pam handed me seven folders from a stack she'd brought with her and said, "These are your students, Tony. You're fortunate you only have a small caseload of kids."

I agreed. "This is certainly better than the three hundred plus I had as a speech therapist."

Pam's tone turned more encouraging. "You'll enjoy the kids. And their parents are sweet—they really care and appreciate what teachers do. You'll enjoy knowing them. They're very serious and concerned about their kids."

The second day of the so-called in-services, again the three of us showed up, and again, no one else did. We decided to utilize the time to prepare the classrooms for the kids. The rooms were completely filthy. Sue and I went to buy a broom, a mop, and some soap. I stopped by my house to get some old rags and towels. Somehow it felt good to prepare the rooms. We spent time writing welcome signs on each of our doors. At the entrance of my door, I wrote, "Through this door pass the leaders of tomorrow." Pam seemed more amused than impressed by my inspiring message, saying, "Tony, you are too much. I love you."

Since Pam was quite an artist, she drew pictures of animals on the blackboards and the walls of my classroom. She drew flowers, trees, and grass. I told her to please sketch a river flowing toward where I would stand at the front of the class. She laughed and obliged. Now I was home. The three of us worked as a family. Our efforts reminded me of the days when Mom expected us to work as a team. Becoming building custodians was a big task, but an enjoyable one. We stayed fortified with coffee and pastries that Pam contributed for our breaks.

The third day of "in-services" was supposed to be for parent meetings. Sue had one conference at 11:00 a.m. that lasted five minutes. She went shopping after that (any opportunity she had away from the school was a shopping venture for her). At least she had one parent visit: none of my kids' parents kept their appointments. Pam told us that this was common. "Parents work, they have no transportation, and some simply resent that their kids go to a school for *loco* kids. So there you have it." I was taken aback by her indifference, but said nothing. I had to wait and see this all for myself.

With the school now ready to greet our students and the rest of the day free, the same sinking feeling I had when I was failing at San Jose State invaded my soul. I felt empty and meaningless again. I went to the school district office to make an appointment with Mr. Ford. He had gone on vacation and would not return for another three weeks. Felicia wasn't there either. I returned home and tried phoning her. I needed advice and comfort. She was also out of town. Lucky gal! I thought about calling Robert and Paul for lunch but decided not to. I didn't want to continue the negative conversation we'd had the previous week about my assignment. I was trying to avoid them altogether. I really couldn't find anyone to talk to about my dilemma, so I decided to do something I often did when I was at my wit's end: buy vegetables. It wasn't just about the produce: I found it relaxing to drive out to one of the nearby farms and visit with the farmers. That day, I told them about my new role as a teacher. They warmly congratulated me for such an important job. That year, I would be back to see them frequently. In fact, we worked out an arrangement for me to harvest my own vegetables and pay them whatever I thought was fair. Fresh, affordable food and friendly conversation all in the same place: it was one good thing I could count on anyway.

The morning school finally started, only two of my students and their mothers showed up. I began to wonder if the parents had not been able to find the school, or if they decided not to leave their children in this despicable place. Though the girls came from different families, they looked like twins. One was Hispanic and the other Caucasian, yet they had exactly the same stocky build and almond-shaped eyes with skin folds underneath. Their tongues stuck out a little from their small mouths, and their speech was nearly unintelligible. I was fascinated to see that they had a lot of the same features as Diablito from back in the placita. I also noticed that these mothers, like Diablito's, seemed to be on the older side. These children had Down's syndrome.

I was at a total loss as to where to begin, so I introduced myself and asked the women to share anything they wished with me. I had to remind myself that part of my job as a special education teacher would be to establish a partnership with the parents. Anything they could share with me concerning their children would be important to me. The mothers seemed to know each other well and were willing to share just about anything with me in each other's presence and in the presence of their children. I wondered how long the kids would tolerate waiting around. Anticipating this, I'd laid out toys, crayons, and paper on a couple of desks. The girls' interest in these things lasted less than ten seconds. Then they just wandered around the room for over ten minutes. Going outside was out of the question: the yard was still overrun with weeds and thorny brush and infested with grasshoppers. It wouldn't have been impossible for snakes to make their home in the overgrowth. Even I wouldn't venture out there. Anyway, the only playground equipment was an old rusty slide that was falling apart. There was no escape from the hot sun except a crooked old mesquite tree that would barely do the job.

Doris Bender, the mother of the Anglo girl Cindy, soon proved to be the more outspoken of the two that morning. "No one in this district gives a damn about my child. Did you see the schoolyard? Look at these rooms. Are you prepared to teach these kids? I mean, do you have a college degree? The last person that was here had gone to college for one year. He didn't even last as long teaching here. Then we had someone else, and that person quit too. I'm disgusted." She turned to the other mother and said, "You tell him, Odelia. Tell him what we've talked about. He seems like a nice man."

I appreciated the compliment, and I thought I was beginning to see where the mothers were coming from. It was time to transition to more specific questions. I desperately needed to know more about these girls so I could help them. I might only have a precious few minutes with these women before they left their daughters with me. But at the moment, Cindy and Ninfa, the other girl, were making in-depth conversation nearly impossible. They were just too disruptive and unable to find any task to occupy them for longer than five seconds. I needed private time with each of the women without their kids. That's when Doris suggested that Odelia take Cindy and Ninfa out for an hour while Doris had a conference with me. After that, they would switch, and Odelia would get her private conference. It was a remarkably bright idea. Odelia told Doris to take all the time she needed.

All I had in my satchel that morning was a blank notebook and a set of pens, and that's all I needed. I started by asking Doris if it would be okay to take notes as we talked.

She smiled. "Absolutely. This will be a first for me. I trust you, Mr. Carvajal—is that what I should call you?"

"Yes, that's my name," I replied. This was a first for me as well: the first time anyone had truly made me feel like a real professional. "Mrs. Bender," I began, "I want to frame our interview around four different topics: family background, educational history, medical history, and behavioral issues. I'd like to start with family background. You can answer yes or no to any question and expand if you wish. You share only what you want to share. Is that okay with you?"

She was eager to start. "Yes, yes, ask anything you want."

"First, does Cindy have brothers and sisters?"

Doris's response was an immediate "No!"

"Does she have friends, cousins, or kids she plays with?"

"No!" Doris answered emphatically.

I continued, "Does she get along well with you and your husband?"

I knew immediately that I'd hit a nerve. Doris's tone became stern and aggressive. "Cindy hates her father, and her father hates her. One time, Cindy went after him with a kitchen knife while he was drunk. I jumped up from the couch and stopped her. She managed to stab him once on the leg. He slapped her across the face so hard it broke her nose. He didn't want kids. I became pregnant when I was forty-two. He didn't want the baby. So now he feels he's stuck. I love Cindy, but I feel stuck too. He wants to take her to Austin to the school for the retarded there. I sometimes wonder if we should. Have you been there? Do you think you can help us get her in? He is willing to pay. He has a great job as a manager for a big company. He wants her gone—out of his sight."

Well, so much for my structured format. I was trembling by the time we took a break. Doris went outside to smoke. In that moment, I felt completely helpless. I remember hoping that this rathole the district called a school would go up in flames. When Doris came back inside, I suggested we meet again in two days. I had to review my notes and try to come up with some ideas about what she could do. I found it difficult to think about anything worth trying. I could see that the problem was enormous. I couldn't recall any graduate class that had prepared me for this. My appointment with Odelia was more encouraging simply because I realized how fortunate children with special needs are when they come from supportive and loving homes.

Two days later, Doris and I reconvened to continue our discussion. We moved on to educational history, which turned out to be much easier than our talk about family. Cindy had attended a "special school" the previous year and had refused to return. Stubbornness was a major issue with her.

"Why didn't she like school?" I asked.

There was anger in Doris's voice as she responded, "No one likes her. That's all. No one plays with her, she never goes anywhere, her dad hates her and won't take her anywhere—not even out to eat or to the movies—nothing. He's embarrassed to be seen with her. Cindy doesn't like anybody, and nobody can stand to be around her. She farts all the time. She has to wear diapers. I'm sorry. I need to stop. Can I come back next week?" She wept as she started to leave. I told her to call me the following week on Wednesday morning. We shook hands, and she embraced me with a gesture of sincere appreciation.

The next week, Odelia also came back in with Ninfa, almost dragging her daughter through the door. "She's like a mule," Odelia explained in Spanish. "If she says no, it's no. Very, very stubborn. I have to spank her a lot. If I don't, she won't move. Excuse me, sir, do you speak Spanish?"

I assured her that I understood and spoke Spanish well and she could use whatever language she preferred as long as we communicated freely and honestly.

She chose to speak in Spanish. I wrote quickly and succinctly to keep up with her rapid pace. Odelia had been forty-four when Ninfa was born. She had two older boys now in their teens. The boys loved Ninfa, but spoiled her in many ways. They treated her like a baby. For amusement, they'd also teach her bad words, which she'd then repeat to their applause and encouragement. Of course, to get their attention, she kept doing it.

I thought of many things to say to Odelia, but chose to listen instead.

Ninfa's father was a farmer. He was a caring father to the family. He had no education, but diligently worked the soil, planting and harvesting crops year in and year out. I told Odelia that at some point I'd like to meet her husband. She was not very encouraging. "El trabaja día y noche" (He works day and night), she said.

Next Odelia jumped to the topic of religion. "Padre Rolando tells me that we should love and respect Ninfa because God sent her to me to teach me lessons of suffering. She is my cross to carry for all my days. Sir, I never did any harm to anybody, and yet she is my cross." Odelia seemed bewildered. She appeared to want some response from me, but I chose to cut the conversation off there. I felt a surge of anger well up within me. What had this woman been told? I didn't care to hear this bullshit, much less validate it. I told her that someday we should talk about it further and then shifted topics.

It was becoming clear that Odelia's concerns arose out of a mind-set that was traditional in nature and marked by what could be considered naiveté. Nevertheless, with each question, she revealed a valid and thoughtful concern about her daughter. Her next issue of concern was that Ninfa would get married. I didn't understand. "Why are you saying that?" I asked.

"She likes boys and likes for boys to touch her," Odelia whispered. "My son told me he's seen her behave this way."

I was beginning to get it: Odelia was actually afraid that Ninfa would have sex, but to her, sex and marriage were one in the same. "How old is Ninfa?" I asked. Odelia began to launch into the history of Ninfa's birth, but I interrupted, "What year was she born?" I was starting to see why sometimes people asked for just the facts. "Thirteen," she replied. "Sir, please tell me, is it possible for Ninfa to get married and have children?" Part of me wanted to tell Odelia that Ninfa could get knocked up without being married. Again, I chose to abandon the topic for another time.

When Señora Odelia left, she had answered many more of my questions than I had answered of hers. I felt unprepared to respond to her crucial concerns and was almost ashamed that I, an educated professional, could not offer any advice to alleviate her frustrations.

I spent that evening searching my textbooks for solutions to these families' struggles. Even though the textbook on etiology gave me significant insights into the causation of Down's syndrome, it didn't talk about the condition being a form of punishment or a "cross to bear" as Ninfa's mother firmly believed. It was clear, however, that advanced maternal age had a direct correlation to the condition. The syndrome is caused by an aberration in the twenty-first pair of chromosomes. That didn't help much. I needed to know specifics on how to help these kids, but it looked as if I was going to have to find this out for myself. The personal problems that Ninfa, Cindy, and their families faced were difficult and challenging. The more I knew the kids, the more time I spent wondering about their lives. I had to allow time to observe them and meet with their mothers at least two more times.

The following morning, I decided to walk to school. I arrived forty-five minutes early. I was surprised to find Doris and Cindy already waiting for me in their car. I waved to them from the parking lot and opened the door leading into our multipurpose classroom, beckoning them inside. They came in and looked at the new arrangements and décor that we had in the room. I made up an interesting story about the room and how fortunate we were to have a classroom with so much possibility.

"I know we're early," Doris said apologetically. "This girl jumped out of bed very early. The first word that came out of her mouth was 'Cal'—that's what she calls you, Mr. Carvajal. I was shocked. Most mornings I've had to drag her here. I think she's found a friend in you."

"Well, the feeling is mutual," I replied.

Doris suddenly remembered that she'd brought snacks for Cindy and me for breakfast and lunch. She went to the car and brought in a large cardboard box full of food. With one hand wiping her runny nose, Cindy put her other hand in mine and led me forcefully to sit down and have some cold pizza with her. Pizza was Cindy's only definition of a meal: any meal.

That morning, we were expecting other visitors. We had learned that a few more parents would finally be dropping their kids off for school. I would actually have a class. Pam was on hand to introduce me to the new arrivals. Thirty minutes after Cindy had gotten there, three more cars pulled up with kids and their parents. "Uh-oh, the party's over," Pam said. "Here they come!" Three mothers came in, each with a child in toe. As we were introducing ourselves to each other, Ninfa and Odelia arrived. Five students in all for me to teach: I was not ready for this. A feeling of panic and desperation, not a new experience for me, was creeping in. I needed an aspirin. Five minutes later, three more students arrived in a car driven by a harried-looking woman. She struggled to get one of the boys out of his seat. I heard screams and saw a small wiry kid kicking the hell out of her from inside the car. I prayed to God they were not leaving him with me.

Pam reached for my arm and said, "That kid, Edward, will give you a run for your money. He's an only child—his mom is just giving a ride to the other two kids. Neither of the parents knows what to do with him. He was here for only three days last year. The teacher used to call him Boom Boom because of his behavior—it's explosive! Anything will set him off. He likes to climb on top the refrigerator and throw himself off headfirst. He gets a kick out of the trauma. Your job is to keep him safe. That's all. Tony, you have to have a serious conference with his family immediately, or this boy will destroy your year. You should also know that the mother is heavily medicated with tranquillizers and probably other things—anything to keep her from going crazy."

"Well, maybe she'll be the answer to my desperation. I need some of whatever she's taking, right now!" I said only half-jokingly.

Fifteen minutes later, child number 9 appeared at my door with a social worker. This completed the framework for my nightmare. I could see that this child was different from the others, however. There was an alertness in Ricky's bright and roving eyes. His handshake was firm and confident. At first glance, his only abnormalities were three deep scars running along the sides and top of his head. I learned that these were from a surgery to remove a brain tumor. However, I began to notice that Ricky did not have full control of the muscles around his mouth. For this reason, he could not speak intelligibly or completely close his mouth. Drooling was a problem. Apart from these issues, however, he seemed intellectually normal. Sue, who was teaching the kids with milder disabilities, had chosen not to accept Ricky into her classroom. How nice that she had a choice. She was concerned that a child like him would be a bad influence on her own darling students. In fact, she didn't really want the rest of my kids around them either. I couldn't sympathize. *Tough shit!* I thought.

At the end of the school day, Pam came in again to check on me. She was impressed that everyone was still in one piece and wanted to know my recipe for survival. "The famous Boom Boom—that hypermanic kid—only had twelve time-outs outside of the room," I reported. "That and he had to be tied to a chair for two hours. It's what I call advanced behavior management. Other than that, the rest of the group listened to and sang *one* song all day. Have you ever heard 'If You're Happy and You Know It, Shut Your Mouth'?"

Pam laughed and told me that my sense of humor would be the key to my success. In a way, she was right. If I ever got to the point of thinking seriously, even for a second, that I could make a significant difference in the lives of this population, I would have to consider myself insane.

Chapter Twenty

Now that I had a full class, it was time to set up more parent conferences. Because of Boom-Boom's severe issues, he was at the top of my list. To make it easier on his parents, I volunteered to come to their home. I proposed a date for the conference a week in advance to give them time to find someone to watch Edward while we talked. Thoughtfully, they complied with my request. When I arrived at the house, I immediately realized that Mr. and Mrs. Langtry were very comfortable financially. I soon learned that Mr. Langtry was a pharmacist and Mrs. Langtry a nurse. Their living room was elegantly furnished and meticulously organized. In a den off the living room, I could see medical books and journals lining a huge mahogany bookshelf. After we talked for a few minutes, the Langtrys took me to see Edward's room. It was a different story—a total disaster. Toys of all sorts were carelessly scattered across the floor and jammed into the closet. Bread crumbs covered every possible surface, including the bed. The only things that seemed deliberately placed were old crusts of bread on top of the pillows. The Langtrys explained that Edward would hoard pieces of bread and not let them go. He had to have them at all times of day and night. They told me that he would bring them to school in his pockets. "If anyone tries to look in Edward's pockets," Mr. Langtry warned, "they'll have hell to pay. Sometimes just touching him will set him off. I mean that seriously."

I learned from the Langtrys that Edward had appeared developmentally normal until the age of three. He had been affectionate and engaging. He had even started to speak in short but clear sentences. However, soon after his third birthday, Edward stopped talking. He withdrew deep into his own world. He no longer seemed able to engage with his parents or others. This was also when the self-abuse began. Edward's frightened parents took him to childhood specialists in Austin and San Antonio, but were sent home without answers. They still had none, yet were forced to contend with their son's devastating state with no help in sight.

That day, I prayed to God to give these parents the strength they needed to live through this merciless agony. I also wanted to do whatever I could to help. Mr. and Mrs. Langtry asked if, in addition to being Edward's teacher at school, I would give him some private assistance. They would hire me to develop a therapy plan for their son and meet with him once a week. I agreed to come work with Edward through play therapy on Saturday mornings for the rest of the fall semester. Soon after our conference, I began my assignment. Progress was so slow that I wondered if it was happening at all. One Saturday, a truck on the street outside honked loudly. Suddenly, Edward flew into a rage and kicked my face. He loosened one of my teeth and fractured my nose. I had a nosebleed that lasted for two hours. I was just beginning to realize the complex—and sometimes dangerous—nature of my career.

Back in the classroom, things weren't going much more smoothly. In the first few weeks of school, I cleaned several bloody noses, revived a girl who suffered from seizures, and changed the diapers of four of the boys. I totally refused to change the girls. They had to wait until Sue came in during the afternoon. One day, she didn't stop by until after school. She said the room smelled "funny." "No, Susie dear," I corrected, "what you're smelling is not funny. It's the smell of human shit." She made an about-face and left.

After two weeks of this dreadful schedule, I realized that this war could not be fought, much less won. I didn't have the physical or emotional strength to continue. My usual personal resources of romanticism and sentimentality were not coming into play. During the most difficult times in college, when I was confronted with rock-bottom situations, I would hum or sing "The Impossible Dream." But this time, Sancho Panza wasn't coming through for Don Quixote.

I had to get Leo to meet with me. I had called him and left messages on three different occasions. He hadn't returned any of my calls. One afternoon,

I drove to his office and found him sitting at his desk, talking on the phone. He immediately turned to me, said his good-bye to whoever was on the line, stood up, and embraced me.

"Tony, Tony, Tony. You are more than I, or anyone, ever expected. The whole town is talking about you. Edward's parents speak highly of you. You know that they're political giants in this community. Felicia gives me updates on what parents are saying about your glowing work."

I had to interrupt, "Leo, listen. I have an urgent request for you. I've made a list of priorities to review with you that need to be addressed immediately." Leo accepted the list and began to review it, whispering to himself as he read the words. The requests were in order of urgency:

1.) I need an individual to assist me by attending to the hygiene of the students and performing other assorted tasks (e.g., changing diapers, helping at recess to find kids who run away [e.g., Edward]). With the help of this person, I need two fifteen-minute breaks a day from the kids. I need to have lunch by myself and have my own opportunities to "go potty."
2.) I need toys and other instructional materials appropriate for the kids.
3.) The playground has to be cleaned up so kids can walk outside.
4.) The toilet needs to be repaired and the clogging problem resolved.
5.) I need to get kids out of the facility once a week to experience being outside in the community.

Leo showed anger and distress in colors. Now he turned deep purple, then red. I waited until the colors faded before I dared continue. He spoke first, "*Chato, chato, chato, mi amigo—fiel amigo de mi vida* [Buddy, buddy, buddy, my friend—faithful friend of my life]. If you knew how much I struggle to keep everybody happy. I work day and night to keep peace in this community. I get it from all sides. I cannot please parents, the fucking administrators, or even my family, and now this. I need you to help me, *mi amigo*. Help me—don't tear into me."

Leo reached for his handkerchief and was almost in tears. I felt like hell—I didn't mean to make him cry. But tears or not, I needed answers. I had enough tears to deal with in my classroom, not to mention the smelly gifts I was constantly washing out of dirty pants and underwear. Leo hadn't visited my classroom once that year. I felt like dragging him there. If he could spend just one lousy, bloody minute in my classroom, he would at least get a sneak preview of coming attractions for the next sucker who came in after I quit.

I waited for Leo the Martyr to finish his performance. Then I told him I needed an answer immediately. "Leo, I need to resolve my situation. Please don't play games with me." He knew I was not backing down; there would be no negotiating. He finally responded through his veil of tears.

"What do you need right away?" he asked tentatively.

"I need a helper to be with me all day," I sternly replied.

"Let me review my budget with the superintendent," he responded. "By the way, *chato*, Mr. Ford thinks the world of you."

"Is he back from his three-week vacation?" I said, not without sarcasm.

"Yes, he took a few days off after he came back. He came home with some awful flu," Leo said. I decided not to sabotage myself by saying what I was thinking: that flu symptoms can be caused by severe hangovers. Whatever illness Mr. Ford was nursing, apparently, I, and the rest of the district, would just have to wait for his attention.

Two weeks later, I hadn't received a response to any of my five requests. I felt abused, denied, and disillusioned. They had fooled me. I was embarrassed and deeply offended. My task was to move on with what I had. But what I had was nothing.

Paul and Robert continued to be terrific sounding boards. Paul gave me the best advice. One evening after dinner, he firmly laid out his opinion, which came in the form of an affirmation I needed to hear. "Get out of here," he said emphatically. "Don't let those fuckers get the best of you. I wish you knew how awesome and brilliant you are. You have this humanity—*eres sencillo y sincero* [you are simple and sincere]—that intrigues everybody who knows you. People not only like you, they love you. You have a magic I wish I had. Tony, I see you becoming the head of an academic department at some university someday. Don't let these bastards finish you off and abuse you the way they're doing. They simply don't give a shit about anybody.

Finish the year and go. Don't get me wrong, if I could, I'd keep you next to me for the rest of my life—I would. I'll always think of you as the best friend I've ever had. But I'm ready to share you with many others. I want many people to know your gift."

Well, this was a powerful compliment indeed. Unfortunately, it still wasn't too helpful the next morning when I got back to the battlefield.

The first people I saw every morning before everyone else arrived were Cindy and Doris, and this day was no exception. "Cindy still has to see you," Doris explained. "She wants to have breakfast with you. You look tired, Mr. C. Anything I can do?" If she only knew how the system was blatantly violating the rights of these kids.

"No, all is well," I lied. "I do need to see you soon. I have some questions regarding Cindy."

"I can be here by tomorrow at four," she said eagerly.

The next day, Edward was out with the flu. Thank God! With extra time and energy now available, I decided to take the class on an excursion to a nearby grocery store. It now occurred to me that this was one of the few times most of the kids had been invited to a public place. Through my conversations with parents, I'd learned that most of the kids were shut-ins: relegated to life at home and in their own backyards. Even though the parents' intentions were good, shame often played a part in why they secluded their kids as much as they could.

As I went over the logistics of the field trip, I had one significant concern: Julie. Julie was a child with severe brain injury. Her skull had been crushed as a result of abuse by her natural parents. The father, in a rage of anger, had thrown her against a brick wall and left her near death. The mother, an alcoholic and drug addict, was passed out when the incident occurred. The mother's sister lived next door. When she saw what had happened, she called 911 and saved what was left of Julie. Julie's parents went to prison (her father was later murdered while serving time), and her aunt and uncle adopted her.

When Julie was exposed to very bright lights or loud noises, she suffered uncontrollable seizures. She was totally nonverbal and could take only two steps at a time with considerable assistance. When I called her aunt and uncle about my plans for the field trip, I expected them to tell me it was not a good idea. Instead, Julie's uncle volunteered to drive her and to take anyone else who could not walk that far. I felt my heart leap with appreciation. Mr. Robb took Julie and Ninfa in his car. I would set out walking with the rest of the kids. Jokingly, Mr. Robb asked if I was sure I didn't want to ride with him.

Keeping everyone together on the walk to the store was futile. Next time—if there *was* a next time—I'd have to rope them together. When we arrived, Mr. Robb handed me Julie's tiny wheelchair, which she usually used for mobility at school. He said they tried not to put her in it a lot because they hoped to encourage and strengthen her to someday walk on her own. I respected his positivity, but did not agree. Julie was much too frail, and walking was out of the question.

When I was at East Texas, one of the curriculum catchwords was "outcome." The idea was to identify a need in a child, develop a goal, and identify activities to meet that goal. Then you would assess the results of the lesson: the outcome. If that was the language we were using here, then the outcome of this outing was disastrous. The kids nibbled at apples and grapes and then put them back in the bins. They stuffed their pockets—and mine—with candy and gum. At least the excursion only cost me $2.25. When we marched out of the store—to the relief of the appalled clerks—Mr. Robb, who'd been waiting in his car, asked how the kids had behaved. "They were angels," I lied. In my mind, I said, *Never again!*

At least the trip had made some kind of impression on the kids. Evidently, when they got home, they shared the news of their great expedition with their families. I received three thank-you notes from parents for my efforts.

That afternoon after the field trip, Doris arrived at four thirty instead of four. It was uncommon for her to be late. "I wanted my husband to come meet you. He walked away and took off without saying a word. He is so angry at me and so angry at Cindy. I love my husband, Mr. C."

Quite abruptly, I said, "Cindy is a very loving and sensitive child. She must feel the rejection she gets from Mr. Bender. She must know he doesn't want her. This is not helping her development in any way."

"What development?" Doris replied sharply. "She's retarded. The doctor told us she would always mentally be a two-year-old. He believes it, I believe it. You're the expert. Tell us if it's not true. The doctor also said that Cindy will die soon because kids with Down's syndrome have a short life expectancy. If this isn't true, I dare you to tell both of us together." I didn't know the answers, but agreed to meet with Doris again the next afternoon.

After school, before going home, I walked down to the nearby river to sit. I agonized over the possibility that there were no answers to soothe the despair of these parents—no answers for these kids at all. As I became more desperate and my thinking more disordered, I prayed. My prayer was silent and directed only to God. It was for his ears and his heart. "When I have children, please, I beg you, don't send me a child like the ones I teach." I sat by the bank of the river and shed tears for each of the parents.

The next afternoon, Doris arrived early—early enough to be our guest for the closing activity of the day. The kids liked to sing and dance the "Hokey Pokey" and always had to repeat it at least four times. I was sick of it. They really liked the body movements and were proud to have learned the names of parts of their own bodies. There was no observing the game: my only choice was to join in. If I stopped wiggling, they immediately stopped. When I started again, they applauded. We'd go on with our activity until it was time to quit. Each of us had the intuitive gift of knowing when this was. There was no mistaking when everyone felt it was time to go.

Odelia, there to pick up Ninfa, took Cindy to her house as well so Doris could have her scheduled conference. Doris asked if it was okay to have coffee at a nearby restaurant, her treat. I ordered a hamburger, fries, and apple pie for dessert. She was pleased at how receptive I was to her invitation.

"Mr. C., I don't know what to do. My husband's attitude is getting worse as the months go by. He wants to leave me. I don't mean to pile this on you with everything else you have to do for these kids, but I need to get Cindy out of the house."

"Where would she go?" I cautiously replied. "Do you have other family or friends that could take her, at least on a trial basis? Have you spoken to anyone at Social Services? My friend is the local director there. If you wish, we can start with her. Doris, I honestly don't know where else to go for advice. Let's start there. I have a lot of respect for what my friend does. I've seen her deal with very tough situations. May I call her?"

"Please do," Doris agreed. "I just don't want my husband to know. This is such a small town."

I promised her confidentiality and respect for her situation.

"Well, that takes care of my major issue, Mr. C. You seem to be having a great time with the kids. I heard about the big expedition to the grocery store. You are one brave man. Thanks for doing that. Julie's uncle raved about you at church. Odelia was there too, and she told everyone you were an angel."

"Believe me, an angel I am not," I said and meant it. "I doubt if angels get as angry and disgusted with situations as I do. I have nothing to work with, Doris. I need help. I need teaching materials, I need a playground so the kids can run and get fresh air, I need a toilet that doesn't clog up twice a day, I need to have someone monitor Edward's medication. Ninfa masturbates in front of the other kids, which obviously needs to stop. Last week, she swallowed twelve aspirin. My god, she has a weak heart—she could have died! I had to make her vomit. After that, I was so scared that I threw up. I don't have the time for everything I have to do in a day." I was becoming aware of how much I was rambling when Doris burst into laughter.

"You are such a loving man," she said. "You have no idea how much you mean to all of us. You have never complained. That's bothered me. Sooner or later you had to explode just like Edward does. Let me deal with this!"

Someone was actually stepping up to be my advocate. And who better than Doris? With her intelligence and assertiveness, she could be in charge of the United Nations. The following Saturday morning, she managed to get every parent to attend a meeting to discuss the issues. She asked me not to be there because of administrative repercussions. One fact she helped me understand well was that teachers could not assemble parents for political purposes. She thought the paranoid administration would perceive this meeting as a policy violation—an act of disobedience and disloyalty not to be tolerated. What a fascinating and brilliant navigator of bureaucracy Doris turned out to be.

By Wednesday of the next week, Doris had formed committees: one to address each of my concerns. The playground was being cleaned and set up by one group of parents and their friends. A different committee was working on gathering the instructional materials and toys we needed. As for the issue of the classroom assistant, the parents established a rotating schedule to make sure someone was there as a helper each day. I was delighted; less so was Ninfa, who could no longer terrorize me freely, calling me *chango chingao* (fucking monkey) and flipping me off whenever she wished. What lovely manners her brothers had taught her.

Besides the clogged toilet, which the parents were also looking into repairing, only one item on my list still needed addressing: the issue of giving the kids access to the community through field trips. For this, we required transportation, but also interest from the community in meeting and hosting the kids. This would not only provide education and new experience for them, but would make the public more aware of our school and its students.

By the following week, Leo had caught wind of the parent meeting. He called to ask me to stay after school to meet with him on Wednesday afternoon. He wanted clarification on exactly what was going on at "his" school. I suspected that the big cheese's ego had been bruised. I called Doris to see if she would like to join the meeting. She was delighted. "Absolutely. I'll have Julie's dad, Mr. Robb, come with me. Is that okay?"

"Doris, you represent the parents. These are your kids, not mine," I simply said.

When Leo arrived at school, he was shocked to see Doris and James Robb walking around the playground. He sarcastically asked if I had the parents working overtime and if I was paying them for all the work they were doing. "This is your job, you know," I retorted. "Parents are not supposed to do your work." With that, Doris and James came in the room. James and Leo evidently knew each other. They exchanged the typical "Good to see you" greetings and "How are things?" small talk. I introduced Doris. Leo bowed to her and praised her for being such a great mommy. "I have kids too, you know," he said ingratiatingly. "They can sure test you every chance they get."

Doris cut to the chase, "Mr. C. tells us that you need to know all about our organization." I almost passed out. I didn't know the group was considering themselves an organization. I felt like running.

James chimed in, "We're here to provide Mr. C. with any and all materials he needs to make this a good place for our kids. We support what he's doing. All of us see a lot of improvement in our kids." Then, patting me on the back, he continued, "We thank you, Leo, for all your support of this outstanding young man. Mr. C. is just what these kids needed."

Leo was eloquent. His colors didn't even change as he said, "Tony is what we call in Spanish *oro molido*—gold dust. He is the finest: pure and everlasting, glittering and superior in every way. I call him my *chato*, my buddy. I've never known anyone like him. I mean that sincerely." In his own way, I think he did. I felt guilt and shame. I prayed that Leo didn't feel that I was overstepping my boundaries. I didn't doubt Leo's allegiance and respect for my efforts. I did trust him and knew how constrained he was by the politics of the system. He now seemed willing enough to support the parents' efforts to help—especially since it required no extra effort on his part.

After the collective accolades I received at the meeting, word seemed to spread even farther that I was a "saint," which I thought was absurd. I was soon to be recognized as a special member of the Catholic church in Eagle Pass. Felicia called to prepare me for receiving a certificate of appreciation, or something like that, during Sunday morning mass.

Though I hadn't been to mass in years, I arrived at the church early that morning. Felicia and my friend Virginia—the director of Social Services—were waiting to escort me inside. It was the same church I'd wandered into when I'd first arrived in Eagle Pass. I'd always felt nervous in the spotlight, and having attention called to me at church was even worse. The memory of our excommunication years ago invaded my mind. Down the aisle, I felt my knees buckle and my hands get moist. The church was packed with adults and children. I looked around and was thankful that my escorts had thoughtfully reserved seats for the three of us. I still didn't like it. After the priest said the Gospel, he informed the attendees that the homily would be brief. He had a special person to present to the congregation. In that moment, I felt a violent urge to break through the wall, run away, and never return. I did not hear one word of the homily. But when the priest turned to look at me, I had no choice but to snap to attention.

"What an honor and pleasure to have in our midst, in our humble city, a person who truly is the best that God can send us," the priest began in Spanish. To say this priest was eloquent would be an understatement. I wondered if Shakespeare could hold a candle to him. He mesmerized the congregation with elegant metaphors and apt quotes from the Bible. Now he was about to give me a heart attack. Felicia held my hand tightly.

"Señor Carvajal, pase aquí al altar" (Mr. Carvajal, please step forward to the altar), the priest said. I obeyed. As I walked toward the altar, immersed in the scent of candles and incense, my mind returned to my days as an altar boy. The priest told me to face the audience and asked if there was anything I wanted to say. At first nothing would emerge from my mouth. Then I heard myself saying, "Gracias por sus atenciones, este honor, y sus rezos." Then I repeated the same in English, "Thank you for your thoughtfulness, this honor, and your prayers." I don't know why I felt the need to translate to the congregation: the majority in attendance were monolingual Spanish speakers.

On the way out, I asked Felicia, "What in the world was all that about?"

"Ninfa's mother has a lot of clout in the church," she responded. "She is quite a leader in the Women of the Most Precious Sacred Heart of St. Mary's organization. She wanted prayers to come your way."

When we stepped outside the church, many people approached us to congratulate me and welcome me into their humble parish. Several asked me to have dinner with them anytime I wanted—they would be most honored. That I liked.

When Robert and Paul heard about the bestowing of my "sainthood," they expressed their admiration with tones of sarcasm. They each bought me a beer as a bribe to guarantee them a place in heaven. "Don't forget about us when you get there," they mockingly urged.

Now that the entire community seemed to know of my teaching efforts, several people unrelated to any of the kids called the school to see if they could come meet the students and offer support. I had mixed feelings. In a way, I needed as much help as I could get, especially to build the playground. At the same time, I didn't want the school to become a sensationalized attraction for "do-gooders."

Throughout this strange time, I started enjoying and appreciating Robert's company even more than usual. He had valuable social insights that didn't come as naturally to Paul and me. To him, everything in society was political. Robert's theory about the public school system was simple: the system rewarded the incompetent—individuals that seemed to just wander around in a fog year after year. He maintained that these were the kind of folks promoted to the highest level of their incompetence. He urged me to read the book *The Peter Principle*. To prove this embarrassing theory, he had me look at what went on in our own schools.

"If you look around, the tenured teachers are not the best teachers. They're the ones who kiss up to central administration—they're the loyal ones," he explained. "Also, if you look around, most school principals are coaches or were coaches at one point. You seldom see a scholar as a principal. The administration is a club for the jocks. These incompetents are successful because they each have informants at the lower levels. Many times these informants are teachers starving for recognition and security."

I finally said, "Robert, shut up, man. You make it sound as if the system is infested with fungus."

He responded, mimicking Leo, "You've got it, Tony, *mi chato*! In fact, you should be on your guard. I wouldn't be surprised if some of these people were already preparing to get rid of you. You're coming on too strong. You should be subservient and meek: a peon. Watch who you talk to and what you say. Know your friends. I like your image of fungus. You're right on. Whenever there is a fungus among us, I'll just say the word 'fungus.'"

"Did you say 'munungus'?" I replied.

"Brilliant, Tony. Yes, I'll just say the word 'munungus,' and you'll know exactly when to change the subject or keep your mouth shut."

Paul weighed in, "Damn, I like that. Munungus among us. We can make a song about that one. We must be careful not to share the code with anyone, or we'll be suspected and canned."

Chapter Twenty-one

One late afternoon, I was waiting for Paul and Robert at the Moderno Lounge across the border in Piedras Negras. We seldom went into Mexico during the week but decided on this particular day that we wanted a quiet and private place to talk. There were a lot of personal issues we had to discuss over dinner and away from the main areas of town.

I waited for over thirty minutes, but neither of them arrived. I resolved to wait a bit longer. Bored and anxious, I got up from my table and walked over to a piano used for entertainment during the dinner hour. Only three other people sat at the bar, silent and staring around the room at the tropical décor. I sat down at the piano bench and called to mind a song Paul and I had heard two weeks previous at another lounge in this Mexican town. I remembered that Paul had fallen instantly and madly in love with the singer. That song, enhanced by the woman's exquisite voice and offset by the sight of her lovely body, had impressed me so much that I wanted to learn to play it. Awkwardly at first, I picked out the tune until it began to flow more readily through my hands to the keys. All the lyrics came back to me. "Si en algo te ofendí, perdón . . ." (If I somehow offended you, pardon me). The message spoke of love and sincere longing for forgiveness. When I completed my musical interlude, a couple of the people at the bar applauded feebly. I hadn't played to entertain anybody. Before I returned to my empty table, the bartender came over and offered me a drink *de la casa* (on the house). I accepted the offer and ordered a beer. When he returned to my table with the drink, he said that the gentleman at the bar had insisted on paying for it. I waved a gesture of thanks at the man he had pointed out. Next, the man at the bar walked over to my table and asked if he could join me. Awkwardly,

I accepted. "I'm waiting for my friends," I explained. "They're late. I need to get back to town across—"

"I'm Jack Bender, Doris's husband," the man interrupted. "My wife adores you, Mr. C.—as she calls you. I want you to know how much I appreciate the help you're giving her." The man seemed like a real gentleman. I carefully studied his face to see if I could note any traces of evil there. He was handsome: his eyes bright green like Cindy's.

"Wow, this is a real pleasure. I can't believe I'm speaking to Cindy's dad," I said. "She's a delightful child, one of my favorites."

"I'm Doris's husband. I am not Cindy's dad," Mr. Bender responded abruptly.

Maybe I'd been wrong about the green eyes. I surmised now that Doris had been married before. No wonder he couldn't accept Cindy. "Did you adopt Cindy?" I asked. "Did you know she would be such a challenge to raise before you adopted her?"

"Mr. C., I am the father, but I am not her dad," Mr. Bender clarified firmly. "What I'm saying is that to me, Cindy is not a daughter—she can't be, and she never will be. Let me say something to you, you're making things more difficult for her mother and me. We want to find her another home. Doris told me you might be able to help with this. She doesn't keep any secrets from me."

I was ready to put on my Don Quixote armor, get on my philosophical high horse, and go into battle when Paul and Robert flew in the door. Thank God. I waved to them eagerly. Mr. Bender immediately stood and reached to shake my hand. We said our good-byes and parted, expressing civil intentions to meet again soon.

Two days later, Pam came in to replenish my diaper supply. Though she was a great help to me, her anxious disposition was getting annoying. She ran as if she were on a timer and had only seconds to talk. If she took longer, it was to scold me or warn me not to "step on people's toes" or "muddy the water." "Hi," she said as she swept in the door and hugged me. "Stay away from the Moderno Lounge. Are you getting paid to entertain at the bar, or are you a professional teacher? I don't want an explanation, Mr. Piano Man. Just don't."

Gossip sure traveled fast. I guess I wouldn't be accepting any awards of honor for my foray into lounge entertainment. In a way, I was proud that my reputation was expanding to different corners of the world, but I also sensed an invasion of my privacy. I had the right to do whatever the hell I felt like doing. I was not backing down. If I wanted to play a song on a damn piano, I would. If creepy Bender didn't care for Cindy, I did. If the pillars of society were offended by my strategies or the existence of these terrific kids—hiding them from a world they had a right to be a part of—those hypocrites were in for a rude awakening. As long as I had the support of the parents, I would forge ahead.

One theory of life is that you should always be a nice person: always stay positive and ingratiating. This is how I was raised and educated. I was taught that to be humble, meek, submissive, and forgiving were virtues—that these were the only traits of a good person. However, I've learned through experience that I personally do better when I'm royally pissed and feel pressed to take a stand for what I believe is the truth. My emotional juices get churning, and I erupt into action, going to places I've never been before. When I'm insulted or feel taken advantage of, it may take time for me to get truly angry, but when it happens, not even giants can stop me.

Pam's words had left me feeling deeply insulted. But after I'd stewed in my anger for a few hours, it was time to turn that negative energy into a positive outcome. I arranged a meeting of the parents' organization. I then met with Doris and Odelia to ask for their input about the meeting. I suggested a three-item agenda: to come up with a name for our school, arrange to obtain new furniture for each room, and discuss ongoing community access for the kids.

At the meeting, I took my time to present the rationale for my new plans and evoke a sense of urgency around them. The parents were inspired. Forty-five minutes into the meeting, we had decided to name the school Riverside School since it was indeed near a river. Previous to that, it was just known as a school for retarded kids. As for the second item, Ricky's dad would be in charge of coordinating fund-raisers for the new furniture and perhaps getting individual donations. The final item on the agenda, a plan to expose the kids to the larger community, was more intricate. Transportation was a major barrier. I resolved to ask Leo about it.

When I told Leo about our productive meeting, he seemed earnestly pleased, but in response to the transportation issue, he was not encouraging. "I'll tell you right now, *chato*, unless you drive one of the school buses yourself, there's no way of going on field trips. No way. You can't take all those kids in your car. It's against the law!"

Nonetheless, the following week, I saw a huge bus in the school parking lot. It was mine to use. But where was the driver? The anger began to churn again. Well, with or without a professional driver, we were not letting this opportunity slip by. We were going on a field trip today. I decided a nearby park was a good a place as any. I lined up the kids and marched them onto the bus, telling them to be good and listen to Ricky, my special assistant. Ricky, as the highest functioning student in my group, had become my right-hand man. I relied on him often to help me lead the others. I was now almost thankful that Sue had seen it fit to pass him off to me. In turn, he seemed to enjoy his role as assistant teacher and appreciated the extra attention.

It had to be a rainy day. What started as a sprinkle soon turned into a torrential storm. I couldn't find the windshield wipers or the headlight switch. Oblivious, the jubilant kids were applauding me. I realized that my rash anger had inspired a very bad idea. Soon, we came to a large hill. I had no idea how to drive this stupid bus. It had about eight gears unlike the four that my own car had. As I stepped on the gas to make it up the hill, the engine died. I tried to turn it over to no avail. I couldn't move the bus forward, nor could I keep it at a stop. The only way to go was rolling backward down the hill. In desperation, I tried the engine again. This time it worked, but now I couldn't get the bus to shift into gear. I stepped on the break, and the engine died again. I felt the bus sliding backward as the kids continued to applaud. I screamed at Ricky to shut them up. The bus continued rolling downhill until it landed directly in a deep ditch at the side of the road. Everyone was in one piece, thank God, but we were totally stuck. A couple of truckers got out of their semi and asked if we needed help. I pleaded, "Señores, por favor, lleven los niños a la escuela" (Sirs, please, take the kids back to school).

I don't know why I chose to handle the situation this way, but I just wanted to get the kids back to school. As many as could fit, they piled into the semi's cab with the truckers. I made sure Ricky was among them, telling him to show the men the way back to school and to tell Sue that the bus was stuck and that she needed to call Leo. Then I remembered that Ricky couldn't talk. I quickly wrote a note for him to carry. I stayed with the others and wallowed in my defeat. This was known as eating crow. Anger sometimes does backfire.

Chapter Twenty-two

As that fall progressed, it was soon time for Eagle Pass's annual harvest celebration: one of the highlights of the season for the entire community. The main event was a parade with a theme of harvest and bounty. Everyone turned out to watch it, and many in the community participated, including farmers displaying the abundance of their crops. Folks got there early to claim a place to view the grand spectacle. The parade was cosponsored by the mayor's office, the local banks, and the Eagle Pass High School, whose marching band was prominently featured.

Two weeks before the festivities, Odelia asked me if we could prepare a float so the kids in my class could participate in the parade. She and three other parents had discussed the possibility of having the kids make autumn leaves and paste them on a horse-pulled wagon. My farmer friends could provide the wagon—the parents suggested—and would have the name "Riverside School" written on each side.

I was uneasy but proud of the parents for being willing to coordinate the project. I thought it was a great idea and a perfect opportunity for the community to become aware of our school. Odelia wondered if we could get a few of the kids to ride on the wagon. Ninfa, of course, would be one. Doris also wanted Cindy to share in the limelight. Since none of the other parents consented to having their kids ride, it looked like the dynamic duo of Ninfa and Cindy would be representing us. We set to work on the float, Ricky helping me coordinate the making of the leaves. We then fastened them to an old wagon that was ready to fall apart. Next, it was time to prepare our class representatives for their role. We took a dry run around the parking lot in the wagon, practicing to get the kids on and off safely and ensuring they could stay on without falling off. Cindy and Ninfa were delighted and applauded themselves. Ricky and I applauded them as well to show our support.

The morning of the parade, the commotion was worrisome. We lined up among large floats and three marching bands, loudly tuning their instruments. Applause could already be heard erupting from the crowd as the parade started to go by. Our float riders—so excited about their role up until now—were frightened and refused to get on the wagon. Doris and Odelia came forward and explained that the girls would not go without me. This too was problematic since I would absolutely not go with them. I knew there was more than a little hypocrisy in my stance. The bottom line was, I would not be seen with my students, especially not on a wagon being pulled by two cantankerous mules. Absolutely not! I had endorsed the float, sure, but I would not allow myself to be socially damaged. What would people think? "Carvajal has totally lost it!" This appearance would be social suicide.

Cindy and Ninfa were getting more anxious by the second. I was worried they would jump off, so I compromised. I ran and bought plastic flowers from a nearby vendor, gave each girl a flower to carry, firmly grabbed the side of the wagon as it started moving, and somewhat awkwardly began walking alongside it. The kids applauded me. I looked up and saw a pleasant smile on Cindy's face. Doris had placed the blue plastic flower in her hair. It was her favorite color.

I don't remember seeing the faces of anyone who knew me as we made our way down the parade route. Perhaps this was because I purposely never looked beyond the kids. However, out of the corner of my eye, I could see people waving at us and applauding us loudly. Some were calling my name. If only Ramón could see what kind of unwitting celebrity I'd become. Twelve blocks later, we were at the end of the route. The parents were waiting for us with hot drinks and donuts. I walked home, wondering what in the world was becoming of me. When I arrived, Robert and Paul were waiting. They'd already heard about my parade debut. I said nothing and dared them to say another word about it.

As the fall went on, Cindy's possessiveness of me began to grow. Every day she brought to school her blue flower, my gift to her, and it was not to be touched by anyone but me. She got upset when other students approached me or even touched my desk. During snack time, I had to sit next to her and her alone. At recess and lunch, I had to be within arm's reach or she would demand that I sit next to her. It was a difficult situation for both her and me. Doris was also concerned about Cindy's behavior and cautioned that I needed to teach her daughter to be independent from me.

Soon, the new playground was complete, and the parents planned a picnic celebration to dedicate the playground to their kids. Its crowning glory was two swings attached to the branches of the lone mesquite tree, which turned out to be quite solid after all. The parents had trimmed the branches nicely, giving the swing set a stunning appearance. The kids adored the swings, and everyone took their turn. Ricky embraced a new role as swing master, giving each kid a push to get started—everyone except Cindy, since only I could push her. When she was on the swing, no one but I could swing next to her. If I wasn't swinging, no one could even touch the empty swing.

One day, the inevitable happened. I had to run across the yard to restrain Edward. No one could catch up to him except for me. By the time I returned to the playground with Edward firmly under my arm, Cindy had pounced on Ricky and Ninfa. She was dangerously furious that I'd left her. She threw the plastic flower at me, kicked me, and sat sullenly on the ground. No one could touch her. When Doris came to pick her up, she was still kicking and striking at anyone who came close. I told Doris what had happened and how frustrated I was with the situation. She reinforced the notion that I move on and help the other kids. Cindy stared at me with fire in her eyes. The next morning, Doris called and told me that Cindy didn't want to return to school. Worried, I visited her at home several times that week. With the extra attention, she finally responded and came back to school the following Monday.

Thanksgiving break rolled around like a magical gift. I received dinner invitations from several families, the parents' organization, and the church parish. I decided to drive to Dallas instead, simply to get away from the area. When I returned from break, the momentum we'd managed to build thus far in the school year seemed to have dwindled. Ninfa was having serious respiratory complications; Edward's medication was becoming ineffective and had to be changed. Cindy's relationship with her dad had become even worse: Mr. Bender was not willing to come home as long as Cindy stayed.

When I called Virginia at the office of Social Services for advice on Cindy's situation, she suggested we meet with Doris. She spoke firmly, "I have one suggestion you will not like, but I feel this is the only option left for the family." When Doris, Cindy, and I arrived at her office, Virginia was on the phone. She asked if we could wait thirty minutes. After forty-five, she came out, asked us to sit on the couch, and presented her plan. "Tony, I know you're not going to like this one bit, but this is the only solution," she began. "There are two spaces available for retarded children at a facility affiliated with the Children's Hospital of Austin. I believe Cindy should go there. It's a great facility—there's great care. Doris, you can come visit her whenever you wish. Tony, you can even come see her. They have celebrations on holidays and parties for the kids on their birthdays."

I was disgusted and furious at Virginia. "I know exactly what this is," I said. I turned to Doris and looked deeply into her eyes. "Cindy will become a ward of the state. She will be owned by the state to do with as they wish. Doris, we are talking institutionalization. She is not my child, but I would never ever allow this if she was."

"Tony, let's go for a walk outside and talk. Please," Doris replied, her voice filled with urgency.

Since Cindy would not stay back at the office by herself, she walked with us. She wrapped her tiny hand firmly around mine as she always did. Though this level of conversation was too complex for her to understand, I somehow felt Cindy knew what was happening.

"She can't stay with us," Doris began. "I've asked my sisters, and they're not prepared to take on the responsibility. Odelia checked with the church organizations, and no one is willing to take a chance with Cindy. You know the challenge. You know the problem better than anyone else—"

I interrupted, "Doris, you and your creepy husband will do what you want to do, and I know what you plan to do. Keep me out of this. I am totally out of this hopeless travesty." As we were walking back to the office, Virginia joined us. Before she could say anything, I directed bitter words at her, "Well, Virginia, you sure are meeting your obligations to the state. Congratulations. I'm sure you'll get a bonus."

Chapter Twenty-three

Christmas break was a blur. I went to San Jose and bought Christmas gifts for my family. I also bought souvenirs for each of the kids in my class. I returned the same day school started. Among my phone messages were several from Doris, asking that I call her right away. I did not return these calls.

Two weeks into January, the weather was cold and wet. I felt my energy draining away. Virginia came by the school one afternoon after most of the kids had gone home. Ricky was still there, as usual, helping me to prepare the room for the following day. Virginia asked if I could excuse him to go home so that we could talk. I said he had to stay because he had tasks to complete.

"Tony, please listen. Let's go somewhere for coffee. I need your support on this one," Virginia insisted.

After Ricky and I prepared the room for the next day, Virginia and I took Ricky home. He waved in his usual friendly way, and the minute he was out of sight, Virginia started driving with great focus, speaking to me carefully as if she'd prepared what she was going to say.

"The paperwork is ready," she said. "It was an enormous task, but it's complete with notarized signatures. I've made two trips to Austin with Doris and Mr. Bender to look over the facilities. They were very pleased with the setup. Cindy will be able to come home during the summer and spend time with the family."

What a crock! I thought. They'd finally succeeded while I was gone. Sneaky, shameless imbeciles: that's exactly what they were. Shameless, heartless, and selfish: all of them. I felt my tears gushing out. We drove past a grocery store, and I abruptly insisted, "Please stop right here. I have a damn cold. I need medication." We pulled up to a traffic light, and I jumped out of the car, walking behind a building to vomit. I wept. I saw Virginia circle the block looking for me. I didn't go back to the car. I walked the backstreets leading to the river near the school. There I stayed until the rain and cold drove my broken spirit home.

Late in January, Doris came to see me after school. Ninfa's mother again took Cindy with her, giving us a chance to talk. "Mr. Carvajal, please don't make things worse than they are. I hate myself for what I'm doing. I also know there is no other way out of this mess. I wish you could understand what these kids do to their families. We live for them twenty-four hours a day with no hope in sight. I don't know if you know this, but Boom Boom's parents are considering finding a slot in Austin for him too. His mother has taken so much medication that her heart can't deal with it. Their child hurts himself all the time just to feel the blood run down his face. He's a terror day and night. His parents are scared to go to sleep at night. These kids can destroy their parents and everyone else around them. There is no place for them. We worry and wonder what will happen to them when we're gone. Please understand! You've been the best thing that's ever happened to these kids and to all of us. Now please, you have to see our side."

"Doris, I think you need to go," I replied bitterly. "You'll take Cindy to Austin when you choose to, but don't try to justify your shame to me. I have work to do and plans of my own to make."

"Mr. C.," Doris persevered, "we're scheduled to deliver Cindy in three weeks." She said the word "deliver" as if Cindy were a piece of furniture. "My husband would really appreciate it if you came with us. We have to be there on February 11 at 9:00 a.m. We both feel that Cindy will do better if she sees you there."

I felt sick all over again.

When Robert came home, he asked how "the god of the mongoloids" was doing. It was not a jab I was willing to hear. I pushed him and hit him in the face. I drove into Mexico and walked around for over two hours. I expressed my anger and fury to God for giving children like Cindy such hopeless disabilities.

February 11 was a Friday. That afternoon, I went with Doris, her husband, and Cindy to Austin. I drove my own car and followed them to the state-affiliated school where Cindy would live. The dreary, cold, and wet day plunged me into the depths of depression. When we arrived, I got sick just as I had that day with Virginia. Afterward, I went and peered in at Cindy in the backseat of the Benders' car. She was virtually covered in stuffed animals, dolls, and coats. Her nose was even runnier than usual, and the skin around her eyes was red. I knew that she too had been crying.

Cindy got out of the car and wrapped her small hand in mine as we walked into the building. She clung tightly to my arm as we entered the lobby where two huge nurses were waiting to escort her. Mr. Bender simply walked away. We followed the nurses through the institution that would now be Cindy's home. Doris hugged her daughter with a love that only mothers can give, crying until I thought she could not withstand the agony of departure. I prayed to God that she would change her mind. Instead, she turned to me and said, "I'll wait in the lobby while you say good-bye to her." With that, Doris left. The overly assertive nurses stayed with Cindy and me. They would be responsible for taking my precious Cindy into the School for Retarded Children. There, she would grow up without the family, friends, and advocates she had known thus far in her life. She would be deprived of intimate familial love and the beautiful days of life in normal society that she had known with us. I felt myself choking with tears and gasping for air as I embraced her. Instantly, Cindy angrily bit my hand, shoving me away. The bite was so hard that she left an indentation from her tiny teeth in my skin. Beyond a doubt, she knew I had also betrayed her. She walked away with the nurses in total resignation and defeat.

We live in a "no pain, no gain" society. I know through my own experience how much effort and struggle it takes to make headway in life and better one's situation. The hand we are dealt in terms of economic, social, emotional, and intellectual resources helps determine how well we are able to learn and grow from experiences. However, many children and adults with mental disabilities do not have the resources they need to lift themselves out of the devastating options given to them. Children like Cindy rarely have the advocacy or emotional support they require to navigate through life. They are totally dependent on us for support and assistance. Either we make gains for them, or society will relegate them to human warehouses, putting them away whenever they become less than convenient.

The personal rewards I received from loving Cindy and the rest of my kids were immeasurable. However, the anger and disgust I felt toward myself, the parents, and the educational system pushed me farther and farther away from believing that teaching was a place where I belonged. When I returned to my little school, I had finally had enough. I started counting the days until spring break. I took inventory of my teaching hours, called Dr. Armfield, and asked him if I had completed the practicum requirements. He reviewed my program requirements and indicated that, while I had enough practicum hours, I still needed nine more academic hours to complete my master of science degree. I considered not returning to East Texas.

Is there always gain from pain? I don't know, but pain is all I felt. I had given it all I had and was left emotionally wrecked and disillusioned. I had believed that the support the school administration had given me was genuine. Instead, it was a system filled with hypocrites. I had become a tool for their true goal: to isolate and eliminate children that nobody wanted to see or even acknowledge as human beings. I had become part of their stupid game. The romantic fool that I was didn't see the mockery right before my eyes. Mr. English Major, with all his knowledge of great writers, was ill-prepared for the field of special education. It had devoured him.

Two days before spring break, I submitted my resignation as a teacher of the trainable mentally retarded at Riverside School. I was ready for a new journey. I departed without farewells or explanations. I left for personal reasons, and I left with a broken heart.

I drove directly to the state school where Cindy now lived, parked my car, and walked across the campus, observing the ugly dorms where the kids were kept. Again, I left ashamed of myself for not fighting harder for Cindy's rights to be loved and protected. I will forever recall Cindy as a happy child who loved to wear a plastic blue flower in her hair, and I will always remember how she believed that the old tree on the playground, the swings, and I were her sole property.

There aren't many moments in my life that I truly regret. However, my sudden departure from what I considered a long-term teaching commitment evoked in me deep regret. I had abandoned my students and was plagued by grief, shame, and self-loathing. The rashness and thoughtlessness of my resignation compelled me to try to understand where my actions had come from. Yes, it was true that I could no longer tolerate the indifference of the district administrators toward my school and its students. But did this justify my departure? I went through many desperate days of analyzing and rationalizing my reasons for leaving. I talked myself into believing that the entire American school system could not, or would not, ever commit itself to educating children of below-average intelligence or those deemed substandard in any way. This was just the way it was: it could not be changed by me.

Yet I knew that the parents of the Riverside children had placed their hopes in me and had not deserved my betrayal. They had finally found in me someone who would try to answer any and all questions they had about their kids. I had been the one person who had offered a glimmer of hope that their children could someday be accepted into public schools. I had injected optimism into their lives, leading them to believe that their children had personal rights: the right to a good education, the right to be happy, the right to be productive citizens of society. But in the end, I'd done nothing to back up those promises. When the parents had vented their deepest frustrations, I'd been powerless to help them. In the end, I'd simply walked away. The irony of it all couldn't be more palpable than with Cindy's situation in which I, her past protector, had watched as she was tossed into an institution where unwanted and unacceptable children were forgotten.

I realized now that ignorance wasn't always bliss. Despite my desire to truly make a difference for my students, I'd simply lacked the knowledge and training to do so. I'd had little specific education into the etiologies and environmental influences that cause permanent and irreversible mental deficiencies. I observed the complexity of my students' behaviors, their limitations in intelligence, their social maladaptiveness and ineptness, but could not understand the reasons for their intricate learning limitations or abnormal personalities, let alone begin to help them in these areas.

One thing I did now understand was how much my students were subject to discrimination and misunderstanding by others. Just like the "imbeciles" and "village idiots" I had encountered in my American literature books, these kids were often seen by others as surplus, worthless individuals to be put away, out of the sight of the "normals." They were given no acknowledgment as human beings to be respected. Sometimes, the ignorance went even deeper. Perhaps in an attempt to understand or make sense of the mentally retarded, some people even viewed them as specific punishments for crimes against God. Odelia was still struggling to understand what sin of hers had led to the birth of her defective child. I had no doubt that many children were still unfairly demonized with the same sense of superstition and fear as Diablito had been.

I could no longer tolerate the depth of the ignorance, yet I also know now that my decision to leave also came from a bruised ego—from my own intellectual and professional arrogance. At Riverside School, I couldn't have been farther from my dream of becoming an English teacher like Mrs. Pasley. Instead of inspiring promising high school minds to love and appreciate literature, I had spent my days struggling to explain to severely retarded kids the difference between a dog, a cat, and the Easter bunny. How had I gotten so far off track from my goals? I realized that my course had been entirely manipulated by the district administration. I had originally been offered a position teaching high school English: my lifelong aspiration. Instead, strictly on the basis of federal funding allocations, I'd suddenly been made a speech therapist. The district was all too happy to let me out of that job when they found a truly qualified speech therapist. Next, they'd simply, and without asking me, left me to flounder in a position literally just abandoned by another fool like me. Being isolated from the mainstream of any occupation or profession is demeaning. You are not a member of a group: you live behind closed doors and secretly survive with whatever personal resources you can muster. When Robert and Paul would discuss with each other district changes that had been discussed in their faculty meetings, my reaction was to walk away. My students and I were not part of the broader educational system. We existed only for each other, at least until the day someone came to claim our school as a storage facility. In a sense, it already was.

Perhaps what bothered me most about my resignation was that I had admitted defeat. I had fought and clawed my way to every success I'd achieved in life and believed in the illusion that nothing could stop me. Up until now, I'd chosen to believe I could win any war and avoid sinking with any ship. Whew, was I wrong! It was a lesson in humility, but perhaps one that prepared me for the challenges and battles that lay ahead.

After long and weary weeks of talking myself through what had happened, I realized finally that I simply had to accept what was and move forward. I had to stop trying to put the blame on one thing or another when nothing about this situation was black and white. I realized that I'd been terribly judgmental of Doris, making her feel like an unworthy parent. Perhaps both of us were complicit in and also defeated by the established system.

I decided to return to San Jose to become a part of my own family again. Before I left, I thanked Robert and Paul for all the support they had given me. I set out on my journey home. When I arrived, I called them. They were elated to hear from me. Knowing how fragile my emotional state had been when I'd left, they wondered if I'd gone and joined the circus. I told them that I was indeed the leader of the clown gang. Badly needing a sense of refuge, I was glad to be home, but I already missed the constant friendship of my two buddies. They pleaded with me to come back. I could not and would not. Whatever damage I'd created was behind me. I did promise to see them that summer when I returned to complete my graduate program at East Texas. They assured me that I was missed by many people. Everyone was asking about me and wanted reassurance that I was well. Doris had called Robert and asked for my address. Eventually, I received a letter from her, indicating that her marriage to Mr. Bender had ended. They'd decided to divorce just seven weeks after I'd left. I was saddened by the news.

Late that spring, Robert called again, ecstatic to tell me that a school district near Corpus Christi, Texas, had several openings in special education. He said that the pay was enticing as was the proximity to a beach packed with gorgeous babes. The educational reputation of the district was one of the best in the state. I, however, was not one bit impressed and ignored Robert's ridiculous attempts to lure me into another professional fiasco. I was not about to fall into another trap. Three weeks later, however, I found myself taking the bait. It was probably a combination of wanting to see Robert and Paul again and my driving need to redeem myself from the Eagle Pass debacle. However, I promised myself that this time would be different: I was in control. I was willing to rigorously study each move I made from now on and assess the personal ramifications it had on me. This would guide me in every decision I made from now on.

Chapter Twenty-four

When Robert called me that spring with the news of jobs in the Corpus Christi area, he pleaded with me to at least go with him to visit the area before I made any definite decisions about my next move. Early in the summer, after I'd returned to Texas to complete my degree, we took a weekend trip to Corpus Christi, staying at a hotel across the street from the beach. I'd never seen so much water or so many seagulls gliding through the air overhead, crying their loud cries. I thought somebody ought to feed them.

Padre Island in Corpus Christi was a tropical paradise without the palm trees. The weather was quite humid, and the beaches covered with fine white sand like I'd never seen before. The population seemed to consist mainly of tourists. It was certainly a change of pace from Eagle Pass with its strong Mexican influences: that had been something I'd really liked about the small town where I'd taught. Here in Corpus, however, life seemed to come with its own brand of joy. Perfect suntanned bodies swarmed the beaches. Tourists and locals coexisted together, everyone staking out a place on the sand. The yearlong residents seemed to have their own designated spots that they reclaimed whenever the weekend rolled around. Tourist or not, anyone not in beach apparel stood out like a sore thumb. I was one of them. Therefore, my first priority upon arrival was to purchase swim trunks, a couple of huge beach towels, a sun umbrella, sunscreen (the saleswoman insisted I needed it, which I thought was ridiculous), and a six-pack of beer. Settling onto the sand, I was overcome by an instant therapeutic sense of wellness. The ocean breeze, the sound of the seagulls, and the spontaneous music provided by amateur guitar and ukulele enthusiasts were all new experiences for me. There was a general live-for-the-moment vibe among the pleasant and friendly beachgoers that I could appreciate. All these elements were good for my soul. I wondered if this was paradise.

Of course, I did have to peel myself off the beach eventually: I had a teaching interview to attend. My meeting with Mr. Guillen, assistant superintendent of instruction for the school district, lasted for three hours. Mr. Guillen asked direct questions, and I responded with direct information. He inquired about my reasons for selecting this area for a teaching position, and I told him that my roommate had encouraged me to come here because of the coastal environment. He smiled. He delved into questions about my professional experiences in Eagle Pass, and I briefly explained the positive aspects of my time with the students, their parents, and the fun things we did in the community. He smiled twice on that note. After Mr. Guillen had finished gathering his information, he disclosed that the salary for this position would be twenty-five thousand dollars—eight thousand more than I'd made in Eagle Pass. I felt hot and cold prickles run down my spine. I abruptly said I would accept this offer if extended to me. *Hell, I'd even clean up the beaches on Sunday evenings for that much cash,* I thought to myself.

A few days later, I had a formal job offer. Mr. Guillen informed me that my contract would be ready for review and signature the following week. Now that I had the job, it was time to keep my promise to myself before I officially accepted it. The next week, I called to schedule a follow-up meeting with Mr. Guillen. I had to know the exact details of my assignment before I signed anything. I silently recalled my Eagle Pass lessons and thought, *Fool me once, shame on you. Fool me twice, shame on me.* When we met again, Mr. Guillen seemed impressed by my professional conscientiousness and insight and briefed me on my teaching assignment at Dillard Jr. High School in a low-income section of Corpus. Having learned all I could before making my decision, I signed the papers that day.

Now an official member of the Dillard Jr. High School faculty, it was time to visit my new school and meet the administration. As I drove farther away from the beach area, the elegance and beauty of the landscape gave way to low-income housing, empty lots overrun with weeds, and unpaved streets. I found the juxtaposition between the affluent tourist district and this disadvantaged neighborhood appalling.

When I entered the school building, I saw janitors cleaning the halls in preparation for when classes started a month later. The only people occupying their offices that day were the two individuals I was there to meet: the assistant principal and the building principal. I knocked on the open door of the assistant principal Mr. Reynolds. He jumped out of his chair and declared he'd been expecting me. His military crew cut and a handshake that cut off the circulation to my fingers seemed in keeping with his role as school disciplinarian and football coach. I wondered if the motto "Don't mess with Texas" had been inspired by people like him. Fortunately, his smile was broad and welcoming.

Mr. Reynolds immediately took me to meet Mr. Parch, the building principal and big cheese. Immediately, the assistant principal's demeanor changed from that of a rather pleasant host to that of a staunch lieutenant. He firmly introduced me as "Mr. Carbahali," one of the new teachers in special education, making my name sound vaguely Arab. Mr. Parch didn't even look up from his desk to acknowledge me. He asked Mr. Reynolds to show me around the teachers' lounge and take me through the building. As we began to walk out of his office, Mr. Parch spoke to Mr. Reynolds in a commanding voice, "Remind him that the special ed room will not be ready until November. Also review the building expectations I have for teachers. Be sure and stress toilet schedules." The arrogant commander never looked at me. I felt a war looming on the horizon. I told myself not to think negative thoughts: they only create imaginary barriers. I had to be positive. Perhaps the poor man, though a grown adult, suffered from some personality affliction—maybe autism or schizophrenia. I should be more sympathetic and understanding of his situation. I should be ashamed of myself for judging him so abruptly.

With a month to wrap things up at East Texas before my teaching assignment began, I returned to Commerce to complete my master's degree in special education. This final summer of my graduate program had been enlightening: without a doubt the most scholarly significant period thus far in my academic career. I was grateful I had chosen the topic of Maria Montessori's work for my thesis. An important innovator in the field of special education in the early 1900s, Montessori had devoted herself to teaching children from impoverished homes in the slums of Italy. She called her school Casa dei Bambini, and her unique approach involved providing students with relevant activities that mirrored their life experiences, allowing them to develop their own skills at a pace they themselves set. Ironically, from its origins in the humblest parts of Italy, Montessori's method had gained surprising popularity throughout the world and even in the United States, where it was marketed to and embraced largely by families of socioeconomic means. Though the educational philosophy was now becoming "trendy," it also had real merit. I had incorporated it into my teaching plans in Eagle Pass and would now rely on it heavily during my time at Dillard.

In addition to defending my thesis, I had six academic hours to complete during this, my final term. They were on the definition and measurement of intelligence. I learned from the readings that no one seemed to agree on the definition of intellect and that we had few methods of measuring what we could not fully define. The American Psychological Association proposed the use of either of two tools for assessing intelligence: the Stanford-Binet Intelligence Scales and the Wechsler Intelligence Scales for Children (WISC). For whatever reason, the majority of American public schools elected to use the Wechsler scales. This was the only test we learned to use in class. To become familiar with administering it, I convinced my friends and family members with children to allow me to test these young people. The kids themselves also took persuasion. In some instances, I had to pay five dollars for the favor. I promised that if they scored in the genius category, I would make the findings known to their parents and then release the results to the public. If not, all would be confidential.

After completing all my assessments, I scored them, made a profile of the findings, and wrote a brief narrative of observations made during testing. I also made final placement recommendations for each test subject. Anyone who scored less than 85 points on the test, also interpreted as two standard deviations below the mean of 100 points, was considered mentally deficient and classified as mentally retarded. I recommended fifteen out of twenty of my victims to special education. The remaining five who scored above 85 were "normal" on that particular day. Many of my "mentally deficient" subjects were my own family relatives. In my own mind, I had to conclude that the standardized instruments had been erroneous. Nonetheless, some of the test subjects' parents insisted on knowing the findings. I told them that the instrument was flawed and that other tests were in the making. I said the scores had been much too high to be valid. It was a blatant lie.

I took the opportunity to respond to the issue of evaluating intelligence during my written comprehensives. I blasted the stupidity and mockery of using the Weschler scales to measure and define intellect in a human being. I knew for certain that if anyone administered this absurd test to me, my full scale score would be in the borderline retarded range. I stated almost angrily that the items on the test were blatantly culturally biased and should not be administered to children from linguistically different backgrounds or disadvantaged socioeconomic environments. The test was designed to measure academic proficiency and achievement—nothing else. My advisor agreed. He promised that, in time, a new assessment tool would be found. However, he advised me to be cautious and not too outspoken about criticizing approved standards that were impossible for me to change. In the future, I would not end up following his advice.

After a brief graduation celebration with my Dallas family, I left for Corpus Christi to embark on my new professional journey. With a crisp new master's degree in hand, I felt armed with valuable knowledge in my chosen field, which gave me an incredible amount of self-assurance and confidence. This time, I was prepared to design appropriate individualized programs for each of my students. I also resolved that no matter what, I would deal with my superiors with thoughtfulness and tact. I would work within the system to get what I needed. I had finally learned the art of ass kissing—or so I thought.

Chapter Twenty-five

When I arrived at Dillard Jr. High on the first day of school, I expected to find a specially designated parking space with my name on it. The only designations were for Mr. Parch and Mr. Reynolds. Otherwise, it was first come, first park. With the lot almost empty, this did not present a problem.

As I walked into the building, I heard the sound of metal lockers slamming shut. Mr. Reynolds was upset that some of the locker combinations weren't working. I walked over to greet him. He slammed a locker door once more and told me to come with him outside to the parking lot through the back doors of the building. Still upset, he said, "The construction of the three extra classrooms, including yours, isn't finished yet. The crew promises they'll be done by the end of November. In the meantime, you'll have to use this as your classroom." He motioned to a nearby spot in the parking lot.

"Sir," I responded, "this is a bus." I was shocked. For a moment, I thought he must be joking, but I could see by his face that he wasn't. "How am I going to tell my students that this is their classroom? Don't you think they'll be embarrassed to be isolated from the rest of the building? Frankly, *I* am embarrassed."

"Well, take it or leave it," Mr. Reynolds responded. "This is what Parch wants you to do. There are no alternatives. The other special education class for the more severe kids is downstairs in the boiler room."

It was 7:30 a.m. Since class didn't begin until eight forty-five, I told Mr. Reynolds I would return in an hour. I rushed to the district's central office hoping to see Mr. Guillen for instruction. He was just getting out of his car when I pulled into the lot. I waved frantically, and he waved back. I practically threw myself out of my car and stood in front of him.

"Wow, what in the world is going on?" Guillen asked. "This is the first day of the rest of your life at Dillard." He thought he was being cute.

"Not really," I responded, trying to control my anger. "Can you please come with me so I can show you my room?"

"Well, I know your classroom is not completely finished," he responded apologetically. "But I also know that the construction crew is working overtime to get it done."

I was getting furious. "My god, what the hell is going on?" I said, close to shouting. "A damn bus?! What a piece of trash. Is this what you people call a classroom? The kids with severe disabilities are in the boiler room. What kind of fucking deal is this?"

Guillen tried to justify the disgraceful situation. "Well, Mrs. Banks didn't seem to fly off the handle like you are. She has adapted like a real professional and actually made the best of what she has been given for the sake of the kids."

I was beyond angry. "I know," I replied. "I saw how cozy it is. She's brought plants from home and stuck them in the broken old toilets they've got stored down there. Wow, what a deal! By the way, do you know that the idiotic man you guys call a building principal mandates bathroom breaks in alphabetical order? Some kids go in the morning and some in the afternoon. This is the most asinine thing I've ever heard. My name isn't even on the list. Here, take a look!"

"Well, let me call over there about the room," said Guillen. "I'll get back to you." I could tell I was embarrassing him and didn't care. I was embarrassed for all the students and teachers in every classroom in America—and no doubt there were many—forced to contend with similar idiotic rules and insultingly meager allocations.

For now, there was absolutely nothing to do but return to the school. That morning, three kids came out to the bus. When they saw it, they were delighted. In that moment, I hated them and hated their stupidity. I sat in the driver's seat and told them to go home by way of the parking lot. Mr. Reynolds saw them sneak out between the cars and wrangled them back to the bus. He looked at me with disgust in his eyes. During the lunch break, I asked them to leave again. This time, they didn't return.

Sitting in the teachers' lounge at lunch, I felt no common bond with my colleagues. In fact, the other teachers disgusted me. For some odd reason, they seemed to worship Mr. Parch as their mentor, ready to eat up his every nugget of wisdom. They followed his idiotic bathroom-break mandates to the letter. They came in with homemade apple pies, cookies, and candies to feed his ugly face. Some of them were crocheting him scarves and sweaters to wrap around his big round body. Many of these "lounge lizards," as I would come to think of them, seemed to have nothing better to do than sit around complaining about their classes full of slow learners.

That afternoon, as I continued to fume alone on the bus, Mr. Reynolds came by to inform me that Mr. Parch wanted to see me at 3:12 p.m. I was scheduled to see him for eleven minutes. He was such an important man that he had to split each hour down to the minute to find time for his lowly, needy teachers. When it was time for me to confront the king, I was bound and determined to chip away at his vanity.

I didn't get the chance. Mr. Reynolds escorted me into Mr. Parch's office and sat in the only chair available, leaving me to stand and take my thrashing. "Don't you ever again defy me by going directly to central administration," Mr. Parch said bluntly. "This is the chain of command: you go to Mr. Reynolds first. If he needs to, he will then recommend that you see me. That's as far as it gets. You pull this kind of insubordinate stunt one more time and you get fired. Go!"

That certainly didn't take eleven minutes.

Well, I thought, so much for America the beautiful. It was at that moment that I realized dictatorships did exist in this country: in this public school, for example. This scared the living crap out of me. I suddenly felt deeply sorry for the teachers who'd been programmed to believe that this man could rule over them the way he did. I'd been treated with more dignity and respect as a cherry picker than I had since meeting Mr. Parch. Compared to today, those days in the fruit orchards were good and humane indeed.

Again, fair or not, at the moment there was nothing to do but begin teaching. Realizing that this was the school's problem, not my students',

I stopped sending them home and started getting to know them. As the days turned into weeks, we began to fall into a rhythm, centering class discussions around what was pertinent to the kids. They took turns talking about their experiences, each having a chance to say what had happened to them recently or generally in life. Eventually, I started taking my own turn, gradually unfolding my epic tale from the days of the placita to harvesting fruit in California. The students prepared to continue their stories where they'd left off the previous day. They looked forward to their own turn, eagerly awaited the next episode of my saga, and became engaged in one another's stories as well.

From there, we expanded discussions to the world around us, reviewing and talking about articles from the local newspaper. Often, our discussions would center around personal rights and responsibilities. These were things that I knew I needed to instill in these kids if they were to have a shot in life. They thought it was unfair that each right seemed to come with a responsibility. We spoke of the times they had done something that was illegal (like stealing) or unfair to others and why they needed to take responsibility for these actions if they were to be productive and respected citizens. The talk in our "magic circle" flowed naturally. Each day, the intellectual insights of my students stunned me more and more. Why had these kids been placed in special education? Something had gone terribly wrong.

At the same time, there were still students that did have significant learning and developmental problems. One boy, Tommy, presented characteristics that I'd read about in my studies but never actually seen or worked with before. Tommy was a boy who lived deeply within himself. He seemed uninterested or unable to engage meaningfully with others. Instead, listening to music was his entire universe. He had committed to memory a staggering catalog of country-Western songs. They seemed to define his very person—nothing else mattered to him. He knew every tune to the note and every lyric to the very last word. Instead of speaking with me, he'd sing. Eddie Arnold was his favorite. "What's he doin' in my word? We don't need him here in our world . . ." I found Tommy's behavior fascinating. I would be reminded of it later in my career as I worked with other children like him and delved into the unique indicators and challenges of autism.

Week by week, month by month, my class grew closer. We were an island unto ourselves, spending every moment of school on our bus. We even had our lunches there, since we were not supposed to eat with the rest of the students in the cafeteria. The unbearable humidity couldn't stop us, nor could the jumbo-sized gnats, mosquitoes, and grasshoppers attempting to sneak into our seminars. Nothing could interfere with our daily philosophical dialogues. I came to regard my students as genuine friends, and in turn, I felt valued, appreciated, respected, and liked by them. I felt like a real educator. I was also fearful that I was contributing to the educational abuse of these terrific kids by complying with their current situation, which I could see was unfair in a multitude of ways. I was motivated to fight on their behalf.

This was the reality of our situation: my students were literally segregated in a substandard educational facility and directed not to coexist with the rest of their peers. They were instructed not to join the rest of the student population even for lunch. The trainable mentally retarded children at the school, down in the boiler room, had it just as bad. In the case of all these kids, there was no doubt that their basic civil rights were being violated.

Making the situation even more poignant was the fact that of my nineteen students, fifteen were from Mexican American homes, three from African American homes, and only one from an Anglo home. This was obviously skewed since the majority of the school population at Dillard was Caucasian. From what I could conclude as their one and only educator, these students were bright, insightful, and probably put in my classroom on the basis of learning differences that arose from not being part of the cultural mainstream. This, of course, hit close to home for me: I had experienced mislabeling and been deprived of opportunities in much the same way. From my grad school research, I also knew that others in the field of education had begun to recognize this particular brand of discrimination and fight against it. The recent 1967 case of *Hobsen v. Hansen* brought attention to unfair testing and labeling procedures among minority and disadvantaged students in special education. In the same spirit, a professor from the University of Hawaii named Lloyd Dunn had also spoken out against unfair categorization. In his article "Special Education for the Mildly Retarded—Is

Much of it Justifiable?" he asserted that a great disservice had been done to minority children with mild learning problems. Because these children were slow learners, disruptive in class, or had been categorized with low scores on current IQ tests, they had been unfairly placed, Dunn argued, in "self-contained special schools and classes for the mildly retarded."

During my days at Riverside, I had allowed myself to be intimidated into working within the parameters of the established system. But after my important work in grad school, I was armed with knowledge. Responsible educators were waking up to the injustice, and I was intent on showing the district that this was the case. I made an appointment to see Mr. Guillen in order to share my insights. Before I went, I secretly spoke to an attorney who specialized in advising and representing low-income individuals and families. He helped affirm for me how my students' rights were being compromised.

Though I wanted to get my point across to Mr. Guillen, my goal was not an ugly confrontation. I presented my case to him in a simple, nonscholarly fashion. I delicately pointed out how our segregated facilities appeared to be at odds with the Civil Rights Act of 1964, possibly violating the constitutional rights of the students. Then I provided him with a copy of Dunne's compelling article. As he read it, the color drained from his face. As I went on presenting my carefully collected evidence, Mr. Guillen began to lose his professional composure. He grabbed me by the arm and asked me to walk with him to his car. No one should hear. His starched white shirt was now wet—not just with the humidity but with fear. I thought he would be angry, but he was simply petrified. I have to admit I liked the idea of escorting him out of his meticulous and pleasant air-conditioned office. He was struggling for the right words and finally pleaded, "Please, whatever you do, don't tell a soul. We can fix whatever needs to be fixed. Why are you doing this? This could cost you your job forever. No school district would touch a renegade like you. This is the most disloyal thing anyone can do to their own district."

In Eagle Pass, I had been warned several times that "you don't bite the hand that feeds you." I had been Mr. Nice Guy back then. Those days were over. Thinking of my pals on the bus, I took advantage of Mr. Guillen's fear.

I couldn't resist. "One of my new friends is a reporter at the local newspaper. I've been meaning to invite him over for lunch on our bus. I told him it's on the house as long as he brings his camera."

Mr. Guillen politely excused himself to vomit. I knew what he was going through: I'd been there many times. It was his turn to feel the agony of defeat. I could barely keep myself from telling him that no one messed with Texas. Taking pity on him, I decided to offer him a cold drink from an ice chest I kept in my car for just such emergencies. He drank two beers and cried. I drank one soda and smiled. My guardian angels were working overtime.

Just days after my meeting with Guillen, my students were excitedly waiting for me in the parking lot in front of the school. They just couldn't wait to tell me that our classroom on wheels had been removed. When I went into the building to sign in for the day, Mr. Reynolds threw a set of keys down on the table for me in disgust. The keys were for the last room down the hall: we had our own classroom.

It appeared that Mr. Guillen had taken some action after our little talk. Obviously, the venerable assistant superintendent had talked with Mr. Parch, and a classroom had magically materialized. I'm sure he had also painted the details of our meeting in vivid color. Mr. Parch and the rest of his inner circle of staff had no doubt been informed of just what an insubordinate traitor I had become. Well, there was no love lost between me and the rest of them anyway. The entire staff of the school ignored my role as a teacher. Either you belonged to the system, or you were against it, and I guess now everyone knew exactly where I stood.

Now in the school building with everyone else, my class and I felt the isolation more than ever. It was clear that nobody wanted us there. In Eagle Pass, the loneliness felt different: the school itself was set aside for the unwanted. Here at Dillard, the blatant disregard and hostility we received from the rest of the school was that much more piercing. And so we continued to keep to ourselves. Though my students were now allowed to eat in the cafeteria, they found it more comfortable to bring their food back to the classroom, sometimes smuggling in an extra dessert for me.

After the last bell rang at the end of the day, I stepped out through the back parking lot and left.

In this ostracized environment, my students and I made it through the fall and into the winter. In February, the attorney I had consulted, Mr. Connelly, called me in to review the case I had brought to him, which he was now getting ready to use against the district. I had often wondered what he'd done with all the data I'd provided. He had it carefully organized and filed away by date. Included in the evidence were snapshots of my students hanging out the windows of the bus and pretending to be tourists going somewhere special. Other photos featured some of them pissing under the bus, much preferred to waiting around for their assigned bathroom breaks inside the school. I'm certain they were unaware of their celebrity status.

This case was for real, and I had brought it to light. Though totally warranted and necessary, the reality of suing the district sent chills down my spine. I was frantic, panicked, and afraid. "When are you dropping the bomb?" I asked Mr. Connelly. "You know that school is out for spring break in two weeks. Can you wait until then? That will give me a chance to make myself scarce. I don't want to be around when the shit hits the fan."

Mr. Connelly spoke in a gentle fashion, "We'll be gathering our witnesses. We need several parents to testify, several teachers, members of administration, as well as other school personnel such as the psychologists who administered intelligence tests to these students and the school pathologists who evaluated them. You will, of course, be one of our key witnesses." This was not a reassuring picture. I remembered the gangster movies they used to show at the drive-in—how the "rat" was always whacked before he could testify against "the family." What would become of me? My mind took me back to my favorite memories of the placita, my family, Clara la India, my wonderful friends, and my beautiful days in the California sun.

My urge to run made me inclined to immediately begin looking for teachings job in Dallas or California. Mr. Connelly didn't think this was a good idea. Having been officially subpoenaed to testify, I had to be in the area and available for court hearings when I was called. I regretted the mess I had created for myself. I just wanted to fly away with the seagulls and never set foot on the white sands of Corpus Christi again. How appropriate that, in my agony and fear of crucifixion, it suddenly dawned on me that "Corpus Christi" was Latin for "Body of Christ."

The district must have been served with the legal paperwork in late February.

In March, I received a very professional, polite letter indicating that my teaching services would no longer be needed after the current school year ended. I would have no job the coming fall. Since I was not tenured, they could do anything they wanted; no other explanation was given. Reading the letter, I was sure that teaching was history for me.

In the end, neither the parents nor I were ever called to testify. Apparently, there never was a hearing. The face-to-face depositions with the district attorneys that I had been dreading never came to pass because of successful arbitration procedures with the families of the students in question. The entire outcome was confidential. Suffice it to say that the district corrected their "honest errors" and promised new procedural safeguards to avoid such embarrassing and irresponsible practices in the future. They were indeed clever to quickly and quietly maneuver themselves out from under the atrocities they knew damn well they had committed.

For the remaining weeks of school, I focused my attention on my students. We concentrated on writing short sentences and using basic grammar to make ideas clear. They continued to enjoy our personal dialogues as well as my readings of short stories and poetry. I had heard many times how important it was to take advantage of "teachable moments"—situations that allow us to introduce relevant and important subjects to our students. For me, this meant teaching my class about the Bill of Rights, carefully simplifying its concepts for discussion. I was shocked at how well they could understand and internalize concepts such as freedom, liberty, and due process. During one of the discussions, three of the students were bragging about shoplifting, stealing hubcaps, and pouring sand in the vehicle that belonged to Mr. Parch. I reminded them that abusing property that belongs to others and violating other people's rights never results in ultimate justice. I felt strongly compelled to leave them with this message. I never hinted in any way that, come the end of the school year, I would be gone.

Two weeks before the end of school, we planned a whole-day excursion into the city. We made a budget, decided on the sights we wanted to see, and made arrangements for the day to culminate in a three-hour beach party. That Friday at the beach, my favorite musical combo was playing. I asked them if they could dedicate a song to my class. Eagerly, they agreed and sang "What a Day for a Daydream." They sang it once and then repeated it, asking the kids to sing along. Jimmy, our singer of the group, chimed in and sang from the depths of his happy heart. The trio accompanied him as he belted out, "What a day for a daydream, custom made for a daydreamin' boy. And now I'm lost in a daydream, dreamin' 'bout my bundle of joy." The applause from all my students and the nearby beachgoers scared the seagulls away. The mellow, happy song—perfect for the day—will stay with me always.

The Monday of our last week together, my class and I talked about the trip, speaking of what we'd learned, our favorite moments, and what we might have done differently. The kids' only regret was that the day had been too short and that I hadn't sung a song for them. The next day, I rushed to a music store to get the sheet music for "What a Day for a Daydream" and sang it for the kids while picking out the tune on my guitar. They joyfully sang along. Several teachers came in to listen and applauded as Jimmy, the student who'd been most difficult to motivate, once again sang and jived to the song. "And even if time ain't really on my side, it's one of those days for takin' a walk outside . . . I've been havin' a sweet dream, I've been dreamin' since I woke up today . . ."

The final day of class, the kids insisted that I read a story. With great difficulty, I read *Good-bye, Old Sam. Hope You Find a Happy Home.* The story spoke of a duck who had to move from a familiar and pleasant neighborhood pond to a faraway lake. Reading the story made my throat tremble with sadness. I would miss my nineteen terrific friends and take with me always the memories of all we had learned and shared together. Being with them had enriched my humanity in ways I had never expected: probably more than any other event in my life so far. Now it was time to say good-bye and hope that wherever life took them, they'd find safe and secure waters just like Sam.

In May, I said my final good-bye to them and everyone else I'd known that year. I also reluctantly bid farewell to teaching for what I thought was forever. The system was not made for a malcontent maverick such as I. My lessons from the case against the district taught me that to accomplish what I needed to, I would have to go higher than the classroom. The entire system needed to change, and I wanted to be a part of it. My path seemed clear: law school would be my next venture.

Part Five: Camelot

It's true! It's true! The crown has made it clear
The climate must be perfect all the year.
A law was made a distant moon ago here.
July and August cannot be too hot
And there is a legal limit to the snow here
In Camelot.
Camelot! Camelot! . . .

In short, there's simply not
A more congenial spot
For happily-ever-aftering than here
In Camelot.

—from the song "Camelot,"
lyrics by Alan Jay Lerner

Chapter Twenty-six

Change was in the air, and it was time to embark on a new professional path. With that would come a new locale: my goal was to be admitted to law school at the University of Colorado at Boulder. My particular interest in CU evolved not from its academic reputation in the area of law—which was excellent—but from the gorgeous scenery of the Rocky Mountains. I promised myself that someday I would witness the beauty of this land. I prepared and submitted my admission application. Now all there was to do was wait. In the meantime, I decided to leave Texas once more and return to San Jose during the first two weeks of summer. I needed time to recuperate from what felt like my second major failure in the educational system. I would return to California by way of Colorado and check out the Boulder campus while I was at it. I would drive through Texas, stopping wherever I wanted besides Dallas: I couldn't face explaining to Ramón yet another of my futile attempts to be a successful teacher. I planned to stay overnight in Colorado and visit Rocky Mountain National Park. I had always yearned to see Bear Lake where Lucille Ball and Desi Arnaz had filmed their outrageous comedy *The Long, Long Trailer*. I remembered how impressive and beautiful the mountains and lakes of Colorado looked in that film: that Minelli sure knew how to direct a movie. Watching it, I'd been mesmerized by the power and beauty of nature. I had to see it for myself. If all went according to plan, I might live just a few miles from it all!

The drive did me good. I was a good driver and knew how long I could safely go without a rest. I had also learned from driving long distances that a vehicle got better mileage if not overloaded with too much weight. I was thoughtful not to fill the gas tank more than halfway—that was my clever strategy.

Before leaving the Texas Panhandle, I stopped at a run-down gas station in the middle of nowhere to refuel. A very sleepy and bored guy came out. He didn't look very excited to have a customer. He yawned as he spoke, "How much gas do you need?"

"Just four gallons is all I need," I definitively responded. "I don't like to drive with too much weight." I was almost pleased that I probably sounded quite smart. While the man filled my tank, I got out and walked around the edge of the dusty lot. Fearful of rattlesnakes, I quickly returned.

"Four bucks unless you need anything else," the attendant said. His tone was not exactly solicitous. In fact, he almost seemed pissed at me.

"Sir, I requested four gallons. Not four dollars' worth," I said, a little irritated.

Instantly, the guy attacked, "Listen, you bastard, you pay me four dollars right now! I don't take this shit from you fucking Mexicans. You are all alike!"

I was so shocked that I couldn't respond. I gave him the cash and left without a word. As I drove away, I wondered what had just happened. What in the world had this idiotic man just said to me? I hadn't been trying to steal from him or deceive him in any way. Maybe we Mexicans did have a lot in common: we were a people of enormous pride and self-respect. My mom, my grandparents, and the rest of my family and friends—we were all tough as nails and had hearts of solid gold. If this wasn't what that imbecile had meant, I felt terribly sorry for him.

Instead of dwelling anymore on the insult, I set out alone on the open road. Playing my favorite tunes, I allowed my mind to drift through the past weeks and months all the way back to when I'd first left California with Dale. Internalizing my feelings about everything, I realized that the sum total had been positive. I'd learned a lot along the way. No doubt, some of the lessons I'd learned had been difficult ones. One thing I now knew was that optimism had to be balanced with realism. I had to stop thinking it was possible to singlehandedly find a solution to every problem. Perhaps I'd been in situations where I could have negotiated or conducted myself better, but maybe not—maybe I'd done all there was to do in the role of a teacher. Before I became a teacher, no one had explained to me that my job was to be subservient and meek, but this had quickly proven to be the case. You did what you were told, and that's it. You trained your bladder to release not as needed, but when the boss required—literally, in the case of life at Dillard. Perhaps things would have worked out better for me if I'd simply realized the limitations of my role and not taken my professional status as a teacher so seriously. In the case of both school districts I'd worked in, the chain of command had been fixed. No one and nothing could change that, especially not a lowly beginning teacher.

I drove on, and when I'd worn myself out with all my self-analysis, I turned my attention back to my music. I sang out loud with the songs, pretending to be Tony Bennett for one hour, Frank Sinatra for the next, and Perry Como after that. After a while, I'd switch to Spanish music, listening to the boleros my friends and I had grown up with. These were songs of profound emotion that usually spoke of either staying forever with those you loved or leaving them forever. Some of my friends, like Robert and Paul, had given me mix tapes as farewell gifts, which, as I listened, conjured powerful memories of our days together. Now and then, I'd turn the music off completely and sing the songs Mom used to sing to us as kids. As the memories and emotion poured out of me through the songs, I marveled at how powerful music could be for a mind that needs to remember and a heart that needs to heal.

Behind the wheel, in the solitude of my car, I let myself indulge fully in my memories, knowing that when I arrived at my destination, I didn't plan on going back to inventory regrets of the past or lament what I'd left behind. My energies would shift toward finding out what the future held: for my profession and my life. Whatever happened, I knew that law school would lead to territory I'd never seen before. Even more than this, I believed it would give me what I craved most right now: success. I set a singular goal for myself: I would be the "king of the jungle," just as I'd been as a child playing at the river. This time, no one would stop me. After all, I had two degrees in higher education and more to come. In my mind, I dared a highway patrolman to stop me and ask me for my license: I would flash my diplomas and intimidate him. Fast-forwarding a few years from now, I imagined myself as a corporate attorney. I'd use my intellect to design my own legal team. I'd live on the East Coast where the hustlers and the money grabbers lived. I would travel the world on my own plane and visit exotic locales. I would invest in stocks and bonds. I would wear only dark suits, brilliantly starched white shirts, and red-striped ties to accentuate my power. Nobody, absolutely nobody, would mess with me.

In my excitement, I must have been stepping on the gas because before I knew it, I saw blue and red lights flashing in my rearview mirror. Maybe the highway patrol had caught onto my mental dare. Whatever the case, I was pulled over. Instead of flashing my diplomas, I produced my driver's license. Without too many words, the officer produced for me a sixty-dollar speeding ticket. Then I was free to go, returning to my dreams of grandeur.

My mind was so busy as I drove into Colorado that there wasn't much room left for navigation. I missed the proper exit to Boulder, and by the time I realized it, I was way off course. I couldn't even find a place to turn around. I finally took an exit marked for a town called Greeley. The exit seemed to lead onto another small highway going a different direction entirely. This definitely looked to be a road less traveled. I figured I'd eventually turn the car around when I saw an opportunity and get back on track. And yet something kept me driving on. I don't know what it was, but it couldn't have been the smell: the closer I got to Greeley, the more the pungent aroma of manure seemed to waft in through the vents. This was farmland and ranchland. Soon, I was driving through the outskirts of town. I was passing by a large department store when my Chevy suddenly made a loud noise and died. I saw heavy smoke billowing from under the hood. I knew I was in trouble. Panicked, I looked around as two cars drove slowly past. The drivers—obviously farmers or ranchers—waved at me, which was a good feeling. No one stopped, however. I quickly jumped out and walked toward a department store called Gibson's. In the huge store, less than ten people were shopping. Hopelessly, I looked around for a public phone to call heaven knows who.

As I passed by the camera and small electronics department, I spotted a handsome, rather bored-looking clerk. I asked him if he could direct me to a public phone. Pleasantly, he invited me to use the phone behind the counter, if it was a local call. I asked him if he knew where the closest filling station was. He chuckled. "In this town, everything closes on Sunday. We're the only store open because we're outside the city limits. You'll have to wait until tomorrow. Is there some kind of an emergency?"

I started to panic. "Well, my car just broke down in front of the store. I need to get it fixed so I can move on."

Clearly, I'd at least added some excitement to the clerk's dull afternoon. By now, he thought it was really funny that I'd had luck rotten enough to break down on this deserted day. Still, his concern was genuine. "My advice is to call a cab and go to any of the motels two miles south of here. You can get the car serviced tomorrow. Actually, I'm out of here in twenty minutes. I can drive you in that direction. I'll leave you at any motel you want."

I thanked him and said I would wait outside. Ten minutes later, he walked out. I showed him my car, packed with all my earthly belongings. The first thing was to get the car out of the street. To do this, the clerk got in his own new car and pushed me forward toward the curb. I now realized that on top of everything else, I'd been driving for who knows how long with a flat tire. Then I jumped in the clerk's car, and in no time, we were driving toward the area where the motels were situated. During that brief amount of time, I mentioned that I was certified as a teacher and had taught four years in Texas. Once we got to the motel, I thanked this man profusely for his kindness. He shook my hand and said, "Oh, by the way, my name is Mel Lane. I got your first name, but it's Tony what?"

"Carvajal," I responded emphatically.

"Tony Carvajal," he repeated. "That's a strong name. In the morning, just walk across to any of those filling stations. They'll help you. If you have time to kill while you're waiting for repairs, take a cab to Colorado State College—it's two miles from here. I'm the coordinator at a school on that campus. Once you get to campus, ask anyone where the Lab School is. I'll show you around. Don't mind the smell around here. It's the smell of money."

The next morning, I got a tow to the service station where my car was declared dead. Apparently, I had overlooked the fact that automobiles require oil every year or so. I'd simply neglected to tend to the minor obligations of regular service. With all my legal preoccupations over the past year,

I wondered how many other important details of my life I'd ignored. It looked as if I'd have to say good-bye to my old Chevy here in Greeley and buy another used car before heading out of town.

For the time being, I decided to take Mel Lane up on his offer and find my way to the college for a little walk around. When the cab dropped me off, I saw a beautiful, quiet campus as pristine as a monastery with manicured lawns and old brick buildings. This being a Monday morning of the summer term, students were out and about, making their way to and from classes or simply hanging out on the lawn. Typical student stuff, but this group was unlike any I had ever seen before: they were all white. The campus population seemed more glaringly Anglo than even East Texas had been. Strange, yes, but I took it in nonchalantly. I was only here to amuse myself before going to buy another car and getting out of town. I had enough cash to make at least a hundred-dollar down payment on any vehicle I wanted.

As promised, I was easily directed to the Lab School, whatever it was. As I walked into the building, all the faces I saw were equally white, including that of the receptionist. To her, I announced, "I'm from another planet and here to see Mr. Lane." Pleasant and welcoming, she laughed joyfully and practically danced her way into an office to inform Mr. Lane that I'd arrived. She asked me if I wanted coffee or anything else. I was surprised: monasteries didn't usually serve chemically enhanced drinks.

Mr. Lane emerged from his office looking as pleasant as he had the previous day. He greeted me graciously, thoughtfully asking how the car situation had turned out. Then he gave me a tour of the school, which would not be in session until the fall. Though the school was on a college campus, it was in fact for children. *Somewhat oddly,* I thought, *two distinctly different student groups were taught here.* On one side of a long hallway were classrooms designated for children with emotional, mental, and physical handicapping conditions. On the other side were classrooms for academically "gifted" students. This second group was made up primarily of the children of professors at the university, their spots reserved years in advance. This seemed odd. Apparently, the criteria for giftedness here were directly related to the educational and professional status of the parents. It struck me as blatantly unjust. But no reason to get worked up all over again: I had bigger fish to fry now. I was on my way to a new life in law school. Perhaps someday I would address issues like this: someday when I was actually the one with the power. For the time being, I would just relax and enjoy Mr. Lane's company.

Before I knew it, it was four in the afternoon, and Mr. Lane's wife called to check on dinner plans. She invited me to join them for a meal at their home. I quickly accepted: I was sick and tired of eating in the car. Before we left the school, I called my motel and extended my stay for another night. Tomorrow I would move on to see the mountains.

Mel's wife, Jane, was delightful. Tall, fair, and brunette, she was just as striking as her husband. She and Mel had known each other since childhood, both from neighboring Iowa farming communities. They explained that they had married when they were just seventeen years old, making me feel like an old bachelor at twenty-six. They spoke of the small towns where they were raised, and I told them about the placita and my days in the California sun harvesting fruit just like we were having for dessert. They were very impressed.

After three hours of nonstop chatter, it was time to go. Mel and Jane urged me to return for dinner the following evening. I was touched by the invitation, but explained that the bears were summoning me to their lake high in the wilderness of Rocky Mountain National Park. I guess it sounded fun to my new friends because they insisted on driving me there and joining me for the impromptu excursion themselves. I excitedly welcomed them.

The Rockies were even more splendid in real life than I could've ever imagined from the movies. The drive from the flat plains of Greeley into the forested foothills and on into the jagged, majestic cliffs of the park took my breath away. We spent the sunny afternoon walking around Bear Lake, taking in the awe-inspiring scenery. We sat on a huge boulder overlooking the water and had a picnic of delicious chicken sandwiches. Mel and Jane really were two of the kindest people I'd ever met. My detour to Greeley had been well worth it after all.

Of course, this didn't change my plans to get on the road as soon as possible. The day after our mountain trip, I went around Greeley searching for a car to buy. The task was not as simple as I'd hoped. The financing was the problem: although my credit was fine, I was, after all, unemployed. It seemed the only option would be to rent a car with appropriate references. When I reluctantly shared my dismal status with Mel, he insisted that I use the other car he and Jane owned until we could resolve the dilemma. I accepted conditionally: they'd have to allow me to pay them ten dollars a day for their trouble. They refused any payment and, instead, insisted that I stay with them until I had things sorted out and was able to reimburse them. But when would this be? What was it about my situation that was to change while I wandered around Greeley? It was all very confusing to me.

Five days later, I got my answer. Mel informed me that a position had unexpectedly become available teaching special education at the Lab School in the fall. They needed to fill it immediately. He said the position was mine if I wanted it. He and Jane had been discussing my situation with each other since meeting me, and Jane had become determined that I stay in Greeley. Now they had their bait to keep me there.

This was not the first time I'd felt like running. How had I ended up in this little town with this job offer seemingly dropped from the sky? How had a simple drive through "Colorful Colorado" gotten my life off track again? In the end, I did not run. I walked to the central office of the district and signed yet another contract for a nine-month school year. It was just one year. After that, I would definitely pursue my plans to become a famous attorney and make a lot of cash. Nothing and no one would block my aspirations this time. After all, I was the master of my own destiny.

Chapter Twenty-seven

The day I signed my contract to teach and was thus officially employed again, I immediately went and purchased a new car. It was the very first new car I'd ever bought. I negotiated and got a great deal on it because it was a bright shade of orange that no one else wanted. Well, it would come in handy come Halloween: I'd be the most festive guy in town.

For now, it was the beginning of September and time for school to start. I was hardly surprised when the school administration switched my teaching assignment at the last minute—it had happened before. Instead of teaching at the Lab School, I was placed at an elementary school in the far northern part of town across the railroad tracks. This neighborhood was inhabited mostly by Mexican Americans, and therefore, the student population at Park Elementary was largely minority. Since most families in the area were less economically advantaged than those in the center of town and didn't have transportation to get their kids to public schools in these areas, they were in a sense racially segregated by default.

As in Corpus Christi, I was assigned to work with the "educable mentally retarded." By now, I knew this was merely a generic label that could mean many things. In fact, it could mean any child with a serious learning problem, whether legitimately mentally retarded or not. Therefore, my first task was to familiarize myself with the individual educational, medical, psychological, and social background of each child by going through his or her cumulative folder. The more I read, the more I realized that planning for instruction would have to be multidimensional and guided by the unique needs of each student.

The first task at hand was testing, which helped me gather all the additional information I could before deciding how to teach. For this, I administered both individual and group achievement scales, just as I'd learned to at East Texas. While I knew to take the results with a grain of salt, it was still a place to start. All this I did in my first week with my class of eighteen students. The next week, it was time to set the tone for our time together. In my own experience as a student, it had always made me feel more at ease to know what was coming next: to have a syllabus or a general plan of what to expect and what was expected of me. With this in mind, I shared with the students the schedule for the current day and the upcoming week. We began to establish a routine. Mornings were for language arts (reading, writing, and speech) and math. Afternoons were dedicated to aesthetics and kinesiology: in other words, art, music, and physical education. Despite my love of music, these were definitely not my strong suits. I pleaded with the art and music teachers at the school to come in and assist me so the students could benefit from their talents and expertise. I was impressed by and grateful for their willingness to help.

Our Mondays through Thursdays were firmly set, with our Friday schedule contingent on how the students performed and behaved during the week. If they completed all their assignments with positive outcomes, then on Fridays, we would invite special guest visitors, go on field trips, or watch movies of my selection. One Friday, we watched *The Wizard of Oz*. I was amazed at the lively discussion I was able to draw from the kids after the film. They loved it so much that they asked to watch it the next three Fridays in a row. Because it was one of my favorites too, I had to oblige. It was during that month that I discovered that yet another one of my students had a gift for singing. Like Jimmy on that day at the beach, Olympia simply came alive as she sang, suddenly belting out "Somewhere Over the Rainbow" in front of the entire class. Some of the other teachers poked their heads in the door to listen. Her talent amazed me. I was even more excited by the confidence and assuredness I saw in her as she did what she loved.

In that first month of the school year, it was also important to get to know my students' families as I had learned well from my days at Riverside. I invited the parents of each student in for a planning conference. Though I carefully wrote and phoned each family, my attempts yielded no results: the parents simply couldn't or wouldn't commit to a date. The school principal

Mr. Eckhart was an outstanding and genuine administrator, and though he was very supportive of me, not even he held out much hope for the parents coming in. He advised me to go visit them at home instead: that was the only way. I could do that: I'd been a master of home visits in Eagle Pass and rather enjoyed the delicious dinners the parents had graciously shared with me in the process.

My first visit was to the Rodrigo family. Their sons Anthony and Stephen were both in my class. They were partially blind as a result of congenital syphilis and suffered related problems such as severe dental decay. Their mother, Mrs. Tayes, didn't seem overly concerned about her children's special needs or about the origin of their problems. She freely admitted that she herself was on medication for syphilis and that her own mother happened to be as well. I left angry that the severe "retardation" of this woman meant these boys would have to pay the price of poor health for the rest of their lives. I wanted to do all I could to help them, but this was new territory for me: I had to secure resources for the partially sighted. Dream principal that he was, when I approached Mr. Eckhart about the matter, he immediately made some calls. Within three days, a specialist for the visually impaired was in contact with me. I wondered how Eckhart and Parch could exist on the same planet.

Eckhart also made sure I felt welcomed by the Park teaching staff. During the first weeks of school, all my focus was on getting to know the students. Perhaps out of habit, I chose to have my lunch with them, either in the classroom or the cafeteria. Seeing this, the principal suggested that I needed time away from the kids—at least a thirty-minute lunch break—to shift gears and converse with the other teachers. The idea was remarkable: for the first time, I was being mainstreamed! Joining the teachers for lunch, I got to officially meet many that I'd merely seen during the week of teacher orientation. I began to hit it off with many of them, and our lunchtime soon expanded to social gatherings after school. Then those times expanded to getting together on weekends. My growing social network turned out to be perhaps the most delightful aspect of my new job.

It helped me solve my housing situation as well. Within a month of school starting, Jim Bensler—the fifth-grade teacher—and I found an apartment to rent together close to school. He was especially excited that he'd easily be able to come back to school to cheer on his students at afternoon sporting events. I admired his dedication and genuine interest in the kids he taught. Very soon, we realized that a few other young single teachers lived near our complex. This expanded our social scene. It was this way that I met my first girlfriend in Greeley, Joan Harrison, a first-grade teacher at another school. For his part, Jim soon met Janice, a fourth-grade teacher living nearby.

On weekends, a group of us would often take off for the mountains where we'd relax, hike around, and, when the winter rolled around, ski the beautiful peaks of the Rockies. Jim and a few others could ski the high trails while I stayed on the bunny hill with the small kids, colored balloons tied to their ski caps. Nonetheless, I was proud to be learning and felt incredibly fortunate to have access to this magical winter wonderland. So far, Colorado really did seem to have the best of everything—just like they said about Camelot in that musical. I wondered if someday soon I would be fortunate enough to meet the noble and righteous knights of the round table. After our skiing expeditions, my friends and I would gather for pizza and beers. Jim and the others would recount their horrific near-death experiences on the slopes, and I'd remark on the delightful time I'd had with my toddler buddies. As the evening wore on, the conversation would often turn to teaching: to our students and our roles in educating them. Since most of the others taught traditional students, they were eager to know more about my students and expressed admiration for my dedication. They were willing to help me out in any way: if I felt overstretched, they offered to take some of my students into their own classrooms for an hour a day to give me a break. I found this gesture remarkably thoughtful.

Fortified with the firm support of new colleagues and friends, I continued to make my way through the most urgent of my home visits. My next stop was to Jerry Mendoza's home. Jerry had several disturbing behavioral tendencies bordering on the psychopathic. One day at recess, he somehow found and caught several small kittens and tied them to a stick. Next, he built a fire and roasted them alive, to the horror of the students looking on. He seemed to enjoy not only the act of killing, but the process of death and decay. At one point, the students began to complain about a terrible smell emanating from the vicinity of his desk. After a couple of weeks of these complaints, it was time to find the source. I waited for the kids to go to lunch and then lifted the lid off the top of Jerry's desk. The strong, putrid smell of decay assaulted my nostrils. I peered down and saw the carcasses of three birds, each at a different level of decomposition. To my horror, I immediately recalled how over the last few weeks, Jerry had often stuck his head inside his desk and grinned a smile of absolute pleasure.

Urged by Mr. Eckhart and the building nurse, I went to Jerry's home to confront his parents. I went unannounced since all attempts to arrange a meeting had been futile; I doubted that the notes I'd sent home with Jerry had ever made it there. Now I could see that a pickup truck was parked in the driveway. I parked my car in front of the house, walked to the front door, and knocked. No response. I walked around to the back door and found it half open. I knocked again, but still no response. I poked my head in a little and called for Mrs. Mendoza. Nothing. I could see into the kitchen where several whiskey bottles and beer cans were strewn across a table. I opened the door wider and took a few tentative steps inside. Suddenly, I saw a woman coming directly at me with a kitchen knife! In complete fear, I identified myself as Jerry's teacher. I felt myself trembling and perspiring as I apologized for my intrusion. "You son of a bitch!" she stammered, "You're trespassing! I'm going to kill you!"

At that moment, a very drunk and very naked man came staggering out of the bedroom. He slurred, "Hey man, you wanna party?"

Mrs. Mendoza turned around and yelled at him, "Get back in there, you drunken bastard." At that moment, I took off as fast as my legs would carry me, sprinting out the back door with the fear of God in my soul. I jumped into my car and realized that I didn't have my keys: in my panic, I must have dropped them inside the house! There was no going back: I ran the few blocks back home. That was the absolute last and final home visit I ever made in my entire professional career. The next day, I called a locksmith to make new keys for my car.

As for the other students' families, at that point it would be meeting with me at the school or nothing. Mr. and Mrs. Clayton, Olympia's parents, agreed to meet me at school one weekend. They both worked evenings during the week. The Clayton family was one of the few black families in town. They'd been in Greeley for three years. When we met, their first comment was unexpected: they asked me what in God's name I was doing in Greeley. Mr. Clayton solemnly stated that minorities were not welcome in this community and that, in fact, Greeley was the most racist place he'd ever been to. "We live in a trailer park where poor Mexicans and white trash live. We have no garbage service, running water, or grocery stores around to buy stuff when we need to. When we go into any store, the clerks follow us around—afraid we'll steal. We can't even go nowhere to eat."

Mrs. Clayton told her husband to be quiet. "Mr. Teacher here don't need to hear your babble," she warned.

I respectfully disagreed with her. "I just arrived here from Texas. You're actually the first black family I've seen here, and I'm surprised. Is there a Mexican community?"

Mr. Clayton jumped in, "Yep, I told you they're across the way with the white trash folks and us. You should come over for dinner sometime and meet some of 'em."

I sincerely liked the idea and thanked him. I told them that I would call them later to plan it.

"Don't bother to call," Mr. Clayton said. "No wires in our area. Just send a note with Olympia. By the way, how's she doing?"

This was my perfect entry. "She's a great kid—funny and very pleasant. I'm curious to hear more about her from you."

Mr. Clayton seemed caught up in the last subject. "I tell you, Greeley is a racist people. They tell you to your nose. Signs all over the damn place."

Mrs. Clayton interrupted him again. She had a clever flare for keeping the conversation on track. "Olympia is our only child. She's always seen trouble in school because of her slowness. She is good friends with many of the Mexican kids around home, but in school, some teachers don't know how smart she can be. God bless that child."

Mr. Clayton interrupted again, "Teachers don't know shit from Shinhola when it comes to her learning. They're stupid. No one likes for her to sing. As a child, she'd sing and sing just like a little bird. She learned all the words to every song all on her own."

Though I was enjoying myself with the Claytons, it was finally time to reach an end to our meeting. "I really like what you're telling me about Olympia," I said. "I want to know her better. Soon, I'll send a note home with her, and we can plan to meet again." I stood up and thanked them for their visit. Mr. Clayton extended a firm handshake. As they were leaving, he reminded me that the dinner invitation was open anytime.

After each conference, I'd scribble notes for the student's file, hopefully to use in developing an educational, social, and even health-related plan for each student. In Olympia's file that day, I wrote, "Olympia is an extremely overweight eleven-year-old African American child. She is gifted with a radiant and gregarious personality. She has a talent for music and likes to sing. She has a strong and engaging voice."

It was true: students and teachers alike enjoyed listening to Olympia's powerful alto voice. I liked just hearing her contagious laughter, which resonated through the halls when she thought something was funny, which was most of the time. The sound made the day a little happier. The only teacher who seemed to have a problem with Olympia was Mrs. Morris, who taught third grade. Often, when Mrs. Morris was on hall duty and Olympia was coming back to our classroom, this teacher would scream at the girl to hurry up and get back to class or she would "color her white." Maybe then she would follow directions, Mrs. Morris would add. It was not just I but other teachers who heard these comments from Mrs. Morris.

If there was a play to be performed at school, Olympia was usually assigned the lead role. If singing was involved, she would participate without reservation. One day, they announced a singing contest at our school. Olympia, of course, entered and urged everyone in the class to come and clap for her in case other kids forgot. No one needed convincing: my class loved school assemblies and special programs. We were first in line to get into the cafeteria for the show along with Mr. And Mrs. Clayton, who showed up thirty minutes early. As the program got underway, Mr.

Eckhart introduced the twelve students who would be performing. When he announced Olympia, my entire class, with the help of her parents, gave her a standing ovation. When it was Olympia's turn to perform, she walked onstage, took a glance at her corner of supporters, and smiled at the piano and flute accompanists, indicating that she was ready to begin. I wondered what song she had selected. During the previous weeks, I'd asked her if I could come to one of her afternoon rehearsals. She'd said no, that the song was a surprise for me and all the other teachers who liked her.

Now with all eyes on her, Olympia began to sing, "Somewhere over the rainbow, way up high, there's a land that I heard of, once in a lullaby . . ." As she sang, she looked across the audience, drawing us in as if she had a sincere message of determination and hope to impart. As the piano and flute danced along in harmony with her voice, the song resonated through the cafeteria, now transformed into a magical space. "Birds fly over the rainbow, why, oh, why can't I?" The final lines of the song echoed in our ears and hearts. When it was over, everyone cheered for Olympia, students and teachers alike, recognizing her for the star that she was.

Just like all my students, Olympia needed and deserved success, especially since she faced plenty of obstacles. Her obesity went hand in hand with severe asthma. Her mother insisted that she not participate in any physical activities that compromised her health, which she said were the doctor's orders. The school nurse tried to do what she could for the situation, dedicating herself to changing Olympia's sedentary lifestyle as much as possible as well as improving her eating habits. Along with this, I continued to be concerned about the social opportunities available to Olympia and the other minority students in my class, who faced life in a city where racial lines, as I was learning, were staunchly drawn. Mr. Clayton's critical words about the bigotry in Greeley echoed in my head, and people like Mrs. Morris were proving his point. Just how deep did the racism go? Was I refusing to see or acknowledge its extent, just as I had when I was a boy in Del Rio?

One day I was on lunch duty, watching the kids eat their sack lunches outside. I noticed that one of the students—a Mexican kid—didn't seem to have anything to eat. "Quieres parte de un burrito? Está bien sabroso. Yo lo hice" (Do you want part of a burrito? It's pretty good. I made it), I said. He took off like a bullet, and I heard him jokingly tell some of his pals that I spoke Spanish and ate burritos at school. This incident perplexed me. And as I became set on finding out more about the racial situation in this town, I began to ask questions of the parents I met with during conferences. When I shared with them the puzzling episode at lunch and asked for their take on it, several made it clear to me that speaking Spanish was not allowed in school and that eating burritos was a private matter. If you did, it became clear to people that you were a Mexican. What the hell was going on in Camelot?

As I was still learning in my life, there were all kinds of discrimination. And I was discovering that my students at Park were subject to a similar kind of discriminatory categorization as my students at Dillard had been. Just as I struggled to understand why many of my students—most of them minorities—at Dillard had been placed in special education, the same was true here. It was clear to me as time went on that Olympia and several of her classmates simply didn't belong in special education and that they were being cheated out of their rightful learning environment as a result. It all came down to testing: if you didn't meet national standards of competence on the Weschler intelligence test, you were placed in special education. In my classroom now, just as in Corpus Christi, the children seemed to fall into one of three groups. The first group tested between 55 and 70 on the Wechsler scales. They typically displayed severe mental impairment (often accompanied by other physical impairments), poor academic skills, and poor social skills. These kids came from a variety of socioeconomic and cultural backgrounds. This was the only group, in my opinion, that justified placement in special education. The second group was made up of those who scored between 70 and 80 on the Wechsler scales, showing specific deficiencies in reading, writing, verbal language, and math. They were generally at least two grade levels behind in school and often had behavioral problems. These students usually came from less economically advantaged homes that were other than Caucasian. Often, the predominant language spoken at home was not English. Then there were the children with intelligence scores between 80 and 85. These were simply individuals with linguistic variations or reading delays. Interestingly, those in this small group often came from Caucasian homes. In the case of both the second and third groups, I simply could not understand how these students were ever placed in the same classes as students with significant mental retardation. The lumping together of all these different levels into one classroom meant that overextended teachers, busy tending to the more severe cases, were not able to give other students the attention and inspiration they needed to truly thrive.

I had enough familiarity with this pattern by now that I didn't waste time going to Mr. Eckhart with my opinion. After all, he was the first administrator I'd known who actually seemed interested in hearing me out. Mr. Eckhart shared my frustration, but said his hands were tied. "You see, Tony, there is nothing anyone can do. These kids are placed by the district strictly on the basis of the score they get on the IQ test."

I persevered, "Kenny, that is illegal. I saw this practice take place in two school districts in Texas. The fact that it's done over and over again doesn't make it right or legal. Kids like Olympia should be with their peers in a regular classroom with regular teachers. But no one does anything about it, and we can't either? Well, then, the least we can do is remove that damn sign on my door that says Educable Mentally Retarded. Who the hell thought of that one? This is so stupid and unfair. Damn it, I'm angry!"

I felt like a broken record, playing the same lamenting song, feeling the same desperation I'd felt in Corpus Christi, and realizing that arguing was absolutely futile. I walked back to my classroom and through the door with its irksome label. The regular classroom teachers probably thought it referred to me as well. I fell back into the familiar feeling of isolation.

These poor kids and their parents were victims, thinking they were getting the best possible education out of the American public school system when, in fact, this was a total crock. Once again, the hard reality hit me: if I didn't do something for these kids, nothing would be done on their behalf—they'd be utterly forgotten. And so I resolved that if I was all these students could rely on for their diverse needs, I'd try to do whatever I could for each and every one of them. The curriculum I was given did nothing to address individual needs, so I set about designing my own for each group I identified and each student within that group. For my efforts, Mr. Eckhart was there to lend me outstanding support, and my kids responded remarkably well. I began to see academic and social growth in them that was nothing short of significant.

Eckhart became a true advocate: something rare and wonderful in a director. But for every good apple, there always seems to be one who is intent on spoiling the barrel—a munungus among us, if you will. Usually, a group of wonderful teachers who treat students and parents with dignity and compassion are able to compensate for the dead wood. But the rot can seep in and do its damage through deviousness, hatred, and cruelty. When I first arrived at Park, I knew that sooner rather than later, I would spot the one teacher who would attempt to destroy what the true educators were striving to develop in their students: self-confidence, empathy for others, and a love for learning. It should come as no surprise that this teacher was Mrs. Morris.

One Monday morning, as I was going past the third-grade classroom, I heard Mrs. Morris's loud and commanding voice. "Stay away from those weird kids, especially that nigger girl," she warned her class. "I don't want any of you to become like them. The more you're around them, the more you become like them. I don't want any of you close to any of them."

All I heard was evil. All I saw was red. I felt utter agony and disbelief. So what did I do? I peeked through the door and waved. I didn't deign to yell, give this woman the finger, or even speak. Neither did I report her to Mr. Eckhart or to my colleagues. I had seen this type of abusive behavior toward kids so often by so many cruel and insensitive teachers that I decided that there was no point in reporting her. The damage Mrs. Morris had done to her students in telling them these lies was irreversible. The effect she had on everyone at the school was horrendous and inexcusable. Yet like many of her ilk in the educational system, she kept her job and continued to spew her bile. People like her would never completely go away. And so it was my job to educate my own students about their worth, their rights, and the fact that there would be people in life they'd have to deal with who wanted to bring them down, to see them fail, and to keep them separate.

For myself, I knew that there was evil and monstrousness in the world: there always had been and there always would be. That's why civil rights legislation had been passed in our country: to protect citizens against this and make discrimination illegal and punishable. I gained a new admiration for those individuals responsible for moving America forward in this spirit of equality and human dignity, even if it had to be done through litigation. Litigation, as I was fast learning, was often the only path to true social change. The practice of mislabeling in special education was just such a case. There was no other possible solution: the abuse was too blatant and the long-term developmental, social, and emotional damage to the kids too great. I was coming full circle to the same conclusion: my place was in law.

In the meantime, I was committed to teaching for the year. I also resolved to enjoy as much as possible my days in Greeley and accept with gratitude the many fantastic educators and friends I'd already met here. There were good days after all. One morning in late November, I woke up to find the entire city covered with a thick white blanket of snow. I decided to walk to school, bringing my camera along and snapping pictures of the wondrous scene to send to my family and friends in Texas and California—poor, deprived things. I kicked and danced my way through the powder, even sampling a little for breakfast as I sang a premature rendition of "It's Beginning to Look a Lot Like Christmas" all the way to school. That morning, it seemed to me that the very idea of Christmas must have originated in Greeley. I waved to every person and dog I met along the way: I'm sure I looked crazy. I thought again about Camelot. Today, Greeley seemed like that ideal village: a place where love and goodwill triumph and where any problem facing the land could be solved by King Arthur and his knights. I sang as I walked, "It's true! It's true! The crown has made it clear. The climate must be perfect all the year. A law was made a distant moon ago here . . . . The winter is forbidden till December, and exists March the second on the dot . . . . The snow may never slush upon the hillside. By 9:00 p.m., the moonlight must appear . . ."

Perhaps Greeley was truly as racist as Mr. Clayton said: I'd seen some evidence for myself. But for now, at this very moment, there was not a place more splendid than Greeley, Colorado.

Chapter Twenty-eight

My romance with Greeley in the wintertime extended through Christmas break. Luckily, my bouts of snow-induced elation hadn't gotten me thrown out of town quite yet. Oddly, it was one of the first Christmases that I didn't think much about going home to California. Over the holidays, Mel Lane approached me with an offer. He asked if I would consider transferring to the Lab School for the spring term. I would be relieved of my obligations at Park and immediately take a position that had just become vacant, teaching high school special education. I would not only teach, but also be an example for students at the college who were pursuing degrees in special education. They would attend my classes and observe the teaching methods I used on a daily basis. In essence, I would be their assigned practical mentor, helping them develop the teaching tools necessary to be successful in the field.

I said no. Enough was enough. Each new offer I took simply got me farther away from my clearly structured goal of pursuing law school. I had a confirmed interview yet to do at CU Boulder. I could not jeopardize that opportunity: it was the chance of a lifetime and one that would open up an entirely new career for me.

Mel didn't press the issue, understanding my rationale. He and Jane seemed content to just enjoy the winter holiday with me. As the snow continued to fall by the foot, most days I'd walk to their house to visit and feast on some of the best meals I'd ever had. Driving in the snow wasn't working out for me. Each time I got behind the wheel proved disastrous. I'd skid on the ice, plunging deep into ditches or slamming into a tree or parked car. Daily, it seemed, I'd rely on several kind souls to bail out my car from a snowdrift. I couldn't get the hang of stopping properly. One day, I skidded directly through a school crossing. Luckily, there were no kids around, and the crossing guard scampered out of the way in time. I even very lightly rear-ended a police car driven by a very sympathetic officer who let me off with a stern warning. I wished my family could see just how brave I was to even attempt driving here. But heroics aside, I eventually decided it would be safer for me and the rest of the good people of Greeley if I left my car home and set out on foot.

Over our leisurely visits and meals, Mel spoke to me more about his role as principal at the Lab School as well as his current efforts toward earning a doctorate in special education at Colorado State College. His long-term goal was to become an administrator of special education somewhere in Colorado. As for my own teaching role, he encouraged me enthusiastically, saying that everyone who'd visited my classroom at Park spoke highly of my natural gifts in teaching. He told me sincerely that he thought I had strong potential to become a college professor. I immediately felt uncomfortable: this was a compliment too big to accept. I realized perhaps I wasn't the crazy one after all.

As winter slowly crept toward spring, my thoughts began to turn more intently toward Boulder. Nonetheless, I kept my promise to make the most of Greeley, the remainder of the school year, and my social life. I continued to go out and do things with my network of friends and found myself casually dating: nothing serious—after all, I'd be hitting the road soon. I began dating a woman named Beverly who lived in Denver. One weekend, she drove up to Greeley to go to a party with me. It was a party like many others, except that she'd brought her roommate along. And just like that, the guardian angels dropped down for me the most beautiful and elegant gift I'd ever known.

Beverly's roommate was a pretty petite woman who I would soon learn was from Iowa but Irish in heritage. Joanie's blue eyes seemed to glow with a love that no one could miss. I was immediately intrigued by her joyful, ingratiating personality. This was the first time I'd been so fascinated by someone outside my culture since my sad affair with Carol at Sul Ross. We immediately connected and ended up talking for much of the night. Beverly, probably for the best, was busy visiting with others and did not notice my fascination with her roommate. I learned that Joanie was completing a nurse practitioner program at the University of Colorado in Denver. We spoke of our families, our dreams and aspirations, and the good and bad times we'd encountered. We laughed as we shared the funny times we'd known. I spoke in detail of my early days by the placita and the river. She was fascinated by my background; I thought hers was more intriguing. She'd been a church volunteer in various poor areas in Mexico. She spoke of her family in Arizona with endearment.

After several hours at the party—most of which I spent talking to Joanie—and a terrific steak dinner, she and Beverly returned to Denver, and I walked back to my apartment. I walked and thought, and thought some more, about our encounter. I recalled Joanie's graceful ways and that she'd spoken to me in excellent Spanish! "Habla español, caballero? Qué guapo y elegante habla usted. Qué maneras tan finas tiene usted. Yo quiseira conoserlo mejor" (You speak Spanish, sir? How handsomely and elegantly you speak. What fine manners you have. I would like to get to know you better). Going over it again with pleasure, I thought, *Damn, she's awesome! And she's nuts about me!* I had to settle down and remember that I was dating her friend. Realistically, this was probably one of those silly chance encounters that didn't mean much. Not only did she live in Denver with a woman I was supposed to be dating, but she was busy with school and work. I doubted I would ever see her again.

Weeks went by. The cold days of spring suddenly gave way to brilliant warm weather. Beverly and I still got together from time to time, but she was focusing her dating efforts in Denver. Two months after Joanie and I had first met, I saw her again, this time at a pool party hosted by the same mutual friend. I couldn't keep my eyes off her. Unfortunately, this time it was she who'd brought a date. Maybe her good-girl act had tricked me the last time: clearly, she was a flirt. I'd heard that Irishwomen were that way. I thought the guy she was with was socially awkward and shy—not a bit debonair like me. The guy didn't even seem to know how to swim, and I was sure he couldn't speak eloquent Spanish. Joanie and I, on the other hand, were both natural swimmers and social butterflies. I wondered if she had been raised near a river as I was. She plunged into the pool, and

I plunged in right behind her. We'd swim a lap or two, then stop to chat at the edge of the pool. Her date never had a prayer. I was in my natural glory: perfectly comfortable with the party, the water, and resolved to not let Joanie out of my sight. Yet the day ended like the evening we'd first met, with no opportunity to talk about meeting again.

Summer was now here, and I remained in Greeley. I was still seeing Beverly occasionally when our schedules allowed for it. It was she who usually made the trip to Greeley to see me. One evening, we agreed I'd drive to Denver for our date. I wasn't looking forward to the trip: any drive beyond Greeley limits was a new and frightening experience for me. I wasn't familiar with the rest of the state at all. I arrived after a harrowing ninety-minute journey feeling exhausted and terrorized by the confusing highways and heavy traffic of Denver. I walked up to the apartment and rang the doorbell. Unexpectedly, Joanie answered the door. "I'm so sorry, Tony, Beverly had to go back to work. She tried to reach you to say she wouldn't be able to make your date. She felt awful. Please do come in. Can I get you something to drink? Have you had dinner yet? We have some delicious spaghetti . . ." She seemed to genuinely feel bad for me, and I could tell she was embarrassed by the situation.

I had to interrupt and end this embarrassment immediately. "Are you free?" I asked.

"Let me get my coat," she responded.

That evening, the two of us went out for dinner to a jazz club. The conversation flowed just as it had before, but tonight, there was no one to pull us away from each other. The talented vocalist performing that night began his repertoire, and we danced. Soon, he began a Burt Bacharach number popular in the day that I'd heard many times before. But tonight, it opened the doors to my heart. "How can I show you I'm glad I got to know you, 'cause I've heard some talk, they say you think I'm fine. This guy's in love and what I'd do to make you mine. Tell me now, is it so, don't let me be the last to know . . ."

That's all it took. The distance between us melted away. So did our prior relationships and the obstacles in our busy lives. Soon after we began dating, I accepted the position at the Lab School for the fall. Eight months later, in spring, Joanie and I were married. It was a beautiful church wedding—we were both from Catholic upbringings—and the most nontraditional reception anyone in Greeley had ever attended. The honored guests who traveled to be with us included our parents, siblings, and Robert and Paul from Eagle Pass. Also in attendance were Mel and Jane, of course, and many of my students. We didn't have to spend a cent on entertainment: at the reception, Mom banged on the piano for three hours straight, playing all the songs from my childhood. "Cielito Lindo" was the special hit of the day. I thought Mom's lungs would burst wide open as she belted out the song with every fiber of her being. She sang like a woman who possessed all the happiness in the world. I loved my mom that day.

Mel and Jane were delighted to see me finally "nailed down" and also settled in Greeley for the foreseeable future. Joanie's grandmother had surprised us with a wedding gift of money to use as a down payment for our first home. Mel and Jane, clever as they were, found a home for us on the block behind their house.

When I made the choice to stay in education, perhaps it was for no other reason than that the pieces of my life—the pieces of the puzzle—had begun to fit together, and this teaching opportunity felt like one of the pieces I needed. My elusive dream of becoming an attorney had faded—yet if someone asked me now when the most fantastic days of my life were, I would say that these had been the best ever.

Chapter Twenty-nine

My new married life and the most rewarding teaching job I'd ever had were two dreams that came true. My first semester teaching at the Lab School was more challenging and exciting than I'd ever expected. I was in my glory. I would have my students for a full three years: throughout their high school education. As in my previous teaching positions, getting to know each individual happened over a matter of weeks. As soon as I knew who was who, I began delving into their cumulative folders, gathering information about their backgrounds. Every day, we grew a little closer. They and their parents would become my best advocates and friends.

On top of this, professors from the college were looking to me to help educate their students by example. Special education majors rotated continuously into our classroom to observe me working with the students. I prepared every day not only for my own class, but for the numerous college students who came to observe, scrutinize, and learn from my teaching approaches. The admiration and esteem I received in this role from professionals in higher education was extremely uplifting and energizing. However, the daily reality of it could also be draining and uncomfortable. There was no interaction built into this process, so I merely tried to ignore the fact that observers were constantly present, taking notes on my every move to write reports for their professors. Though difficult to take sometimes, this was what I'd agreed to when I'd signed my contract. As for my own students, many had been in this fishbowl learning environment for years and, quite accustomed to it, were usually prepared to behave and perform at their best. Even on days when I knew they were tired of the parade of visitors, they managed to tolerate the system.

In addition to teaching at the Lab School, my attention soon turned to other endeavors on the Colorado State College campus. I was asked to teach a college-level course on curriculum and methods in the afternoons. To add more excitement to this time of growth, I decided to apply for admittance into the doctoral program in special education at the college. Applying was Mel's suggestion. He'd been accepted a year before we'd met and was working diligently toward his own degree. Though his plate was certainly full, he felt that taking classes while working as an administrator served a dual purpose, one role informing the other. He was sure I'd be able to handle the simultaneous roles of teaching and learning in much the same way. I admired Mel's dedication and ambition tremendously and respected his guidance. I readily obtained my graduate entrance exam scores from East Texas State as well as several letters of recommendation. Mel assured me that Dr. Vander, the director of the Lab School, would make sure I was admitted into the program. Vander was also a member of the faculty in the College of Education and could serve as my graduate major advisor. It all seemed a natural matter of course. Mel's advice proved solid once again: I was admitted into the doctoral program within days of applying. I would take two four-credit classes each quarter over the next three years and earn a cumulative GPA of 3.9.

Mel was one of those fine friends who pushed me to the next level in life. Of course, for every person as generous and caring as this, there are usually a few who want to knock us down. Mrs. Collin's junior high classroom was right next to mine. The students in my class had been in hers previously, and she claimed she had taught them everything they needed to know. Now, Collin believed, my substandard teaching was destroying all her precious work. She always seemed to have one ear open to my classroom and would constantly poke her head through the door to point out deficiencies in my methods. To her, a deficiency was any method that deviated, however slightly, from the Life Experience Unit Approach, the educational philosophy developed by the Lab School over the years. This model emphasized incorporating new concepts into the context of the students' daily lives, and as such, it shunned the use of any commercial instructional materials. Dr. Vander supported this approach, so to Mrs. Collin, it was set in stone. To her, the use of traditional textbooks was just asking for trouble. In my experience, this didn't make much sense. I preferred an eclectic approach to teaching, incorporating whatever methods and tools worked for my individual students. I knew that each student's ideal learning style was different and unique: some thrived on communication and constant affirmation; some preferred to work autonomously and in their own solitary space. Some, but by no means all, responded well to the Life Experience Unit Approach. I was well versed in the benefits of this approach, which had its roots in the work of Montessori. However, Montessori herself acknowledged that children must learn at their own pace and in their own way. To me, the Lab School's strict methodology, as vehemently defended by Mrs. Collin, could be just as limiting as any other singular model.

The more I stuck to my guns on the subject, ignoring Mrs. Collin's condescending "advice," the more she had it in for me. I became a personal affront to her: the source of disorder and havoc in her life. To add insult to her injury, my irksome existence wasn't something Mrs. Collin only had to face at the Lab School. It so happened that she also taught a section of the same course I taught at the college: Curriculum and Methods. Shockingly for her, more students registered for my class than for hers. In fact, when my class was full, students often complained and requested that I teach another section at a different time. Her ego bruised, Mrs. Collin was about to declare all-out war.

I was shocked when Mel came to me with a warning to be cautious of Collin. She evidently had a maddening tendency to run to Dr. Vander with a list of grievances against me, attempting to prove my incompetence and unwillingness to conform to the system. And Collin's opinion, according to Mel, did hold weight with Dr. Vander. Lackey that she was, Collin was something resembling the "king's" right hand. And King Vander was powerful indeed. He controlled an enormous amount of federal funds for both the Lab School and the College of Education. As such, he presided over not just the Lab School's staff but the faculty of the graduate school as well as the professional teams of the speech clinic and vocational rehabilitation center. Obedience to the king was absolutely bottom line, and Mrs. Collin played this game to a tee.

My worry began to grow. One night, I dreamed that Vander was sitting on a throne proclaiming his power. "Anyone who disobeys me loses his head," he proclaimed. "The traitor will be publicly executed and his head tossed into the Camelot snow to be eaten by buzzards." When I awoke, I immediately called Mel. He was no consultation. He warned me that Mr. Vander had the power to fire me with the snap of his fingers. Mel also said it was time to talk about a lot of things that were happening at the Lab School. Embarrassedly, he admitted that the teaching staff was considerably annoyed by our friendship, believing I received preferential treatment in getting hired and maintained as a teacher. I was offended and repulsed by such accusations. This was simply trivial bullshit, and I chose to ignore it.

Despite my new agonies at work, teaching was no longer my whole identity. Other things were now more significant. What mattered most was that, for once in my life, I had a woman I truly and completely loved, who loved me in return and would stand by me for the rest of my life. She gave me a new foundation of stability and confidence, and her family—especially her wonderful mother—added to this emotional security. I knew for certain that their genuine love and support would always be there. I was already coming to realize that my new ventures in higher education would require all my resources as I learned to address conflicts as they arose. It was reassuring to know that I now had even more close family to rely on through it all.

Our family grows in age and maturity. Jenny, born in 1970; Carmela, born in 1974, and finally, a boy, Marc Anthony, born in 1976

Our family

My grown children.

Later marriage after 39 years and retirement celebration

Chapter Thirty

For Joanie and me, one of the top priorities in our lives after marriage was to start a family. Six months after we were married, we found out that we were expecting our first child. We were both thrilled and ready to begin a family, which we had both always hoped to do.

I had some strong opinions about what our first child would be named. I wanted America for a girl or Marc Anthony for a boy. After taking an informal survey among friends and family, I learned that the name America was not too acceptable to people. It seemed okay for the name of a continent, but not for a sweet, small, and precious child. As for Marc Anthony, people found it too Roman, conjuring up images of emperors and Cleopatra. That's why I liked it.

The Lanes were as excited as could be about the imminent arrival of our little one. They too were expecting a baby, due just a couple of months before ours. Practical mothers-to-be that they were, Joanie and Jane urged me to put the naming project on hold and get busy preparing the baby's room. I was instructed to assemble a baby crib that we'd bought on consignment. I was told to paint the walls of the room without spilling all over the carpet. Though we didn't know the gender of the child, I wanted to paint the room blue since I could sense it would be a boy. Joanie and Jane wanted pink for their own illogical reasons. The weeks rushed by and, soon, only two months remained for the name-that-babe contest. I had precisely marked on my calendar the exact day the baby would arrive. I was keeping meticulous records of the voting. "America" was gaining favor almost two to one. "Marc" without the "Anthony" was an almost unanimous win. I still hadn't gotten around to assembling the crib, but I figured there was plenty of time.

Soon the Lanes' baby arrived: a big healthy baby boy. We were at their house constantly to marvel at him and imagine that someday soon our kids would be playing together. One Saturday night, four weeks before our due date, we arrived home from having dinner at the Lanes. Three hours later, Joanie calmly informed me that her water had broken. I had forgotten what exactly that meant but knew it meant trouble in Camelot. I was paralyzed with fear, so much so that Joanie thought she should be the one to drive us to the hospital. My male ego kicked in and refused to allow such nonsense. I called Mel and Jane, who advised me to stay calm: Mel would come by and pick us up. No way, I said, this was my role. They made me promise to ask the doctor for something to calm me down and help me get through the night.

Jennifer Ann, not America, was born at five on a snowy Thanksgiving morning—the first Thanksgiving Joanie and I had celebrated as husband and wife. I was in the delivery room to welcome my daughter into the world—almost a month early. No wonder I was so confused. After regaining my emotional equilibrium, I was gallantly escorted out in a wheelchair. I think my wife was okay too. I was a proud papa. I had witnessed the miracle of birth. I had a brand-new daughter. No one would ever take this away from me. I would never allow her to get married and abandon me. These were the most precious moments that I would cherish and remember for the rest of my life.

I loved showing off my new daughter to everyone and was pleased that my students and their parents were getting to know not just me but my family as well. Likewise, I was once again learning the different personalities and motivations of each of my students. I reinstated the How and Why Club of my childhood, inviting the class to ask questions and engage in an open discussion about issues of concern to them. The students challenged me with questions about jobs, money, love, and marriage. They were certainly better students than my brothers and sisters, who would run off on a whim to climb trees or take a dip in the river. Appreciative and excited, my current students yearned to learn something new each day.

They were particularly concerned about jobs: how would they get one and what skills did they need? Just as I'd had at a young age, I wanted them to have practical entrepreneurial experience. We needed an activity to help them take the subjects of math, language, social skills, and practical skills like cooking and apply them to adult life. So we converted the classroom into a mini coffee shop for faculty and staff where we served and sold baked goods and breakfast burritos we had made ourselves. The students conducted their business in a corporate fashion. Some exhibited leadership sensibility to the point that it was almost frightening. I found myself singing a familiar tune: how in God's name had they ended up in this special ed classroom?

Of course, it once again came down to the cursed IQ cutoff. Many students had been tested and placed in special ed at the beginning of elementary school and were never reevaluated. Such students were then stuck in special classrooms for their entire educational lives. In some cases, physical disability seemed to be the cause of slight learning differences that did not even constitute learning delays. Timmy was afflicted with congenital spina bifida, Steve and Michelle had cerebral palsy, and Charlotte had a congenital heart problem. Another boy was deaf in one ear. Clara was placed in the group because she was extremely overweight, and her grandmother, with whom she lived, could not speak English.

Peggy was a prime example of a student who was being held back by her placement in a special classroom. She had scored in the low 90s on the Weschler scales—just at the cutoff for special ed. But in many ways, Peggy was extraordinary. When she had something to say, she articulated her perspective with deep conviction, her glowing eyes compelling us to listen to whatever she had to say. An individual with superior passion and alacrity, Peggy wanted to dedicate her life to the service of children, working to eradicate poverty, hunger, and disease. She also dreamed of becoming an educator to make a difference in the lives of kids. Many times she said to me, "Mr. Carvajal, my heart demands this of me. Will you help me? There are so many things I want to do. You yourself tell us that the sky's the limit. I want to know the sky." Individuals who are mentally retarded do not evolve to the level of social consciousness and ambition that I saw in Peggy. She had more motivation and aspiration than any student I'd taught in my college classes.

Peggy had an identical twin sister who was also part of our group. Debbie had similar scores on the Weschler but lacked her sister's tenacious passion. Though she had comparable academic skills, Debbie did not seem to share her sister's ability to persevere through tasks she found difficult. Debbie was pleasant and congenial, but socially more awkward than Peggy. I soon learned more about the girls' background through a conference with their mother, a nurse. One factor that she believed might have led to delayed learning in her daughters was trauma at birth. Her labor with Peggy and Debbie had been complicated and drawn out, potentially causing oxygen deprivation to the brains of both girls. Peggy was eventually born first; Debbie's birth had been delayed even more. In addition to their slight learning delays, Peggy and Debbie both exhibited some hyperactive behavior when placed in stressful situations. Sometimes I wondered how this was different from other people: I had certainly been there many times before.

Other students in my classroom were placed there due mostly to behavioral issues. In several cases, I could barely identify a problem. Ross's issues seemed to amount to running too fast and being hooked on basketball. Doug, an adopted child, was perhaps a cocky Casanova, but his only compulsive tendencies appeared to be playing guitar and singing. Admittedly, there were students with more severe behavioral problems. Cody was severely emotionally disturbed. During the four years he was in my classroom, I tried several times to have him psychologically evaluated. I was never successful. Each year, his state seemed to worsen, making it difficult to see what his future would hold. Senior year was typically a time when students worked with a vocational counselor to explore possible avenues of employment. Each student was placed at a job site appropriate for him or her, and we would evaluate progress and performance. Cody was placed at a local diner. Within the first month, the diner owner called to tell us that he'd called the police and filed criminal charges against Cody for spraying insecticide over the lettuce. Cody had apparently gotten upset with his manager for scolding him to wear a hat while washing dishes. He'd misplaced his anger on anyone eating at the diner that day. Luckily, a coworker saw this and immediately reported the incident to the manager. He was immediately taken into custody and required to undergo psychological treatment. Cody was later released to return to my group. Two months later, he got married to one of the other students in my class. They were unprepared for the marriage, and it was later annulled. Cody's inability to cope with this failure created a major psychological setback. Six months later, he killed himself with a shotgun stored in his parents' home. The tragedy of this outcome spoke to the fact that some of these children needed substantial psychological help that I could neither provide nor acquire for them.

Sometimes, I felt as if there were only a handful of students in my class who actually fit the description of who I was hired to teach, which were children with mild mental retardation or significant learning disabilities. There were, however, four students who were more severely developmentally impaired. These four exhibited similar traits: they were deficient in their ability to reciprocate socially, seeming to live in a world of their own. All four also displayed significant language abnormalities, principally echolalia, the tendency to vocalize words or phrases repeatedly. The problems of these children fit under an umbrella that years later was defined as pervasive developmental disorders (PDD). These disorders include autism, among a few others.

One such student, Mark, was originally diagnosed with minimal brain damage. His mother thought otherwise and tenaciously searched for a proper diagnosis. After numerous visits to Children's Hospital in Denver, Mark was diagnosed with autism spectrum disorder. Some children are afflicted more severely than others. Mark was considered mildly autistic. He had great difficulty adapting to social situations or making any lasting friendships in school. But while he struggled with basic learning tasks, he would fascinate the college observers and me with his atypical pockets of intelligence, such as an uncanny ability to recall intricate facts and data he'd heard or read only once. His incredible memory and compulsion to keep reciting these facts took me back to my days in Corpus Christi when Tommy would sing for me his astounding array of country songs.

Another one of these four students at the Lab School, Mike, was equally disengaged socially and emotionally. He always brought to school with him a boom box and had to have it with him every minute of the day, everywhere he went. There was no taking it away from him: he would become extremely upset. If he was so much as asked to reduce the volume, he would literally attack himself, scratching so viciously at his eyes that he inflicted significant damage. Needless to say, I only tried to tell him once. Mike brought memories of the notorious Boom Boom from the Riverside School, whose uncontrollable tantrums always drove him to inflict physical pain on himself.

Though at the time these idiosyncratic behaviors were beginning to be understood as indicators of autism, no doctor could explain to the parents why their children had these problems. As the children grew older and their progress remained minimal, the parents were agonized—their lack of answers leading to frustration and even rage. To date, although the medical and scientific communities continue to make serious efforts to isolate the specific factors that lead to autism and PDD, the causation remains virtually unknown.

All these students, with their diverse needs and abilities, made it into my Lab School classroom, and I set about the impossible task of being the best teacher I could be for each one of them. But I couldn't keep my opinions to myself. The more I realized that the placement criteria at the Lab School was just as illogical if not more so than anywhere else I'd taught, I began to speak out—it was simply my nature. Of course, Mrs. Collin didn't hesitate to run to Dr. Vander to tell him I'd been blasting the system. An emergency conference was called. As my major advisor, Vander threatened to delay my date for taking oral and written comprehensives. It was also within his power to approve, or not approve, my graduation from the doctoral program.

When it was time to take them, I failed both the written and oral comprehensives. Whether my work deserved a failing grade, I don't know. I do know that my performance was affected by the pressure I felt knowing Vander would be evaluating me with the most critical of eyes. I felt finished and humiliated. Mel consoled me, saying, "Don't feel too badly. You'll be better prepared next time. I need to take my comps next semester. Let's get serious and study together." I knew that wouldn't help me one bit: my problem was the very presence of the one person that I knew was out to get me, no matter how I performed. So psychologically intimidated did I feel in front of Vander and the entire comp committee at this point that any ability I possessed to do well on the tests had been compromised. I could not even try.

In spite of my demeaning experience with comps and the fact that my doctorate seemed farther away than ever, I was determined to create something unique and exciting for my students. An opportunity came during social studies class. Though during math and reading the students worked in groups according to skill level, everyone came together for social studies. The students enjoyed this class where we would freely discuss ideas about life and personal experience. One day, I allowed them to choose between four topics of discussion: poverty, boredom, music, and "going steady." They chose boredom. Our discussion revealed that many students didn't like the Lab School and were tired and bored of all the visitors coming in and out of the classroom all day long. The subject came up of getting away for a field trip—so far away that they wouldn't even go home at the end of the day. We all got wrapped up in the idea. I encouraged them to brainstorm places they would like to go, just to see the expression of boredom on their faces transform into hope and enthusiasm. For my part, I took it to another level, suggesting faraway destinations that were simply impossible, perhaps just to prevent anything from getting nailed down. Our discussion continued throughout the week. I couldn't help myself: I talked about Washington, DC; Hawaii; Mexico; Ireland; France; and Italy. I discussed the cultural and historical context of each place, none of which most students had ever heard of or would likely ever go. The whole week, salutations of *aloha, bon giorno, buenos dias*, and "top o' the mornin' to ya" echoed through the hallways of the Lab School.

In reality, Dr. Vander allowed only preapproved field trips within a fifty-mile radius of the school. I eventually had to come clean with my students. When I explained this to them, their faces fell. Even a sixty-mile trip to Denver was out of the question. And yet we continued the discussion as if our field trip would take place in some alternate universe where the rules did not apply. We reserved our discussions for when observers were not in the room, and we could engage in our delusions freely. We developed an unspoken rule to shut down the topic when visitors were around. One day, we went so far as to vote on the field trip location: too much talk and no action never got anyone anywhere. We consulted *Robert's Rules of Order* for a step-by-step guide to conducting a formal meeting. Motions were made, seconded, and eventually, polling took place. The final destinations on the ballot were Hawaii, Disneyland, or Washington, DC. Our nation's capital was the winner. Instead of celebrating, my heart filled with agony. I knew this entire exercise had been a scam I'd created to awaken my students' dying souls. So now what?

Chapter Thirty-one

When I arrived home that day after the vote, I fessed up to my wife, telling her that my kids now believed we were all going on a trip to Washington, DC. She thought I was totally insane. When I called Mel, he said I would be assassinated. Soon after, he called me back, asking me to meet him at school the next morning at six thirty. Then the phone started ringing off the hook with calls from elated parents wanting to know all about the trip. The kids had wasted no time in telling them. The families wanted me to plan a special evening meeting so everyone could get together and discuss this exciting venture. That night lying in bed, my eyes didn't close once.

The next morning, Mel was waiting for me in the parking lot. He said Dr. Vander wanted a conference with both of us. As I sat looking at Vander from across his desk, I'd never had such a long opportunity to observe "the king." He did not look well. His body seemed inflated and swollen, his face pale and sweaty. I was shocked to see that two of his front teeth were missing. Usually Vander spoke with his mouth partially shut, but today, it was wide open. He was so angry he trembled. He commanded Mel to speak for him.

"Mr. Carvajal," Mel began formally, "there is a policy in place that field trips are allowed only with prior consent of the administration. These field trips are restricted to a radius of fifty miles. This has been clearly defined."

I was surprised at Mel's official demeanor. He spoke in an icy cold, almost reprimanding tone, "I understand that not only have you neglected to get approval for this trip, but that you have already started sharing information about it with parents."

Dr. Vander interjected here, "How far are you in your doctoral studies? Do you realize how this could affect your program?"

I turned to Mel and asked him what this field trip had to do with my academic progress. He avoided my question, staying instead on the subject of the field trip. He had to prove his loyalty to his boss. He spoke to me but stared at Vander the entire time. "Dr. Vander wants you to call this whole thing off. It's not going to work."

"I'll have to keep my promise to the parents and get their input," I responded.

Vander jumped in, "Oh no, no, no, NO! You don't understand. The discussions stop right here and now." I really thought he was going to have a seizure. With some effort, he hoisted his prune-shaped body from his chair and stormed out the door.

As soon as Vander was out of sight, Mel turned and informed me that I was in deep shit. I looked out the window and saw my kids arriving one by one in front of the school. Tears began to roll down my cheeks. I wondered how I was going to mend the impossible situation I'd created. What had I been thinking? I'd managed to compromise the many good things I'd been able to accomplish with my class over the past year.

That day and for the week that followed, I could sense a shift in how I was regarded. I knew I had become the talk of the school among the staff and administration for all the wrong reasons. Even my university professors seemed to ignore me. My best advocate, Mel, was noticeably silent. He looked washed-out and unwell.

One early morning at 3:00 a.m., I jumped out of bed and told Joanie that I was taking the kids to DC during spring break—on my own time and our own dime. This way, it wouldn't technically be a school trip. I didn't have to ask permission from anyone as long as I had the consent and support of the parents. At that moment, I really believe my wife was ready to commit me to treatment for mental illness. The next evening, Joanie, Mel, Jane, and I schemed ways to raise money for the trip. With airfare and room accommodations, we figured each student would require about seven hundred dollars to bring along. We'd also need money for me and perhaps one other chaperone. We would, of course, need additional funds for meals and transportation, not to mention tours and entry into all the places we wanted to go. All told, we should ideally have about twenty thousand dollars for the trip. Raising this kind of money would be no easy task, but as far as I was concerned, it was possible. The next day during social studies, the topic I offered was "Leavin' on a Jet Plane." With the mamas and the papas playing in the background, I revealed to my class that the trip would be a go. The students erupted in elation. Their excitement could be felt across campus. The news spread like wildfire. By the following evening, almost every parent had approached me to share ideas about raising funds.

Talk about incorporating life experiences into our learning. Our math lessons began to focus on the concept of budgeting. Our history lessons covered the birth of our nation and its most influential presidents. Our reading lessons centered around the sites we would be seeing in DC. Each student was assigned a role in preparations for the trip. There were two treasurers, three social coordinators, and five public relations specialists. There were also students in charge of transportation planning, wardrobe considerations, and room assignments. It was a joyful time for us all.

As for fund-raising, however, reality soon set in. Two weeks of bake sales and raffles netted us $23.80. I could see the disillusionment on my students' faces as they counted our nickels and dimes each day. I couldn't keep my guilt at bay. I began to feel desperate for a solution. One day after class, I set out north from Greeley to Fort Collins, about thirty-five miles away, to ask financial advice from an acquaintance there. On my drive, I realized that in my distracted state I hadn't eaten all day. I stopped at a place called the Red Steer Restaurant in a little town called Eaton. My mind clouded in depression and hunger, I climbed onto a barstool and ordered a burger and a beer. The secluded dark atmosphere of the place suited me just fine. The bored bartender asked the usual uninteresting questions: "Where are you from? What brings you to town?" He simply wanted conversation. I took advantage of his cordial mood and, for some reason, spilled my guts to him, telling him all about my students, my promise to take them to Washington, DC, and my hopelessness about the whole situation. I told him that I was at the point of totally giving up since there was no way on earth to raise enough money.

As I was finishing my meal, a gentleman came and sat next to me at the bar, offering to buy me a beer. He said he'd overheard me talking. "I want to see if I can help out in some way," he said, asking me for my home address so he could send a donation. "Wow, sir, that's generous of you," I said gratefully. The bartender said he would also send a small donation. I left the restaurant feeling that people were generally good and that kindness was alive and well in Camelot.

The next morning as I was getting ready for school, I was still recalling my pleasant visit with total strangers at the Red Steer. Suddenly, I heard the roar of a big truck outside the house. I didn't think much of it until I was ready to go. I stepped onto the front porch and found a note on the door. The note read, "Good Luck and Best Wishes, from Kenny Monfort." Then I heard a *moo*. I peeked around into the backyard and couldn't believe my eyes: an enormous cow looked back at me. *Well, I'll be damned,* I thought. Mr. Ken Monfort, CEO of Monfort Beef in Greeley, had been the man I'd talked to the night before at the Red Steer. Monfort had practically put Greeley on the map, revolutionizing the beef-producing industry for the entire country.

Joanie was less impressed than I at our unique gift. "Take that smelly, noisy animal away before our landlady kicks us out," she commanded.

I didn't think I'd ever again take an animal to school after Jackie, but that morning, I walked the cow to the Lab School on a rope also donated by Mr. Monfort and parked it on the lawn outside our classroom. When my kids and the rest of the students in the school saw the enormous animal, they cheered. Then all hell broke loose. Five minutes after the cheering erupted, Mel called me over the school intercom. Vander wanted to see me. The conference was brief. Vander's toothless face was stone cold. "See this pencil here, Mr. Carnival," he said flatly. "It will be very sharp when I read your dissertation."

I knew I was finished. I just hoped I hadn't compromised Mel's career as well. He was much too genuine and noble to be punished for my mistakes.

That evening, I called the parents in for advice. I had 100 percent attendance. We talked through the situation as it stood. Their ideas were practical and brilliant. First and foremost, they agreed that the trip should be during spring break: they would give their permission without reservation. The next topic was our rather uncommon donation, now grazing on the Lab School playground. They suggested that we slaughter the cow and sell the meat. Harsh though it may sound, this was Greeley, prime ranch country, and beef was what cows were for. Being from a farm country myself, I saw this as a fine idea and one that exemplified the solidarity and motivation of our group. In fact, one of the students' fathers was a farmer and volunteered to properly slaughter the animal and butcher it. We decided we would then freeze the majority of the meat and later use it for a huge beef burrito fund-raiser.

After our cud-chewing friend met his noble end, we discovered we had a surplus of meat: much more than we could use for our cooking project. So we immediately organized an auction to allow our friends and supporters to bid on some of the fine—and not so fine—cuts of beef. All the kids were there. The bidders, who knew where the money was going, were extremely generous. The ears of the animal alone earned us one hundred dollars. The feet brought in two hundred dollars. The kids cheered and applauded, excited to see how well our group efforts were paying off. Finally, it was time to auction off the tail. One rancher, a relative of one of my students, bid three hundred dollars. The cheers grew louder and louder. Another rancher outbid him at five hundred dollars. The gavel came down, and the winner walked to the microphone, declaring that this was "the most expensive piece of tail" he'd ever had. The crowd roared with laughter. The kids, thank God, missed the innuendo.

Next on the agenda was to cook and sell the enormous amount of meat sitting in our freezer. Joanie and Jane went to work. They seasoned and partially cooked the beef in twenty-pound batches and set it in the refrigerator, ready to use in tacos and burritos. The kids then sold tickets around campus for our sit-down Mexican dinner, some even speaking in front of college classes about our project and goal. We then set up our inviting one-night restaurant and served the meals to everyone holding tickets.

As they determinedly plodded away with our fund-raisers, the kids continued to inventory our earnings with meticulous care each afternoon.

It wasn't long before they reported net earnings of $22,580! Our cow had been a godsend, not just for the funds that it generated, but for the renewed sense of purpose it gave us to get out into the community and acquire other private donations.

When Vander realized that the trip was actually becoming a reality, he insisted that we include his wife, son, and secretary as our guests using money out of our own budget. Not willing to rock the boat on this one, I complied, though the kids realized it was unfair. In spite of this, they excitedly planned our agenda and carefully considered what we'd need to take along. We had enough money to give each student a small stipend to buy essentials for the trip that they didn't have at home. School at this point was absolutely central to everything they did. Maria Montessori was right on: the thing is to teach what is relevant in the lives of students in a prepared environment.

The day I thought would never arrive finally did: we were scheduled to depart for Washington, DC. Mel was my right-hand man: he'd be coming along to help me manage the kids and everything else along the way. The Lab School teachers, professors on campus, and, of course, parents were all there to give us a warm and emotional send-off. Everyone was in tears: the parents, the students, Joanie, Jane, and me. It was a departure of mixed emotions: elation and anxiety. Most kids had never been away from home even for one night. I promised the parents that their children would call every evening. As for me, I felt my own nervousness about keeping everyone safe and accounted for in an unfamiliar big city. I needn't have worried. The kids were on their best behavior the entire time. Our agenda was jam-packed with the usual stops: the Capitol, the Washington Monument, the Lincoln Memorial, and the Smithsonian. But the highlight of the trip was our visit to the White House where we got to see firsthand where so many leaders of our country had lived and worked, making vital contributions in the direction of our country. Our excellent tour guide was very impressed by the courtesy and manners of our group. My students were proud of themselves, and I was beyond proud of them. Each evening, we'd go back to the hotel, eat our dinner, and, exhausted, tumble into bed by nine.

Chapter Thirty-two

When we returned from our triumphant tour of Washington, DC, the parents were elated to see their kids. That night, Jane and Joanie took Mel and me to our favorite restaurant for a well-earned homecoming dinner. Over our nice meal, however, Jane dropped a bomb on us: she had heard rumors that Dr. Vander would not renew my teaching contract for the following year and that my doctoral program had been terminated. I stepped out to vomit. My gut told me she was right. Though there had been nothing Vander could do to prevent the trip and though he had sent his family along for the ride, I could sense just before we'd left that his anger and resentment had reached a new height. But how could I possibly lose my job and any hope of reaching my educational goals all at the same time? The platitude suddenly seemed truer than not: when it rained, it poured.

One thing I was sure of was that Vander couldn't deny I'd finished my course work for the degree and even some additional electives. Nonetheless, that week, I went to the graduate school office to request an informal check on my credits for graduation. When I met with Mr. Rease, the dean of the graduate school, my worst fears were realized: he informed me that I was twenty-four quarter credits short of the requirements. What? How could this be? I had taken two four-credit classes each quarter for the past year. Rease said there was a clear policy: graduate students employed full-time are not allowed to take more than six credit hours each quarter. I explained that all the graduate classes offered were for only four credit hours, so logically, I would have taken two at a time. "Listen carefully to what I'm telling you," Rease said sternly. "You've violated the graduate school policies more than once." At this point, he took a pen, listed the classes I'd taken each quarter, and deducted two credits from each quarter. I felt my body jump with shock. "Dr. Rease," I said, the blood boiling in my veins, "you're telling me that I cannot graduate because I have too many hours, but that I have to take twenty-four more hours in order to graduate. Please explain the logic of this to me."

Rease simply pushed the huge directory of policies toward me across his desk, stood up, and walked out. Collin, Vander, and the rest of them had finally gotten their way: I was demolished. I left the building in the deepest despair and anguish I'd felt in my entire adult life. Yes, I'd experienced failure before, but now it was different: it wasn't just me who would be victimized—my family would too. The salary I'd hoped to make in higher education would have allowed me to start saving for my baby daughter's education. Now that dream might be taken away, and this was what hurt the most. All I could think was that it was time to leave town. Camelot smelled plainly of hypocrisy.

After summer vacation, I was excited to experience a new school year with my students. Unfortunately though, the turmoil over my program continued into the fall and winter months. The graduate school still refused to acknowledge my credits, and I continued to be convinced that, should I retake them, I would not be issued a passing grade on my comps. Regardless of the foulness that was going on with my career, I still enjoyed the Christmas lights with my daughter and was pleased with the time that we spent with family and friends that visited during the holidays. We hosted Ramón and his family for Christmas. "Are you all set to graduate with the highest degree you've ever wanted?" my brother asked proudly. "You've accomplished so much." It was unbearable. I could not bring myself to share with him the private hell that I was going through. What Vander was doing to me was cruel and unforgivable. I hated him and Collin. I wanted the earth to open up and swallow them both. The day my brother and his family left, I told Joanie that we had to leave or I would die. "There is absolutely no point in postponing the inevitable. We need to get out of here. Where? I don't know, but if I stay here one more month, I'll have a heart attack. Let's talk to someone about selling the house." Even Mel and Jane, who fought so hard to keep us in Greeley, shared our frustrations and agreed that we should probably make a new start somewhere else. For both my wife and I, it felt as if we'd sacrificed everything for a life that now meant nothing. We could have gone anywhere; we'd chosen to make a home in Greeley. Clearly, it had been a mistake.

Though every day now felt like torture, it was nighttime that scared me most. I couldn't sleep and would wander through the house: down to my basement office, then outside to the street, then back to my office again. One night when I'd finally managed to fall asleep in my office, I woke myself up sobbing and choking. Desperately, I got on my knees and prayed to the God I'd known since childhood, my patron saint Our Lady of Guadalupe, and all my guardian angels to help me. I surrendered my pain to them and pleaded for relief. I also prayed that they get the tyrant Vander out of my life so I could finish my program and then get the hell out of Greeley. I awoke in the morning to the sound of my precious daughter hungrily demanding her breakfast. I rushed up the stairs with tears still in my eyes. Joanie was already up. She invited me into her arms and consoled me. At that moment, I needed her more than Jennifer did. Suddenly, I felt relief sweep over me. Whether it was the prayers, the crying, or my wife's loving embrace, I felt a spark of hope that perhaps leaving Greeley would give us a new start as a family.

Two weeks to the day after my emotional breakdown, Jane called Joanie from the hospital where she worked and told her that Vander had been brought into the emergency room. He'd had a massive stroke while sitting at his beloved desk. The paramedics had whisked him away, but he'd been dead on arrival. In complete shock, I sank to my knees once again, this time with guilt in my soul. In my heart of hearts, I knew I was to blame. I was angry at my guardian angels for going overboard with my request to get Vander out of my life. I didn't necessarily want him to go that quickly or in that way, but he did.

To add an extra bit of irony to the situation, my class was asked to sing at Dr. Vander's funeral mass. They would perform two songs: "What I Did for Love" and "On a Clear Day." They were well prepared and knew the songs perfectly, having performed them on two other occasions. Their talented music teacher Mrs. Waterman taught them to feel the lyrics and music and sing with their hearts wide open. It was agreed upon that when it was time for the songs, I would go up with my students and introduce Mrs. Waterman before they began. When the moment came, however, my knees wouldn't stop shaking. I didn't think I could stand. My students looked at me anxiously, ready to follow me in their usual mode. They already knew where they needed to stand. I willed myself up, and we walked to the front of the congregation. Ms. Gibson's words years earlier echoed in my ears. "Look at your audience. Don't look into their eyes. Look at their foreheads, and you won't get as nervous. As you speak, turn your head from side to side so that it seems you are speaking to everyone. Imagine you're talking to a group of friends. Otherwise, the message will be lost."

The advice didn't help: after all, what message did I have? Standing up there, I scanned the room, meeting each attendee square in the eye. Everyone who was anyone in Greeley's academic circle was there: past and present college presidents, vice presidents, deans, members of the board of trustees, college faculty, and all the Lab School teachers. Everyone was in black. There were many tears, both real and phony. Mrs. Collin's wail could be heard above the crowd. I began, "Thank you for being here to celebrate Dr. Vander's life. Also, thank you for all the respect and admiration you've had for him." I felt like a hypocrite. I knew I had to shut up, or I'd be next to be struck dead. When the funeral service finally ended, and everyone headed for the nearby reception, my family, my students, and I slipped out the back door. Though guilt and confusion still lingered in my heart, the overwhelming emotion I felt was liberation.

For the next two weeks, I walked around shell shock. I know I showed up to school and taught my students, though I can't remember what. I asked Mel to take over my college classes temporarily. Then my guardian angels came through again, this time with a little more finesse. Dr. Kolstoe, a member of my doctoral committee, called to inform me that Rease had been advised to restructure my committee. Two weeks later, I was asked to attend a meeting with the new committee to review the status of my program. The meeting lasted forty-five minutes, and that's as long as it took to get me back on the road to graduation. I was instructed to retake my oral comprehensives, present my dissertation proposal, be ready to defend my dissertation in three months, and apply to graduate in five months. In a flood of relief and joy, I came home to share the news with Joanie. We celebrated with Mel and Jane over a steak dinner. Mel had reason to celebrate too: he would be graduating with a doctorate just one semester after me.

Then it was time to buckle down. On top of my other obligations, each day became a constant struggle to meet my deadlines for graduation. I had a lot of work to do on my dissertation and a limited time to do it. The topic I chose was the development of self-concept in children. Fortunately, I had already completed an enormous amount of research on the topic for the courses I had taken toward my second major in professional psychology. I worked on my dissertation night and day. My wife typed the first complete draft, and a professional typist did the final one.

Eventually, the day I had started to doubt would ever come was here: it was the morning of my graduation. I awoke to one of the most serene and beautiful cloudless skies I had ever seen. All that went through my head were my students' voices. "On a clear day, rise and look around you, and you'll see who you are . . ." I'd completed my task at last. I'd stumbled and fallen many times to get to this point. Now the coast was clear. At the ceremony, I waited and waited for my name to be called. When I finally heard it, my entire being lit up with pride. The moment had finally arrived. I walked across the stage, blew a kiss to my family, solidly shook hands with Dr. Rease, and thanked God for giving me the strength and fortitude to persevere through so many disappointments, setbacks, and difficult times. In retrospect, even the bad experiences now suddenly seemed significant and important. As I took my final steps across the stage, I was astounded by the thunder of applause and cheers coming from the bleachers of the stadium. My mother, brothers and sisters, my Dallas family, and my students—both from the college and the Lab School—roared so loudly that my tiny daughter recoiled in the arms of my wife. Little did she know that tomorrow would be a new day and a fresh beginning for the three of us. I could hear Mom's scolding words: "Tu siempre haces lo que te da la gana" (You always do whatever you feel like). This time, she must have been pleased that I'd done just that.

My students had more reason to celebrate: they too were graduating after completing their senior year. They had been my students for the last three years, and I was so proud of them as were their parents. They themselves were ecstatic. They had completed their own goals, meeting the requirements for graduation as defined by the state of Colorado and endorsed by the school board—or so I assumed. It wasn't until we were making preparations for the ceremony that I got a close look at the diploma they would be awarded. It verified their completion in a special education program, nothing more. Flying high from my own accomplishment, I was once again grounded by bitter reality. After so many years of being segregated from their peers, this was a final insult: none of my students would receive a legitimate high school diploma. There it was in black and white: they were being told in no uncertain terms that they were handicapped and always would be, lest they begin to think otherwise. This stigma imposed upon them would continue to denigrate them for the rest of their lives, and for that, I felt truly sorry.

Chapter Thirty-three

I could hardly believe it: I now had a doctorate degree in education. Reaching this personal and professional goal did feel good. However, I realized now that I was used to living my life in a state of turmoil. It never seemed to stop. I went from one struggle to the next, talking myself into believing that all that mattered was the attainment of the goals I had set for myself since leaving my placita years ago. Although these goals were definitely important and something of value to me, I had obstinately compromised my mental and physical health many times and in many situations in order to reach them. Only now did I begin to realize that perhaps my true search had never been for prestige, money, or titles: it had been for the thing that would truly make me feel complete and at peace with myself. All this time, I'd been looking for those elements in life that would complete me as a person. After all the years of looking, I finally found what this was for me: the blessings a family brings.

One by one they arrived. Jennifer first, setting the stage for the other two. Three and a half years after, we received our most precious Thanksgiving surprise, our next significant gift arrived—this time the week of Independence Day. The holiday was loved nowhere more than Greeley where preparations were made a whole year in advance for a huge rodeo, fair, parade, and fireworks show. All around town, the streets were lined with flags, balloons, and steamers in red, white, and blue. It was a special time when friends and family gathered to acknowledge and celebrate the many blessings and freedoms we enjoy living in America. Just two days before the Fourth of July, our second daughter, Carmelita, declared her freedom by arriving into the world. Our second precious daughter felt like wonderful compensation for the past few difficult years we'd endured. Carmelita also became a living baby-doll for Jennifer. From the moment we brought Carmelita home from the hospital, Jennifer rarely left her side, constantly looking over our shoulders and observing intently as we rocked, fed, bathed, and changed the new baby. All Jennifer wanted was to help and love Carmelita. For this reason, my nickname for my eldest daughter became Adore. Her constant loving care for her sister was so unique and endearing that, for me, Jennifer would remain Adore from then on.

For Carmelita's part, it didn't take her long to realize who her devoted nanny was. Very early on, every time the baby so much as heard Jennifer's voice, she would squeal and then peep in mock distress. Adore would, of course, run hurriedly to Joanie or me, urgently notifying us that the new baby was peeping. Thus, Carmelita's name became Peepers as far as I was concerned. Adore and Peepers: nothing and no one could match these treasures. My wife and I had been blessed.

One month after Carmelita arrived, my sister Maggie called to inform me that Mom was on her way to Colorado with all her belongings. The reasons for her relocation were twofold: she had decided that it was time to come live close to her granddaughters, and her physical condition was declining due to diabetes, which required close medical attention that she was not getting in San Jose. I immediately panicked and wondered if we had sufficient room in our home for Mom to live. I wondered if she would miss the rest of the family in California. I was also worried that she would not be able to adapt to the different climate of Colorado, especially the harsh winters. As in the case of many who have suddenly found themselves living with or close to their parents after years of autonomy, there was also an element of concern about how this would affect my own family's daily lives and routines. At any rate, Mom had made up her mind, so if you could call this a case of life giving us lemons, we would learn to make lemonade. And plenty of lemonade we made. Mom became our nanny for the girls. Joanie's part-time work as a pediatric nurse practitioner allowed her to be with the girls much of the time, but now Mom was available at the drop of a hat when Joanie and I needed to tend to our professional commitments or have a bit of social time with friends.

Soon after Mom arrived, we were able to purchase a small home for her just a few blocks from ours. She was elated. The girls now had someone very close by to spoil and love them like only grandparents can. And there was another advantage I'd never considered before: having Mom around exposed the girls to their roots in a culture they might not have known as fully otherwise. Each day, Mom soothed them with songs in Spanish, entertained them with Mexican folk tunes on the piano, and prepared them meals of tortillas, beans, and tamales, giving them an experience growing up that was richer than my wife and I could have done alone.

About two and a half years after Carmelita's debut, we gained our triple prize. Six years after I had first anticipated him, my son Marc Anthony was finally home. He was an instant celebrity. The poor guy never had a chance of escaping the smothering love of his sisters, grandma, mother, and father. Everyone had their own way of fawning over him: Adore took on the role of speech therapist, Peepers became his entertainer, and Grandma would hold and rock the boy endlessly until he was well past tired of being held. For as much thought as I put into the naming of my son, you wouldn't think he'd need a nickname, but I finally found the perfect one. A few years after Marc was born, Pope John Paul II visited Colorado. He was a man of God who connected to the hearts of many, teaching that there is no right way to pray, as long as you do, and that prayer, though it may take courage, is always possible. The enormous sense of jubilation and devotion felt during the pope's visit inspired many artists to express their love and appreciation for such a beloved holy man. One gifted musician composed a powerful song that spoke of the Pope's humanity, sincerity, and loving ways. The song was called "Amigo" (Friend). When I heard this artist perform the song, the lyrics seemed to speak to me not only of the pope, but about the gift of my own beloved son. And so, Marc became Amigo. He was the "friend" of the family and would remain so for all his growing-up years and beyond.

Now our household was complete, and Joanie and I marveled at the home of love, laughter, and new adventure we created as a family. This was contentment. My favorite pastime became playing pretend games with all three kids. We would climb onto the bed and pretend it was a huge boat. Hungry crocodiles and sharks circled all around, but we were safe on our vessel. Wearing a costume eye patch and holding a rubber dagger between my teeth, I would vow to my crew that nothing would ever harm them—not while I was around.

Chapter Thirty-four

I never knew a time when I didn't want to be a teacher. Maybe I was one before I was even born. When I started the How and Why Club for my siblings and friends all those years back, I somehow knew it would be a success. And from that first rudimentary act of playing educator, I knew my love for teaching would last forever. Since then I had thought many times about diverting my path to other careers, but I would invariably find myself once again surrounded by students. This pattern would continue.

By this time, I had completed ten years of teaching in the public school system and earned my doctorate in special education. Colorado State College was now known as the University of Northern Colorado (UNC), and I was invited to apply for a professorship in the College of Education of this newly transformed institution. That week, I was also offered a professorship at San Jose State University. The school that had terminated my major in education because of my "significant foreign accent" years ago now wanted me to teach its best and brightest. The irony wasn't lost on me. I thought about it for ten minutes and then declined.

Dr. Bruce Broderues, the dean of the College of Education at UNC, was honest and assertive in encouraging me to apply for the professorship in the School of Special Education, which would be a tenure-track position. He shared with me the evidence the university had already collected supporting my qualification: glowing comments from professors who had assigned their students to observe me at the Lab School and excellent letters of recommendation from the various school districts I'd worked in earlier in my career. I couldn't help but feel honored to be invited to join the faculty of the university, but the resentment I'd built up for the administration because of Vander and Rease was still fresh in my mind. Hadn't I just months earlier vowed to get the hell out of Greeley for good? Wasn't this the only way to ever put behind me the miserable times I'd recently lived through? For once in my life I had options: to stay or go. But which was the right choice? I discussed my quandary at length with my wife, my mentors, and my dearest friends, and finally realized that the positive factors of taking the position far outweighed the negative ones. Chief among the positives was that I would be a professor at one of the most prestigious schools in the nation in the area of teacher preparation. The choice to be at UNC was also the right one for my family. There was certainly progress to be made in Greeley in several areas, but it was also the place where we now had many friends and wonderful support. This was the place Joanie and I wanted to raise our children. When I finally agreed to the job, little did I know it would span the remaining thirty-four years of my educational career.

Many things ran through my mind the week I was solidifying my paperwork. For one thing, my new position would afford me the authority to teach and act with autonomy, free from the watchful eyes of secondary school administrators and skeptical teachers. I was particularly thrilled that for the first time in my teaching career, I would have the freedom to take breaks whenever I wished and even have lunch with my family or colleagues—no more mandatory lunch duty for me. This was too much happiness. Of course, when I finally signed on at UNC, I was not free from anxiety. By now I knew that each position and institution came with its own brand of bureaucracy and power play. But I could handle it; I thought I'd been through enough struggle throughout my education and in my professional career to know I could survive just about anything. I also convinced myself that the worst of it was over. *At my current level,* I thought, *the hurdles in store for me would be minimal.* Every hire document I signed assured me of the principles of shared governance and academic freedom at UNC. I felt energized in knowing that I was free to teach my students to recognize the political games that infest the educational system without asking for permission or forgiveness from anyone. It was important to me to alert this next generation of educators that although this profession was a noble one, they should be prepared to encounter arbitrary and capricious barriers from various sources and deal with them as they came. I shared plenty of examples with my students. They knew that my life experiences, both positive and negative, provided me with substantial and honest insight.

Perhaps one of the insights I continued to gain as I worked in higher education was that inflexible, singular philosophies simply don't last. I noticed that no matter who they were or what they stood for, deans in the College of Education didn't stay around too long. During my first four years as an assistant professor, we changed deans three times. Each of these leaders came with their individual biases and platitudes—their vision of the perfect teaching model. Each of them imposed their own definition of "quality" on their staff. Some stressed teaching while others believed principally in community service. Almost all believed their professors should publish at least one article per year. We didn't worry too much about each new model: we just waited for the next dean to come in and change the name of the game again. I usually complied with the publication expectations but chose to focus on the areas that I personally valued most as an educator: teaching, advisement, and service. Through the years, I managed to excel in all three.

The transformation of Colorado State College into UNC—a change that occurred right before I began my professorship—was not insignificant. It was the beginning of an extremely long and frustrating period in which the university struggled to define its new image. Colorado State College had been dedicated to the exclusive mission of teacher preparation, and for that, it had been nationally renowned. Now it would be a university with diverse departments and majors. Its clear focus would thus be blurred by multiple agendas that sought to accomplish everything and by awkward and clumsy mission statements that nobody accepted or even understood. The administration was bound and determined to change the profile of the university come hell or high water—even though the quest for identity seemed to grow more elusive with each change. As the institution morphed into something larger, some of the established programs were pared down or eliminated entirely. There was simply no room in the new budget model, the administration claimed. Over forty professors, most tenured, were unceremoniously fired—simply asked to clear out their offices, return their keys, and leave. So much for due process: what the lunatics in charge were doing seemed just as arbitrary and meaningless as any policies I'd lived through in the public school system.

The administration's tactics were simple and single-handed. The faculty was never brought into dialogue about anything that was going on, but merely had to suffer the casualties. Professional consensus in the spirit of shared governance was never on the agenda. As a result, disdain and anger among faculty and students echoed through every corner of the institution. Almost all agreed that the injustice and devastation brought upon the lost professors was unforgivable.

Unsurprisingly, in the months immediately following the loss of their jobs, quite a few professors suffered ill health—some even heart attacks. The stress and turmoil in their professional lives had to have been a contributing factor. Some didn't survive to witness the legal battles that lay ahead for the others. It took over ten years for the courts to render a decision in favor of the abused professors. Soon after, the university had to award these individuals for personal, financial, and emotional damages suffered as a result of their job termination. The university was censored by the American Association of University Professors for violating the tenured rights of professors. By that time, the damage had seeped through the moral fiber of the institution. Morale was at its lowest ebb. Complete trust and the spirit of good will could never be recaptured. I know in my heart that if the cluster of administrators who caused this devastation had realized the impact their decisions would have on the long-term image of the university, they would have more respectfully utilized the tenets of shared governance to find solutions instead of reacting so rashly and unfairly. The consideration of diverse input from the professors and students of the university could have saved the soul of the institution.

Though much of this was in the future, in that first year of my professorship, the atmosphere of change and chaos immediately became my new home. I already sensed that I would have to find ways of living within it. As anger and turmoil about the direction of the university mounted, the faculty attempted to insulate themselves by gravitating toward their respective corners and departments and not looking outside. The School of Special Education was no exception. During the next few years, we as faculty defined for ourselves the mission and values that would guide us if we were to survive. We chose our own leadership: those individuals who would guide us through difficult times, listen to our diverse perspectives, and support a respectful environment where we could openly dialogue, learn from each other, and sometimes agree to disagree. When directors were assigned to us by the upper administration who did not respect us or our mission, their stay was short lived. We nurtured a community built upon mutual respect and thoughtful regard for each other and for our students. Eventually, we also realized that the only way to truly protect the integrity of our special education division and still provide support to the university at large was to step out of our comfort zone and take part in university-wide committees, sharing our findings and perspectives with others. We realized that this was the only true way to avoid adding to the destructive blunders of the university, past and future.

As we developed the tenants of our division, the expectations for the faculty continued to evolve. Instruction, scholarly publication, and service on university, local, state, and national boards always played a role. Student advisement, unfortunately, was not regarded with the same importance. Though the requirement of posting and maintaining office hours was outlined multiple times in a professor's contract, it was never stressed as a priority by any administrator. As a result, plenty of offices were dark and empty most of the time. It was therefore mainly through my own prerogative that I consistently maintained my office hours and made myself available to students who needed advisement. I couldn't help but remember all the times I wasn't given the same counsel in my own education and the frustration and desperation that I'd felt as a result. I never wanted my students to feel that way. Thus, within the changing agendas of the UNC system, I made my place and my mark. And this is how the years passed.

Chapter Thirty-five

One day, four years after I started my career at UNC, I was sitting in my office reviewing a graduation application for one of my students when an apparition from the past appeared at my door. It was Peggy, my philosopher friend and student from the Lab School, standing there smiling at me. We embraced with genuine affection and immediately began recalling all the funny and joyful times we'd shared in our class. We remembered our weeks of fund-raising for Washington, DC and the poor, doomed cow I'd walked to school with me that day. We remembered all the fun we'd had on the trip. We laughed so hard we were soon in tears. Neighboring faculty looked in on us, curious to know what we were on and where they could get some. We talked and talked for the better part of an hour until Peggy finally came to the purpose of her visit.

"Dr. Carvajal," she said, suddenly serious, "I want to be a teacher like you. I want to work with kids like Larry and Debbie and Mark who need a lot of help, like you gave us. I want to teach them how to be nice people and how to be happy."

"Peggy, you've always impressed me and inspired me," I interrupted, eager to praise her. "You were always concerned about social issues. I remember you promising you would do anything you could to stop poverty and help children who were hungry. I also remember how you planned our budget for the trip to Washington. You were one of the best kids in my class."

But praise wasn't what Peggy had come to hear. "I'm not a kid anymore, Mr. Carvajal," she said with a twinge of disappointment in her voice. "I'm a woman—a person—who wants to be a teacher. Can you help me? Remember you always told us to believe in ourselves and that the sky was the limit? Do you remember? I remember you told us how you went to junior college and that there were people who helped you. I remember that then you went to another college where you broke Juliet's balcony. Then you said you finally went to another college and became a teacher. Do you remember?"

Peggy remembered it all better than I did myself, and as usual, her argument was passionate and persuasive. All the encouragement I'd given my students to fight for themselves and become whatever they wished was coming back at me. I was stunned. Peggy was challenging me to face up to my teachings and promises, and she was not about to let me off the hook.

"Yes, I remember, and I'm thankful you do too," I said, trying to gather my thoughts. Peggy was right: I had to live what I'd taught. I had to help. But she also needed to know the reality of the situation. "Peggy, listen very carefully to what I have to say," I began. "Yes, the first step is to enroll in junior college. Take the sixty hours of general education classes and complete the associate of arts degree. Once you've done that and have earned the credits you need to transfer to UNC, we'll talk about your admission."

I don't know why we think time can be measured by calendar months: sometimes it seems to go so much slower or faster. Before I knew it, Peggy was back at my office door, smiling and waving a large envelope at me. She had completed her associate of arts program with a GPA of 3.4. She wanted to know where and when to start her new program. Taken aback by her efficiency and not exactly sure what came next, I told her to enroll in nine hours at UNC the first semester, repeating three classes she'd taken at junior college—speech 101, English 101, and history 101—to make sure she had these concepts. If she passed each class with a grade of C, we would continue with her admission to the teacher education program. Telling her this, I could feel myself participating in the higher education game, making her jump through arbitrary hoops. Did I too want to slow her progress? I'd promised myself I'd never do this after all I'd endured as a student back in San Jose.

It hardly slowed Peggy down. One semester later, she appeared again at my door with a transcript indicating three Bs. I honestly didn't believe she would do so well. I felt surprised and then overwhelmed with guilt for not insisting she belonged in a mainstream classroom years ago. What in the world had we done to this individual? She was more determined and resilient than any student I'd known at UNC. I told Peggy I would process her application to the teacher education program, but that I couldn't be her teacher or advisor. She smiled and agreed.

"Peggy, I don't want anyone to say that I am giving you special treatment because . . ." I stopped. I was embarrassed and ashamed of my games. She was an intelligent and compassionate human being and had the right to pursue her dreams. The fact that we had cheated her for so many years was unforgivable.

Peggy followed my advice and stayed away from me. For two years, I didn't hear from her. As far as I knew, she was busy making her way through the program. Then one day, her mother called to make an appointment to see me. Mrs. Kinley had always been one of the most outstanding and supportive parents in my group. Her daughters were her top priority, and she showed it through her love and devotion. When we met, Mrs. Kinley informed me that Peggy's degree program was in danger of being terminated. Peggy had been asked to attend a conference with seven professors in the School of Special Education. Mrs. Kinley wanted me to be there. Not completely understanding the situation, I nonetheless told her I would definitely attend.

As we all sat around the table on the day of the conference, it became clear what was going on. Peggy was now involved in her clinical work for the program. Her clinical supervisor had been in this position for years and, in fact, remembered Peggy from her days as a student in my classroom for the educable mentally retarded at the Lab School. This supervisor had notified the rest of the department about Peggy's past. They acted as if they were exposing a dirty crime. All seven professors bombarded Peggy with a third-degree interrogation. "Where did you go to school?" they demanded. "Who was your teacher? What classes did you take in high school? Did you graduate? When?" I'd never seen any student subjected to this kind of scrutiny. I was in shock.

Understandably, during the interrogation, Peggy lost it. She broke down in tears and walked out. Mrs. Kinley and I followed. That was the end of the so-called conference. For all Peggy's determination and perseverance, it had come down to this. They had won. Soon after the meeting, the committee recommended the termination of Peggy's teaching program. For her efforts at UNC, Peggy would be awarded a nonteaching bachelor's degree. She would never realize her dream of becoming a certified teacher.

It is one thing to review and recommend the termination of a student's program after carefully considering the evidence. It is another to disregard the hard work and inarguable success of a student in light of mild learning challenges that the student has proven time and again she can overcome. But perhaps what bothered me most about the situation with Peggy was witnessing the way in which her program termination was handled. No one—not even struggling doctoral students—was ever subjected to the level of abuse as a student and as a person that Peggy endured that day. I vowed I would never be a part of this cruelty. And yet as a professor at this institution, I was implicated in it. As the months and years went by, I struggled with this: how could I tolerate being a part of a system that had been so brutally insensitive to Peggy and surely to others as well?

The spring break after Peggy's dismissal, I was eager to get as far away as possible from a campus that had already begun to show its ugly side. We decided to drive to Dallas as a family to see my brother Ramón and clan for a few days. I took everyone out to dinner to celebrate our reunion. My brother and his family were elated to see us. By this time, they'd added a new daughter to the family, Laura, who was around Jennifer's age. Ramón's girls were up to their usual fanciful games: they pretended they were going on a date with the most debonair guy in town. I played up the role by wearing plenty of cologne for them.

However, amidst the celebration, there was worry. My brother looked very unwell. He had lost a considerable amount of weight since I'd last seen him and looked tired and drawn. Mary Ellen seemed anxious. When she had a chance to speak with Joanie in private, she confided that Ramón was ill. He seemed to be struggling with a virus from which he couldn't recover. Though he didn't talk about it, on several occasions Mary Ellen had noticed blood in the bathroom after he'd used it. When Joanie shared this with me, I was gripped with worry. One evening, as the kids and I were planning a surprise night out for dinner, Ramón came in through the back door. When I reached out to embrace him, his body was cold and sweaty. He said he was exhausted after a long day at IBM and had to rest before dinner. He slept for four hours. Scratching our fancy dinner plans, we had a pizza party and later went out for ice cream.

On the drive back to Colorado, Joanie and I were consumed with worry about Ramón's health. Upon our return, I immediately called him. I simply wanted to hear from him exactly what was going on. He responded in his usual terse and macho way, saying that he was fine and that his sickness was no big deal. In reality, the situation was serious. A few weeks later, the family called with his diagnosis: colon cancer.

I returned to see Ramón several times after his diagnosis. The disease and the various procedures used to control its progression took a horrible toll on his body as the weeks went by. Seeing him suffer so profoundly, I begged him to get a second and third opinion on treatment. Each effort resulted in futility. Despite my denial, the end drew near. The week that would be his last, I sat at Ramón's bedside at the hospital. Tears streamed down his cheeks, but it was he who tried to console me. "Listen, bro, stop worrying. We sure had fun together. I always liked playing cards with you even though you're sneaky. *Eres muy chueco, hermano. Te quiero mucho* [You're very sneaky, brother. I love you a lot]. Yes, it's tough to leave my girls and this earth. Watch over them for me, will you? I don't want to go, but it's not up to me. *Lo que el señor mande. Todo está en sus manos* [Whatever the Lord decides. It is all in his hands]."

I left Dallas that week in the most profound agony I'd ever felt in my life. When I arrived home from the airport, I received the call. My dearest brother, terrific husband and beloved daddy, was dead. I immediately returned to Dallas for the funeral. His wife and daughters were inconsolable. I don't care what anybody tells us about grieving and healing. Perhaps we do move on, but a part of us goes with the person we loved. The day we buried Ramón, he took pieces of our hearts with him. His family would never completely heal from the loss. The loss of a loved one does, indeed, hurt forever.

Soon after my brother's death, I experienced another painful loss. My precious and loving cousin Estela also succumbed to cancer. During the days of our youth, there wasn't a person alive who could have broken the bond of our friendship. In our high school years—whether at school, the drive-in, or anywhere else—Estela was always by my side to advise me and look out for me. And as the years went by and we grew into adulthood, Estela continued to care for me and I for her. Though she remained in Texas, we kept in close touch. No matter what was going on, she always made me feel important and loved. She was my "Estela by Starlight," just like the jazz song.

During the last week of her life, Estela called me from Del Rio to say good-bye. "I'll be watching out for you, you hear!" she declared. We cried, and I told her I would miss her. I said that I wished she could find a cancer specialist in San Antonio. "Those fuckers don't know shit!" she yelled back in response. "My entire body's been burned by their fucking treatments. I swear my brain tumor grew daily from each damn one of them. Honey, Tony baloney, *becero* [calf], I'll be okay." Then in Spanish, she said, "God already has a set of huge beautiful wings ready for me. I'm ready to be in his arms. You are a beautiful and kind person. I am going to thank him for having placed you in my life and for having known you. I will wait for you until we meet again in the arms of our Father. For now, take care of yourself and know that I've always loved you, my dearest brother." Estela died three weeks later. I still think of her each time I happen upon a drive-in theater or see a huge bird flying overhead. Just like Ramón, Estela embraced her farewell from this earth with peaceful resignation and faith.

The loss of Ramón and Estela over such a short time challenged me to choose between succumbing to despair, depression, and isolation, or prioritizing my family and moving forward in the spirit of hopefulness, tenacity, and courage. I chose my family. Ramón would have expected this of me. Though he himself had struggled with his own depression at times, he had always come back to caring and loving his family. Estela too would not have wanted me to veer from my goals. And so I chose to continue my search for what would fulfill me and justify my part in this world—as a professional and as a person. Both my cousin and my brother also helped remind me that perhaps there was something greater—God's love—that would be with me no matter what happened.

But keeping faith in God or even in myself was not easy. Year after year, the policies and expectations set by the university—policies that were supposed to be important to me—struck me as trivial and uninspiring. I forced myself to comply with these meaningless standards but knew I also had to address the values that held meaning for me. I published enough in the academic field to comply with the requirements set for professors and ignored the rest. Teaching, student advisement, and community service were my passions, and pursuing these priorities was the only way I could personally continue to survive in higher education. These, beyond a doubt, were of utmost importance to me.

Having chosen to pursue these tenants of my work, doors started to open to more opportunities. I began to receive invitations to evaluate and consult on programs at universities or serve as a keynote speaker at academic gatherings throughout the world: Canada, Ireland, Ecuador, and Tunisia. These experiences provided me with the professional oxygen I absolutely needed, renewing my energy and vitality for my work. Similar engagements at universities and public schools throughout the United States also added welcome variety to my regular teaching schedule. After several years of rewarding travel, consulting, and speaking, it was time to add the next thing to my self-made professional agenda. I had to discover the next phase that would provide me with fresh challenges.

One afternoon, while I graded papers in my office, the president of the university Dr. Peter Hendrickson entered my office and asked if I had a few minutes to visit with him. I was shocked to see him and wondered what in the world I could do for him. He quickly came to the point of his visit: he had a professional opportunity to offer me. Dr. Hendrickson explained that he needed someone to serve as a buffer between the university faculty and himself. He confessed that the faculty was very upset with him, and he needed someone like me—whom they trusted and saw as a peer—to serve as a liaison in the role of executive assistant. I immediately agreed with him that the faculty had a negative perception of him and that he needed someone to help him with public relations. I also bluntly stated that I didn't think I was that person. Out of courtesy, however, I told him that I would consider his offer, discuss it with my family, and call him within a week's time. Immediately after receiving the invitation, I spoke with Mel and some of my other colleagues. I received mixed reactions. That evening, I talked with Joanie, who assured me that she would support me in whatever decision I made. The very next day, Hendrickson called me and requested an answer. I was afraid to let the prestigious position slip through my fingers. Against my better judgment and wisdom, I accepted.

I wasn't sure if this was the next phase that I had hoped for or not. My first year in the president's office was a socially and politically rewarding time for me. I did seem able to embrace my duty of garnering support for the administration. Though I was now juggling my role of administrator with a still-busy teaching load, I began to consider my position as executive assistant as a permanent career option. However, no sooner had I begun to feel these positive hints of fulfillment than I realized Hendrickson had more in store for me. With so much already on his plate, he was compelled to reassign me to other facets of administration that I definitely did not want to consider.

Just as I was growing impatient with my professional role, my guardian angels came forward. One of my esteemed colleagues from the University of Colorado, Steve, invited me to attend a luncheon hosted by the governor of Colorado. In attendance were educators and policy makers from around the state. That day in his talk, the governor addressed a topic that rattled the very core of my social conscience. He spoke of a crisis in our public schools: youth were dropping out at an alarming rate, leaving school and not returning. The subject was not new to me: I'd read about the intensity of the problem in professional journals, but it had mostly been theoretical. I, like many, had ignored it. I felt a twinge of shame for dismissing it as somebody else's problem.

After the governor's talk, I perked up and started rambling to the others at my table about the many ways we could address the problem. I observed how the teachers in my own high school had worked closely with their students' parents and the rest of the community, a model I'd adopted when I became a teacher. I was talking fast and furiously when suddenly the woman to my right addressed me. She was a finance officer in the governor's office. She said, looking at me intently, "We have unspent funds for innovative demonstration programs," she explained. "If you want to experiment with any idea you might have, I simply ask you to write me a two-page concept paper, and I'll get it approved. Ninety thousand dollars is not much, but it can get you started. So dream on, and send me a proposal and a place to deposit the funds." Steve kicked me so hard under the table that I wondered if I'd be able to walk again.

I was in total disbelief, but the finance officer was still talking, confirming what I'd thought I'd heard. "I promise we'll send you the start-up money if you promise you'll be serious and show us how you can develop a program that can address this awful situation. The governor is right. We have a crisis in our schools."

I couldn't help myself. I reached out and hugged her, kissing her cheek at least five times. Then in my joy, I turned to Steve and hugged him ten times harder, practically breaking his ribs. I had to get even for that kick.

On our way back to Greeley, Steve and I were ecstatic beyond belief. The barrio kid in me was on fire. I wanted to give these kids every opportunity I'd been given and many, many more. Just as my enthusiasm for education was running at low ebb, my awesome angels were back in action again.

Chapter Thirty-six

Steve and I immediately set to work designing our program for students in imminent danger of dropping out of school. It would embrace psychologist Bruno Bettelheim's philosophy that rigorous intervention was at times necessary to impact the development of a child. This might mean removing that child from his or her home setting for a period of time. We recognized that family dysfunction could be a contributor to school failure. If and when this dysfunction was acknowledged by the parents or other caregivers—and, if necessary, by social agencies and the courts—by mutual consent, the child would be removed from their home environment to participate in our program.

So Youth Opportunities Unlimited, or YOU, was born. In some ways, our residential program model was radical in concept. We would recruit fifty to sixty students in the age range of fourteen to fifteen to participate. They would live, carefully supervised, in the UNC dorms, and virtually, the entire program would be conducted on the UNC campus. This program would take place over eight weeks during the summer break.

We soon had a small staff in place to help us with all aspects of the program, from recruitment, to planning, to teaching and counseling. We recruited the participants by corresponding with school counselors from across the state that recommended students they believed would benefit from the program. These were individuals failing because of poor grades, poor attendance, and a generally poor attitude toward school. Some had already dropped out of school unofficially, some were on academic or court probation, still others had been declared runaways by their parents. A significant number of these individuals were involved with drugs and alcohol, cults, and gangs. Once the students were identified, Steve, myself, and the staff did the legwork of traveling around the state to meet with the candidates, their parents, and school counselors. During these visits, we clearly defined the nature of the program to them. Everyone's unconditional commitment was absolutely mandatory. For the part of the students, it was remarkable to see the level of acceptance they had to the idea of leaving home. They were eager to make changes in their lives and seemed to sense this was the only way to do it.

Our experimental program was designed to encourage students to stay in school through a series of structured academic and social experiences. Through these experiences, we would explore their affective reactions to situations and help them develop essential coping skills. The program components would include the following:

1. Courses in language arts and mathematics for which students would receive official high school credit
2. Recreational experiences including group sports and outdoor recreation, social events, and cultural activities involving music, dance, fine art, etc.
3. Work experience
4. Individual and group counseling sessions
5. A culminating activity to celebrate the accomplishments made during the program

As we chose students for the YOU program, Steve and I knew that the youth we would be dealing with fell into two basic categories. The first group was made up of individuals who chose to more or less opt out of the school environment. They were generally quiet about their disdain for teachers and school. They faked enough involvement in classes not to get noticed and attended school sporadically until enough absences accumulated to warrant their suspension. These students generally disappeared from school and were never heard of again. The second group was more disruptive in their school environment. They were usually in some way dangerous in that they placed the health and safety of their peers and teachers in jeopardy. These individuals were openly hostile. In many cases, they were members of gangs, cults, involved in drug culture, or engaging in criminal activity. Suspension of the members of this group often coincided with court action or arrest. They were transferred to detention centers, jail, or prison, and eventually returned to their communities in worse condition than they had left.

Members to these two groups had one thing in common: they lacked a viable social support system. Many experienced dysfunction in their families in the form of neglect, physical or sexual abuse, or alcoholism and drug addiction. Thus, they looked for social and emotional support from peers or fellow gang members who fed and encouraged dangerous behavior and their cycle of addictions. Schools were ill equipped to deal with these multifaceted issues. Teachers, stretched incredibly thin with their educational curriculum alone, had neither the time nor the training to provide a comprehensive social support system for students. That's simply how the system was. In our program, Steve, I, and our staff would be faced with the challenge of creating a new paradigm: one in which we were strong advocates for these kids as well as intercessors creating change in their extremely complex lives.

The dropout problem, once perceived to be exclusively an ethnic minority issue, has more recently been recognized as a problem affecting youth of all demographics. The problem transcends ethnicity, social class, and gender. We saw this firsthand in recruiting for our program. White, African American, and Latino students—both male and female—enrolled in YOU. Somewhere along the way, these young people had stopped believing in their dreams. They were waiting for someone or something to change their minds.

Steve and I carefully chose teachers and counselors, many of whom already worked within Greeley's school district. In addition, we'd recruited a team of mentors—mostly college students from UNC's education program—to supervise and provide personal support to the students as they went through their residential stay. Mimicking the role of a close and supportive family member, each mentor was assigned a small group of five or six students, lending emotional support to them during their time away from home. Along with hiring a talented staff, I recruited my own family to help with the program. Not only did this provide extra support for me, but it also helped them better understand and accept my level of emotional and sheer time commitment to the program that summer. I assigned Carmelita to be a tutor in math and language arts. Jennifer became a mentor for six of the girls in the program. Marc Anthony, who trained and competed in the city swim club, became a part-time swim coach for those who chose that sport as a recreational activity. For her part, Joanie, who still maintained her nursing position in Intensive Care at the local hospital, moonlighted as our "on call" nurse to fill in when our program nurse was not on duty. My entire family understood and supported my efforts, which eased the burden of my absenteeism from the household for those two months. I was legally notarized as a surrogate parent to the program participants that summer with all the rights and responsibilities that entailed. In a way, I took on about fifty extra kids, so I was delighted that my wife and "original" kids helped me to shoulder the burden.

Another thing that was of extreme importance and a learning process for me was how to gather all the support we needed from many individuals and local agencies in order to make our plans work. For one thing, we had to ensure that the academic credit we offered in the program would indeed transfer to the participants' individual schools. For this, we had to have the support of the local district superintendent Dr. Warren to ensure that the public schools were supportive of our agenda on both a state and local level. We were fortunate that this came to pass. Next, we needed the support of those at UNC where the program took place. For this, we acquired the backing of President Hendrickson. We sought the help of different divisions and facilities on campus in offering afternoon employment to our students, thus imparting the idea of professional responsibility and earning income through fair and honest work. These students would work as administrative helpers, child-care assistants, and in various other supportive roles in departments throughout the university.

Despite our best-laid plans, the first year of the YOU program was a nightmare from the very start. There were so many unknowns. When the parents and relatives arrived with the participants in front of the dorms on a Sunday afternoon, they briefly wished them luck and left them with me. Three staff members and I extended our welcome and gave the kids a brief orientation of the program schedule. We also gave them the rules and consequences as if they were listening. They were eager to meet their roommates and see their rooms so they could hang up their memorabilia and connect their boom boxes. The dorm was locked. Frantically, we summoned a dorm assistant to unlock the doors. Once inside, we discovered that the beds in every room lacked pillows and linens. The dorm managers had not been expecting us until the next day. To make matters worse, the university cafeteria was closed. I felt the sensation of real fear creeping into my soul. The most urgent matter was to find a place to feed fifty-five very hungry kids. I immediately called my wife, a seasoned pro in emergency situations. She told me that there was food at home for five kids. Not fifty.

Desperately, the staff of three and I assigned the kids to walk in clusters toward a nearby mall. Miraculously, Furr's Cafeteria was open for business and only a twenty-minute walk from the campus. When we arrived, I went in first and spoke to the manager, who was eager for business and thrilled to accommodate us—at least until he got a look at the group. He was shocked to see an army of over fifty kids begin to gorge their way through the line. They devoured every single scrap on the serving tables including all the desserts. They drank every drop of soda from the fountain machine. After the kids finished the meal, I humbly and nervously walked over to the manager and told him that I didn't have any money to pay for the meals. He was in shock and wondered if I was completely insane. He asked me to explain my absurd actions. I described for him our program and sadly outlined the evening's dilemmas, extending my deep apologies. I promised him with all my heart and soul that I would return the next morning with a university check to cover the expenses plus ample gratuity. I signed an invoice and left my name and the number for the UNC president's office. The manager accepted my assurances, and our group happily walked back to the dorm.

The first year of YOU gave us the opportunity to assess, review, and make changes for subsequent years of the program. However, in some ways, the second year was even more difficult than the first. This was the first time that the staff and I had to deal with kids heavily immersed in cults. We also had a few suicide attempts. Most of the emergency situations in the dorm occurred after midnight, and it was often essential to get the parties involved out of that environment immediately to properly address the situation. On several occasions, I had to take the kids to my home to support them and many times to pray for them. One night, a young woman named Rosie attempted to slash her wrists. She had heard from one of her siblings back home that her parents had permanently left the state without her. They had no intention of returning. That night, I sat with Rosie on the back porch of the house. The stillness of the summer night provided her with the time and space she needed to share her anguish with me.

"Tony, can I smoke? Rosie asked.

I thoughtlessly replied, "Absolutely, but only if you light one for me too."

She lit a cigarette for me. I inhaled very deeply. We smoked a second cigarette and a third and a fourth. I was getting sick. We spoke very few words.

"Wow, I didn't know you smoked," said Rosie. "Can you make rings of smoke?" I immediately replied, "No, I can't. One thing I do very well, though, is choke. Watch me."

She giggled and told me how silly I was. Then abruptly she asked, "Why do you do this?"

"Well, it's not my first smoke," I explained. "I used to smoke when I was in high school and college—"

Rosie interrupted. "No, I mean why do you want to take care of so many of us? We're just a bunch of crazy, stupid kids. I'm not the only one in the dorm who wants to end it all."

My heart stood still. I thought for a few moments.

She asked again, "Why do you want to take care of us? We don't give a shit about you or anyone else."

I had to respond. "You know . . . I don't know. I guess because I too have been lonely. That's how I felt after my dad died. I guess I feel that I could have been like so many of you. I don't know. No one has asked me that question. Time to call it a day—I mean a night. When Jennifer gets home from the dorm, she'll fix you a smoke—I mean a snack. Then you have to go to bed. She'll show you to your room. I know you'll feel better in the morning. Tomorrow is another year—I mean another day."

Rosie thought I was kidding. I was simply emotionally exhausted. Yet I also felt thankful to her for revealing to me something about myself—about what motivated me to try with these kids. For two days after that, Rosie stayed home with my daughter until she was ready to return to the dorm.

After that occurrence, my concerns for the care and safety of the YOU participants tripled. Several had attempted to escape the dorm after midnight while the night counselors slept. I developed a serious preoccupation for the kids' safety and worried that they would leave the facility and never be found. I came up with a temporary solution, however unreasonable. I decided to find a spot from which I could observe the dorm entrance. During the nighttime hours when another escape was most likely, I climbed a tall tree right across the lawn from the building and stayed there, keeping watch until two or three in the morning. I'd remain there long past the time when I saw the light in each room go out and until I felt sure that everyone had surrendered to sleep. I prayed that no one would learn of my ingenious sentry post. One Friday night, two weeks after I began this routine, I inadvertently fell asleep in my tree. Before I realized it, I was tumbling down and landed in front of a UNC night security guard. He warned me that I should stop the practice. I sought other methods of late-night supervision after that evening.

As our summers of YOU continued with a fresh group of kids each year, we worked within the model we had designed while gaining knowledge through trial, error, and experience. In the third year, we added a program that became an immediate success: an outdoor education experience. This included a ropes course, hiking, bonfires, and other team-bonding activities. One evening as everyone was gathered around the bonfire, one of the students, Becca, suddenly broke the stillness of the night with a song. Gently and pensively, she sang something that seemed to reach the hearts of each one of us.

Some say love, it is a river
That drowns the tender reed.
Some say love, it is a razor
That leaves the heart to bleed.
Some say love, it is a hunger,
An endless aching need.
I say love, it is a flower,
And you, it's only seed.

After Becca finished, I asked the kids to share their dreams. Becca immediately said that she wanted to be a singer. The group applauded her, and then others began to speak as well. The dreams they shared that evening, unbeknown to them or even to me at the time, would later be shared with friends and family during the graduation commencement. After the camping experience, the program changed: the kids had grown closer. I had made several attempts before to encourage the kids to bond with each other to no avail, but this experience was the thing that finally broke down the walls and remained most meaningful to them.

Miraculously, we survived our first two years of YOU intact. The program was a success. At the end of each summer, it was the responsibility of the mentors to prepare each student in their group for a formal graduation. The excitement was palpable as they accompanied the kids to purchase formal attire for this momentous event. We tried to make the graduation ceremony as special and memorable—as important—as any high school graduation ceremony. Counselors, teachers, parents, and extended families of the participants packed into the university's main ballroom to celebrate the accomplishments of their sons and daughters. Certificates of completion were presented by none other than the president of UNC himself. Some students gave testimonials and recognized the people who had helped them succeed. The ceremony always culminated in a song sung by the whole YOU group: "The Wind beneath My Wings." Chosen the first year by the students themselves, it became the theme song of the program, adopted by each group in the subsequent summers of the program.

At the end of YOU's five-year run, 339 students had enrolled and participated. Of these, 325 had successfully completed the program. In a follow-up study of the population, we were delighted to find that 285 of the students who completed the program actually returned to their home schools and graduated from high school. Twenty-one of these high school graduates went on to complete a four-year college degree. Their areas of focus included counseling, teaching, nursing, business, criminal justice, and journalism.

Directing a program of this magnitude was an extremely complex and strenuous task. It really did take an entire village. It didn't succeed at every turn, but adjusted and improved with its setbacks. This program stretched me, Steve, and the entire staff to our limits and beyond. But in the end, it was well worth it. We accomplished what we set out to accomplish. We wanted to give a group of individuals the chance to actually feel the sensation of success in their lives. We hoped this would ultimately change their minds about school and move them forward with new attitudes and refreshed commitment. I know we accomplished that. In turn, they taught us that despite the odds stacked against them, they were courageous and beautiful. It was through their effort and willingness to rise to our challenge that the program initially succeeded and continued to thrive. We became their leaders and possibly their heroes, but they were the wind beneath our wings.

Part Six:
Necessary Losses

We strive to integrate a wiser, more seasoned middle-aged self with the youthful zest of the self we are leaving behind. But in spite of our youthful zest, we will have to let go—of our earlier self image. Our season is autumn; our springtime and summer are done. And in spite of the calendar imagery, we won't—whenever we reach the end—get to run through the seasons all over again. Nor can we stop time.

—Judith Viorst, *Necessary Losses*

Chapter Thirty-seven

As the YOU program drew to a close five years after it began, I experienced the darkest period in my life. By this time, my mom's health had drastically deteriorated. Though she'd been living with type 2 diabetes for thirty years, it was now taking a systemic toll on her body. Kidney failure and complications from poor circulation in her legs were chief among these problems. It was evident that her condition would be terminal. A year before, we had moved Mom from her own senior citizen apartment complex to our home so we could better care for her. I knew her end was near during the last summer of the program. The fear I felt about losing her, as well as suddenly having to confront the reality that life does end for all of us, haunted me day and night. I became preoccupied about my own health and the health of my children because of the genetic influence of diabetes in the family. Anticipating Mom's death, I also began to feel again the same terrible agony and despondence I'd experienced the day of my dad's funeral when everyone had returned home, but he was no longer there.

It was very difficult to see Mom struggle to come to terms with the graveness of her illness. Unlike Ramón and Estela, she could not accept the fact that she was very ill. To her, illness had always been a personal weakness—the result of carelessness or disregard for one's own health. How, then, had she deserved this infirmity when she had always tried to stay fastidiously healthy? Her body was betraying her, and this, coupled with the sheer physical toxicity that was building up in her body, kept her in a state of anger and agitation. She placed the burden of these emotions onto me and my wife as her caregivers: now it was we who were responsible for her well-being or lack of it. Conflicted, Mom tried to embrace the principles of her Catholic faith. She spoke often about our lives being under God's control. Many times, I heard her say, "Que se haga la voluntad de Dios. Lo que el Señor mande. Todo está en las manos de nuestro Señor" (May the will of God be done. Whatever He commands. It is all in His hands.). Grappling with these contradictions about what she'd believed all her life, Mom became even more desperate and antagonistic.

As the disease progressed and Mom's health diminished, our situation at home worsened. As Joanie and I struggled to attend to Mom's health and emotional needs, communication and shared time between us and with the rest of the family fell by the wayside. Our professional commitments, not to mention personal ones, were subjugated to the task at hand. The severe emotional and energetic drain of taking care of Mom day in and day out definitely took its toll on everyone. Eventually, it became difficult even from a medical standpoint and even with her private nurse Joanie to attend to Mom's needs. As the weeks passed and she began to show serious deterioration, I tentatively suggested to Mom that perhaps having her stay in a nursing home would ensure she got the best care twenty-four hours a day. The idea shocked and repulsed her. She immediately let me know what she thought of the idea. "Esos lugares son para gringos. ¡Idiota! ¡Mendigo! ¡Mal agradecido! Me vas a correr de tu casa. Hablame a mi familia. Tu eres un pendejo que no vale nada" (Those places are for gringos. You ungrateful, worthless idiot! You're throwing me out of your home. Call my family. You're an idiot and worth nothing.). After that, I learned to never again mention the idea of a nursing home to Mom. I promised her she would stay with us.

After that bewildering summer, I was stretched to my breaking point. Even without the responsibility of taking care of Mom, I'd taken on too much. My mornings were spent teaching two classes at the university. In the afternoon, I had to attend to my responsibilities as executive assistant to the president. Perhaps this schedule would have worked if at this point I could have kept out of the day-to-day operations of the YOU program. But I was still rushing to put out fires every day. Because Joanie worked nights, I strove to be there for my own kids while constantly rushing back and forth to campus. Even after everyone else had gone to bed, Mom needed care. Still harboring resentment about my suggestion of the nursing home, she would barely talk to me anymore. By this time, her foot had become gangrenous. She was in so much pain that she couldn't sleep. Her moans and groans of agony were unbearable. She would scream with pain, demanding her medication and her own doctor. I would run to her room downstairs and try to placate her. I'd administer her pain medication. I'd promise her that Joanie would see her in the morning. Mom had no choice but to accept the medication, but then told me to stay away from her. Though she was under the care of one of the best nephrologists in the state, she demanded to be seen by someone new: someone who knew what they were doing. Even on nights when I may have drifted off to sleep without interruption for at least a couple of hours, gripping fear kept me awake: fear that Mom would have a major setback that killed her.

Mom's pain medication—a combination of morphine and tranquilizers—was the only thing that offered her some relief from the overwhelming pain caused by the gangrene. I administered her dosages to the letter. As the ward of her medicines when Joanie was not there, I witnessed their calming effect. One night, I cleverly prepared for myself a cocktail of morphine, tranquilizers, aspirin, and vodka. I too needed soothing. Almost immediately, it took the edge off my personal hell. The next day, I walked around like a mellow-yellow robot with pleasantly weak batteries, feeling like I could fake a healthy existence for the first time all summer. The effect seemed so helpful, in fact, that it became routine. I would pop a few pills with vodka in the evenings and sometimes in the mornings before my workday began. In this way, I floated through the last few weeks of YOU and continued my new very private rituals in the months that followed.

As August turned into September, it became clear that we simply couldn't continue treating Mom at home. One morning, when Joanie returned from work at the hospital, I told her we had to surrender. Mom had to have round-the-clock attention that we simply weren't equipped to provide. We talked about checking her into the hospital, but when we consulted her doctor, he advised against it. There was nothing at this point that they could do for her there. At least in a nursing home she'd have the care she needed to live out her final days in as much peace and as little pain as possible. Angry and unreasonable, Mom fought us obstinately, insisting on a new doctor who would treat her at home. But her kidneys were simply shutting down. One evening, she seemed at her lowest ebb. We called our parish priest, who came to the house to give her last rites. She survived the night and seemed to stabilize slightly, but our decision was made. We packed up Mom's belongings and prepared her for transport to the nursing home. Knowing that she'd fight us tooth and nail if she knew the truth, I lied, reassuring her that we were going to the hospital where a new doctor would be looking after her. After she was comfortably settled in the nursing home and we'd gone home, it dawned on her that she was not in the hospital for a temporary stay at all. She demanded that the staff let her call us at home, and she did so repeatedly, vehemently demanding that we get her out and bring her home. She screamed at me violently, accusing me of lying and betraying her. Yes, I did lie to her. That was the only way I could get her the medical care she needed. The doctors would not recommend admission to the hospital. I didn't know what to do. I trembled as I told Mom that I was on my way to get her. But I'd lied again. I was not on my way to the nursing home: I was on my way to the bathroom cabinet for some leftover morphine to alleviate the guilt.

Two days later, I returned to the nursing home to visit Mom. "¡Vete!" she shouted. "¡Me traicionastes! ¡Vete!" (You betrayed me! Go!). When my brothers and sisters arrived to be with her during what would be the last week of her life, Mom allowed them in, but she refused to see or acknowledge me in any way. She left this earth gripping and scratching to keep hold of life and refusing to show any hints of love or forgiveness for me. It was early November when Mom finally passed away. Her funeral fell on my son's birthday. In the commotion of everyone getting to the church for the memorial service, his dog Sammy escaped from the yard and was hit by a truck. It was the darkest of days. Leaving the reception to rush the animal to the veterinarian, I prayed for divine intervention. But unlike the day of my dad's funeral, I felt no messages beaming down on me from the sky. My guardian angels had abandoned me.

I tried to talk myself into believing the faithful words I'd heard Mom use so many times in the past: "God helps us during our darkest times. Strong people don't fall apart when things fall apart. Only loss of faith makes us weak." She had convinced me that faith gave us both outer and inner strength, and that with it, nothing could tumble us. She'd spoken of God's mercy and his promise of eternal life. The week of her death, I doubted all of it. In the end, Mom herself had refused to accept God's will. Was there sense to any of it? I prayed from the very depths of my soul for an answer. None came. There was nothing to do but acknowledge my terrible pain and eventually face my own inevitable demise. Like so many times in the past, I told myself, I would confront these realities and move forward. Only this time I couldn't move forward: I had lost control.

The first few weeks after Mom's death were dark and confusing, and although I was in some ways now removed from constant crisis mode, I continued, in my pain, to drink and self-medicate. Yet somewhere, a voice inside me—a voice that still wanted me to survive and care for myself—told me flatly that I needed to find help. Admitting this vulnerability to my wife was difficult, but I think on some level she was relieved to be let in on the situation and see me relinquish my superman complex for once. Being honest and straightforward with my children about my problem and my intention to seek treatment was emotional and scary, but they too were behind me.

A thirty-day residential treatment center nestled in the beautiful Rocky Mountains helped to put Humpty Dumpty back together again. But it wasn't as simple as I'd guessed. I walked in with my titles of professor, director, and administrator and figured I could define and control my own treatment. Meeting with my assigned therapist for the first time, I outlined what I was sure I needed to discuss: all the people who'd contributed to my problems. There was Mom, Dad, and others in my family. There were also friends, acquaintances, colleagues, professors, and teachers all the way back to Ms. Quack Quack. The therapist simply gazed at me with a frozen look. She told me that my plan would start with me and end with me. Period. And that's how it was. Day in and day out, my sessions centered on me, myself, and I: what I thought, felt, and believed. In addition to individual therapy, I had group therapy, spiritual guidance, plenty of time outdoors to exercise, and three healthy meals a day. As time progressed and I got comfortable with those around me, I was surprised to encounter so many people from all walks of life who'd suffered serious setbacks and needed space to heal. I learned from their courage and resiliency and was inspired by their honesty, strength, and unconditional friendship.

The day before I was to receive my clean bill of health from the medical staff and go home, I and the other participants in treatment were required to write a farewell letter to anyone who'd been in our lives. For this letter, I had to explain to this person what I believed he or she had left me—what legacy in my life. I chose to write my letter to Mom. In it, I recognized her for her amazing courage and love for all her children. I knew she had raised all of us the only way she could and with whatever means she had. When thinking of Mom, one memory began to emerge in my mind: the memory of a song I heard her sing and play on the piano after her own mother's death. As I wrote down the lyrics I suddenly remembered so well, I was now addressing my own mom:

> ¿Donde estás corazón?
> No oigo tu palpitar.
> Es tan grande el dolor
> Que no puedo llorar.
> Yo quisiera llorar
> Y no tengo más llanto.
> La quería yo tanto y se fue
> Para no retornar.

> (Where are you, my heart?
> I don't hear you beat.
> So great is my pain
> That I can't even cry.
> I wish I could cry
> But I have no more tears.
> I loved her so much and she left me
> Never to return again.)

At the time of his or her release, each person in the program was required to read to the entire group the letter he or she had written. Afterward, we all walked outside and sat in a circle. We were instructed to place the letters inside an urn, place the urn in the center of the circle, and speak words of farewell. I expressed my farewell to Mom, thanking her for the love, guidance, and support she'd given me all the years of my life. I pleaded for forgiveness for having betrayed her and for my lack of understanding and patience. I told her I was sorry for being such an ungrateful son and asked her to ask God to forgive me. After this ritual, we were instructed to burn the letters. Then one by one, we silently walked away.

The years following my treatment were healing years. In them, I continued on my path of recovery and learned to nurture peace and acceptance for myself. With these new insights, I spent my last fifteen years at UNC. When I wrote my letter of intent to retire, I was truly shocked that I had been in the field of education for forty-three years: nine years in the public schools and thirty-four years in higher education. The afternoon I submitted my letter, I looked around my empty office and wondered, with surprise and awe, where the years had gone. I knew it would feel strange to never again hold office hours, walk these halls, or teach in the lecture rooms I'd used for so many years. I walked into one of these rooms: the very one where I'd given my first lecture thirty-four years ago. I sat at the front, pretending that my last class would soon be arriving and wondering what my last lecture would contain. I remembered everything so well. I remembered the hundreds upon hundreds of students who'd shared with me their loving dedication to teaching children. Each of the papers they'd written and discussions we'd had demonstrated their inspiring and sincere commitment to youth. At the end of each semester, they would honor me with simple but meaningful gestures of appreciation for my guidance and advice and for the impact they said I'd had on their lives and in their hearts. I remembered not only my undergraduate students, but also my graduate students as well, who stalwartly forged through their programs though many traveled far distances from home to campus and juggled school with their demanding teaching jobs and family lives. For evening classes, I had often enjoyed greeting them with snacks and soft drinks, which were enthusiastically received. The cleaning staff had reported me more than once for leaving food crumbs around the room. As my mind became blurred with memories of so many talented scholars and dear students, I suddenly felt a surge of loneliness. The thought of what I was leaving behind caused my heart to ache: it wasn't just a metaphor—it was a physical sensation. I murmured a prayer of thanks for the many ways my students had shared their dreams and aspirations with me over so many years. I would not forget them. I could have stayed there in my reverie for much longer, but the cleaning crew came in to prepare the room for the evening classes. I left hoping they had not seen my tears.

On the way back to my office, I was met by several students and colleagues who had already heard the news. Embraces and best wishes, even though expressed with sincerity, were difficult to accept. I was partly in denial that I had actually thrown in the towel. On the other hand, I felt somehow embarrassed that perhaps I had already stayed too long. With all the people coming at me with the best of intentions, I only wanted to run and hide somewhere and never return.

The last week of my final semester, a group of my colleagues from the university planned a retirement party for me at one of their homes. I was flattered and knew this would be an occasion for everyone to express their well wishes and finalize my leaving. Nonetheless, I found myself dreading the occasion: the idea of this formal good-bye was more than I thought I could take. Joanie tried to soothe my anxiety and remind me that this would be a wonderful way to say thank you and, in a sense, good-bye to special people who had been part of my life for so many years. As the night of the party neared, I found myself thinking about all the genuine and respected teachers and friends who'd passed thought my life, giving me immense support and strength over the years. I also thought about the many dear colleagues who had left before me: some who had died, some who had retired, some who had left for new work ventures. I mulled over these memories with an overwhelming sense of gratitude.

The evening of my retirement party turned out to be superb. My friends had procured an old chair from some flea market and painted it entirely in gold. I had to sit on this golden thrown wearing a specially decorated and bejeweled crown. Then the toasting and roasting began. True to my taste, there were a lot of laughs. There were also meaningful testimonials from people that came from the depths of their souls. I knew I would be terribly lonely not seeing them.

And I was. The first days and weeks after leaving UNC felt unbearably empty. I worried that I'd be unable to adapt to the void. Advice and encouragement came at me from all corners: "Now you're free to travel whenever you want. Now you can open a private school and replicate the YOU program. You should open a restaurant—you'd be a natural. You should lecture all over the world." Only half-jokingly, Joanie suggested I use my green thumb and love of gardening to volunteer as a groundskeeper at the church. "You're still too young to just sit around and do nothing," everyone said in one form or another. Some comments made me realize I was really in trouble. "The folks who hand out shopping carts at WalMart really do provide a rare and most appreciated service." For heaven's sakes! Where was I supposed to turn?

The hopelessness and depression evoked by such mostly unsolicited advice took me back to the agony experienced by Willy Loman in *The Death of a Salesman*. At the time I first read that tragic drama, little did I truly understand what the author was attempting to articulate. I vaguely remember how terribly sad I'd felt for Willy after his company threw him out like an old shoe. At least I had walked away with a comfortable retirement fund, a refurbished golden chair, and a glorified Burger King hat. Poor Willy had never experienced the gestures of love, affirmation, and appreciation that my colleagues had demonstrated to me. And yet Mr. Loman and I did have one thing in common: we were both unemployed. My task was to find something else—something of value to me and me alone—to fill my days.

Chapter Thirty-eight

It took me weeks and months after retirement to realize that perhaps there was no singular thing that would fill my every thought and need in my postretirement years. I'd been so focused on accomplishments throughout my life, but my realizations in the years since treatment helped me focus not just on these goals, but on myself—what brought joy and meaning to *me*. Slowly, I began to see that I could wake up in the morning and do exactly what I wished. I'd have coffee and read the paper, then go outside and tend to the lawn and my garden of flowers and vegetables. I could invite old or new friends over for lunch, then go for a swim or a walk. I could have dinner with my wife and take off on a whim to the movies: I still loved seeing anything and everything, and luckily, she did too. There were always opportunities to help at the church or with charities around town. There were political campaigns to support. There were fishing trips and poker nights with buddies. There were parties to plan at home and plenty of family to visit. Delightedly, Joanie and I welcomed two amazing, energetic grandkids onto the scene: the daughter and son of my Adore. Needless to say, we visited them every chance we got. To my surprise, invitations for speaking engagements continued to arise that challenged me to define the essence of what I had learned in my professional and personal life. These projects helped propel me forward with meaning and purpose.

In this way, my life began to fill with just as much richness as it ever had. Despite myself, I was actually enjoying retirement. However, one day, I received sudden and tragic news: my brother Joe—José—had passed away in San Jose. Diabetes, the same disease that had ravaged the health of my mother and grandmother, took his life too. His disease had been aggravated by decades of alcoholism: the legacy of my father. He had never received help for it but rather lived his life with it. Bouts of severe alcohol abuse and the accompanying violent behavior wreaked havoc on his relationships, including several of his marriages. I was asked to arrange his memorial service and say the eulogy. It was difficult to prepare words of praise for my brother. When I tried to put pen to paper, my thoughts turned to his explosive temper, his many broken relationships, and his self-centeredness. I chose to reframe my thinking and trace his life, stage by stage, to identify its positive aspects. Joe, also known as Prieto (dark skin), had multiple dimensions: a Pat Boone sunny side, a James Bond ladies' man/hero side, and a "Don't Mess with Texas" bruiser side. When you were with him, it was difficult to gauge which persona would surface. Perhaps all of us display similar multiple dimensions throughout our days and lives. Usually our best side can thrive when life is at its best. In Joe's case, this was early on—when my father was still alive. Because of his incredible athletic ability, Joe was admired by the entire barrio. More importantly, he was my dad's super-duper glorified hero. Dad and his cantina buddies would bet on his football games and boxing matches, and the losers—the ones who'd bet against Joe, of course—would have to buy drinks for the entire bar. Considered "most handsome" in his class, a different type of admiration also poured in: from girls. It was endless. I worshipped my brother and was proud of him. My dream was to someday be just like him.

But Joe's life changed the day my father died. Fed by anger and surely grief, the darkest side of my brother evolved. He beat on anyone who crossed his path, including his friends and brothers. He was in constant battle with each and every person who he felt was at odds with him. If you so much as showed a hint of disagreement with him, he would remove your teeth, plain and simple. I wish Ramón would have known this. The fact that he'd often been Joe's punching bag was nothing personal: Ramón was simply there. I know because, after Ramón left, I became a punching bag too. I only fared slightly better because of how skinny and scrawny I was: Joe knew I couldn't physically survive as much abuse. Instead, he mostly ordered me around. I was to be at his beck and call whenever he wished or be blasted with verbal insults or threatened with physical harm. I remember only two major belting traumas. One time I came home three hours after my curfew and Joe made it his business to "discipline" me. The other time I mistakenly clipped one of his toenails too close and made his toe bleed. After that, I learned how to perform pedicures to professional standards.

I may not have had much appreciation for Joe's bruiser side, but I was always envious of his ease with women. He could entice girls, court them, love them, and then leave them. The cycle seemed to be at an end when he met the princess of his life: Dora, with whom he had three children. When they divorced, three more marriages and numerous other children followed. With the exception of Dora and her family, I didn't know these ex-wives and children well, but seeing them at the funeral made me realize how profoundly my brother had affected their lives. Just as I had seen Joe as a James Bond hero in my younger years, I now realized he had also shown this side to his children. They had grown up to admire and respect him in spite of his chaotic ways and seemingly tragic flaws. Despite it all, he had been deeply loved by these children, ex-wives, and our entire family. The memorial service helped us forgive his transgressions and remember the goodness in him. One thing you could certainly say about Joe was that he was never one to shy away from life. He lived it fully. This came across in all the astoundingly heartfelt and beautiful testimonials spoken that day.

Conclusion:
On Becoming a Person

And while it takes courage to achieve greatness, it takes more courage to find fulfillment in being ordinary. For the joys that last have little relationship to achievement, to standing one step higher on the victory platform. What is the adventure of being ordinary? It is daring to love just for the pleasure of giving it away. It is venturing to give new life and to nurture it to maturity. It is working hard for the pure joy of being tired at the end of the day. It is caring and sharing and loving.

—Marilyn Thomsen

The ultimate challenge to define the person I had finally become began just two months after my retirement. Seeming to come just when I needed it most, an opportunity arose that would help shape the next phase of my life. One day, I received an invitation to my fiftieth high school reunion. I considered not going, but I was asked to make the closing remarks at the end of the celebration. I felt compelled to attend.

It turned out to be a wonderful celebration at which I got to see many old friends and reconnect with longtime buddies like Arturo and Robert. At the close of the evening, I made my brief remarks in the spirit of our beautiful early years together in our hometown. As my former classmates and I said our farewells, many challenged me to write a book about our early days in

Del Rio. On my way to the airport to catch a flight home, the idea wouldn't leave my head. But the thought of preparing a narrative that reached back fifty or more years into the past seemed too much of a challenge. Not only that, but making sense of this time in light of all the ensuing years of life experience seemed overwhelming and impossible.

When I arrived back home, I shared the idea with my wife and one of my best friends Jason. They immediately received it with enthusiasm and encouragement. This inspired me to begin ruminating upon and writing a narrative that would become the early part of *Essential Moments*. After nine months of writing, I received another invitation. This time, it was to be the keynote speaker for a community formal event—a Black and White Ball—to be held in Del Rio. The event coordinator asked that my speech be about my personal and professional journey and ultimate success since leaving my dear placita. The opportunity seemed almost prophetic in its timing: much for the material for my presentation was already on the printed page. I knew Ramón, Estela, Mom, and Joe were all plugging for me. They were guiding my path. It seemed that they never gave up on me. I accepted the invitation with a rapidly beating heart: flattered, excited, and already wondering if I could pull it off.

Preparing for the speech presented an excellent opportunity and challenge to broaden my perspective. I wanted to share lessons learned throughout my life in the speech and also in what was evolving into a comprehensive written memoir. My heart was beating again. The planning inspired me to continue identifying for myself the many dreams and disappointments I'd experienced from the time I was five years old to the present. The more complex and ambitious the dreams, it seemed, the more room for failure. I had dreamed of becoming a famous musician and singer, a renowned artist, a pro football player, an Olympic swimmer, a traveler to every corner of the world, a fabulously wealthy man, a teacher, a husband, and a father. In my naiveté, I just knew I was destined for indisputable greatness. Only three of these dreams actually became reality, but what truly great things they turned out to be.

I recalled the specific times when some of my dreams had fizzled and died, and others had evolved and flourished. I thought about my first teaching experience leading the How and Why Club and my wonderful, obedient students whom I rewarded generously with roly-pollies. It was my first inkling of a lifelong passion for education. Each of these memories took me back to my home, my placita, and my river. Sentimental thoughts of my mom and dad, my beloved siblings, great friends, outstanding teachers, and other dear and meaningful people of my barrio swept over me.

The day I arrived in my hometown, Joanie and I joined some of my high school friends on a walk on the bank of my river. Next we walked into my placita, still thriving after all this time—its historic value carefully preserved. I climbed the steps to the gazebo that still stood in the center of it all, imagining myself to be the singer on a day of celebration long ago past, ready to entertain the eager crowd. Somehow, this helped my heart and soul warm to the idea of the presentation I would give that night.

The evening of the ball was magical. Family and friends of multiple generations, dressed in their finest, turned out to celebrate the collective spirit of the community, past and present. While I was reviewing the content of my introduction with Mr. Paz—one of my favorite former high school teachers—he noticed my trembling hands. I was shocked to find myself coming undone after so many years of lecturing in various international settings and teaching hundreds of college students for over thirty years.

After Mr. Paz's brief and thoughtful introduction, I finally gained the courage to face my audience. Ms. Gibson's words, the very ones that hadn't done an ounce of good that miserable day of Dr. Vander's memorial, came back to me. This time, however, I could follow her advice. I paused, looked around the room, and found the loving eyes and gentle, caring faces of those I'd known through so many years. So many friends and family had come from far and wide to support me: Dallas, California, Colorado, and Washington State. Their reassuring smiles let me know they were there to share this moment and this evening with me. It was the perfect setting and the perfect time to tell my story.

I entitled my presentation "On Becoming a Person," the same as the title of a book by psychologist Carl Rogers. I had studied Rogers during my doctoral days and believed that his message was timeless and universal. In his writings, Rogers talks about the importance of unconditional love and acceptance in the formation of an individual's personality. His theory suggests that a person's self-concept stems from how he or she is regarded by the perceivers in that person's life. With each positive experience, that person's well-being grows. After explaining this idea of self-concept, I spent the next ninety minutes weaving the story of how my parents, teachers, peers, and siblings had formed my personality and made it strong, thus contributing to my success.

After the applause, the thanks, and the farewells of this memorable evening were over, Joanie and I returned home. And the writing of *Essential Moments* continued. This book, at its core, is a celebration of the many positive experiences and precious people I've encountered in my life. And in retrospect, even the negative times and people I have known, have been important. Like just about everyone, I've known people who—out of envy, hate, or fear—have attempted to sabotage my efforts through bigotry and betrayal. At times, their ugly agendas were meant not only to impede my success but diminish my very self in the process. Those people have slipped out of my life, and the memories of them have lost their power. Ironically, each negative blow only enhanced my resiliency to confront the next challenge. Today, I recall and value the powerful words of Albert Gore Sr., U.S. senator from Tennessee, when his son lost the presidential election in a dubious election with devastating consequences: "No matter how hard the loss, defeat might serve as well as victory to shape the soul and let the glory out."

Yet just as I learned that first day in treatment years ago, I can't simply blame others for the difficulties I've had in life. Now I can easily admit that I'm not free from flaws either. I know I've often had a tendency to wrap myself up in the lives of others, sometimes to an excessive degree. I also know that, in many instances, I've overcommitted myself to projects and situations without clear boundaries. I've made it through these times through God's grace and with the help of the people who've loved and cared for me. They have been my safety net and given me the resources I needed to accomplish what I have.

Thus, what is essential for me today are not the setbacks, flaws, or necessary losses that I've experienced in life. Perhaps it is not even the outward evidence of professional accomplishment and the accolades that attempt to mark my success. What is left—what really remains—are the strong intimations of love, regard, and acceptance I have received from a multitude of individuals in my life. *Ellos fueron mis rayitos de luna que iluminaron mis cielos en mis noches sin fortuna* (They were the moonbeams that illuminated my skies on the darkest nights). My precious moonbeams include my family, friends, students, and, most recently, my grandchildren—Taylor Maté and Alexander—who have brought the most exquisite and precious kind of love. These are the people who nurtured me and continue to nurture me through the process of becoming the "ordinary person" I am today.

The beloved San Felipe—the high school

Summer of 1955, Tony with best friends on a Sunday afternoon

My high school classmates, Reunion, 2007

**Doctoral Graduation from UNC (after years of struggles)
celebrating with my first daughter**

Christmas, 2001, with two new sons-in-law

Ready to explore Disneyland with daughter Jenny and grandchildren,
Alex and Taylor.

All dressed-up for a wedding—me with my granddaughter Taylor

Enjoying the Seattle lake beach with grandson Alex, 2 years

Family Reunion at San Felipe Black & White Ball, Fall, 2008

**Grandchildren Taylor and Alexander teach Grandma and Grandpa
to Laugh, Love, and Live.**

About the Author

Antonio Carvajal is a professor emeritus at the University of Northern Colorado. He completed a bachelor of science degree in English literature and speech/drama at Sul Ross University, a master of science degree in special education and sociology at Texas A&M University, and a doctorate degree in education at the University of Northern Colorado. Dr. Carvajal has been in the field of education for forty-four years: ten in public schools and thirty-four in higher education. He currently lives with his wife in Greeley, Colorado. They have three children and two grandchildren.